APPRENTICE to the RAIL
A JIGSAW PUZZLE

We Did Our Time at the VICTORIAN RAILWAYS
Not Bloody Pentridge

Dennis Denman   Norm Swanwick

First published by Ultimate World Publishing 2025
Copyright © 2025 Dennis Denman

ISBN

Paperback: 978-1-923583-18-4
Ebook: 978-1-923583-19-1

Dennis Denman has asserted his rights under the Copyright, Designs and Patents Act 1988 to be identified as the author of this work. The information in this book is based on the author's experiences and opinions. The publisher specifically disclaims responsibility for any adverse consequences which may result from use of the information contained herein. Permission to use information has been sought by the author. Any breaches will be rectified in further editions of the book.

All rights reserved. No part of this publication may be reproduced, stored in or introduced into a retrieval system, or transmitted in any form, or by any means (electronic, mechanical, photocopying, recording or otherwise) without the prior written permission of the author. Any person who does any unauthorised act in relation to this publication may be liable to criminal prosecution and civil claims for damages. Enquiries should be made through the publisher.

Cover design: Ultimate World Publishing
Layout and typesetting: Ultimate World Publishing
Cover image copyrights: Petr Vaclavek-Shutterstock.com
　　　　　　　　　　　Image Nest-Shutterstock.com

Ultimate World Publishing
Diamond Creek,
Victoria Australia 3089
www.writeabook.com.au

Apprentice to the Rail – A Jigsaw Puzzle

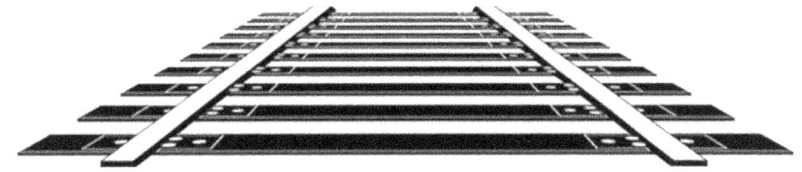

Author – about this book.

it's our history...**that needed to be told.**

This book is dedicated to the memories of young men that commenced as apprentices and forged diverse and interesting careers. Some stayed, others sought greener pastures beyond the Victorian Railways.

> 'When I left the railways in 1968 of the 60 fitting & turner apprentices who commenced in 1958 only three were still at Newport, most were working in private industry'. Tony Davis.

The enclosed stories and information are the assembly of patient research and the contribution by a number of 'old men'. It is an insider's story. Each story is a snapshot of personal experiences within the apprenticeship system in the Victorian Railways and its later names in the context of their work and the economic times. Regrettably the records of many aspects of apprentice training and decisions have been mostly lost and this advertisement in the NEWSRAIL magazine said it all. **Time is Running Out.**

Wanted – for a proposed history of apprentices trained in the Victorian Railways and V/line workshops – stories and recollections from the trade grades in support of the rail industry in building, servicing and maintaining the fleet...we are looking for personal experiences and highlights including the VR Technical College, Newport Technical College and the manual training centres and elsewhere as well as on-the-job training. Your stories may be told in confidence to: Dennis Denman, '61 electrical trade, author Once upon a train, *email djd0409@yahoo.com.au*, or Norm Swanwick, '66 electrical trade, *email normswanwick@yahoo.com.au*

Disclaimer: The contributors who responded to 'Time' and any bias to metal trade apprentice experiences is only chance. The authors warmly thank every individual who believe the Victorian Railways apprentice story is worthy of being recorded and told. Some content from, 'Once Upon a Train' is included. Hopefully these stories will provide a starting point for others.

Contents

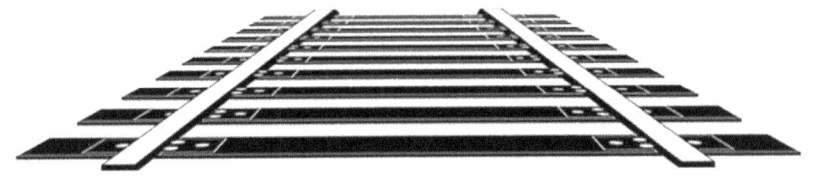

Chapter 1: A Jigsaw Puzzle	7
Acknowledgements	9
Chapter 2: Welcome to the Victorian Railways	15
Chapter 3: Historical Overview	29
Chapter 4: Where Did We Fit In?	35
Chapter 5: The Real World – On the job	39

Jolimont, Newport, Ballarat, Bendigo, North Melbourne, Train Lighting Depot, the Railmotor Depot, the VR Garage, South Dynon Locomotive Depot. North Melbourne Steam Locomotive Depot, Spotswood Workshops, Electrical Engineering & Way & Works Metro/Regional Depots

Chapter 6: A College of Our Own	85
Chapter 7: A World of Change, and Change again	111
Chapter 8: The Manual Training Centres	119
Chapter 9: STA - Scholarships and Awards	133
Chapter 10: The passing of the Victorian Railways	137
Apprentice Honour Roll	143
A Scrapbook History of Apprenticeship Training in the Victorian Railways 1960 -1984	151
Apprentices of the Year	233
Reflections	235

CHAPTER 1

A Jigsaw Puzzle

This collection of stories is to acknowledge the impact of young men who commenced their livelihood as an apprentice in the Rail Industry. Their role has been a continuum from the commencement of the railways in the State of Victoria. It is essentially a Victorian Railway story of the various trade roles essential to build, maintain and service the industry. It may resonate in the sound of welding strikes, in precise engineering as metal is cut by a lathe or the occasional spark. All manner of trades were needed, some designated as core trades and included; boiler makers, turner & fitters, electrical fitters and carriage & wagon builders and their start point was as an apprentice. In many ways our training may be considered a type of jigsaw puzzle, with many of the pieces known only to some hidden paper shuffler deep in the bowels of 67 Spencer Street. What we did know was the term of indenture and our start point. Each period or year based on a time block and relocation memo. Please report to…said it all. So, for those early period apprentices our work experience was nominally time based for the infrastructure and rolling stock of the day.

Later of course with role changes and work equality, some young women joined the ranks and added to the list of achievements.

The authors will attempt to provide some insight into the life of an apprentice in the Victorian Railways and the multiple organisational names changes up to the period of privatisation. We hope to include a wide range of inputs as well as their personal accounts of being an apprentice in the mid-20th century. From the journeys start, from selection and induction to aspects of the learning process along the way; at locations, colleges and workshops long gone. Workshops and infrastructure across the state-wide locations that provided the environments that were our initial and on-going work places. Yet retained in both individual and community memories. A wide array of young men followed the trade pathways while a few based on their first year's results entered either technician courses or cadetships for full-time diploma studies. Some individual apprentices were to become examples of progress to senior positions. The bulk remained in the trade. Others on completion of their apprenticeship saw greener fields and opportunities beyond the brand to forge varying and successful careers. The commercial world lined up for these highly trained talents. Some of these we can share.

My thanks to the many contributors. Significant among them, Norm Swanwick, who had commenced an independent search of aspects of apprentices in monthly staff magazines published by the Victorian Railways and subsequent identities. Stuart Smithwick, Ray Crampton, Owen Murray, Tony Davis, Scott Gould, Harry Stevens, Bruce Nevandt, Andy Barros and Steve Rogers. Special thanks to Owen Waldie for his patience in hours of conversation and memorabilia.

Acknowledgements

Madeleine Midgley, Hobson Bay library, Heritage section.
Kim Burrell, archivist, Victoria University archives, VRTC/NTC/TAFE records
John Hawthorne, editor News Rail
Public Records Office of Victoria, archives, V/Line Employee list 1988, extracts - Workshops Board meetings, No 24,33.39,and 72.
Stephen McLachlan, editor, ARHS magazine A.J. Clark article, Reminiscences of an apprentice at the Victorian Railways' Newport workshops 1959-1963 part of. ARHS Bulletin February 1996.
Prahran Mechanics Institute library Inc. Victorian Railways Newsletters collection
Nick Anchen's, Life on the Victorian Railways, N. Harris extract
Victorian State Library, articles and books collection. A report prepared for the Victorian Railways Board on the proposed Jolimont rail-yard of railway stabling. Transmark. Apprentice Intake 1981 by Recruitment & Employment
Owen Waldie, personal papers, photos and records
Lucie Akers, archivist, Federation University, Mt Clear, Ballarat.
Eddie Butler – Bowdon, part of: A history of the Victorian Railways and their Union. ISBN: 094706858
M.J. Woodford, Swinburne course notes
Michael Meszaros, OAM, sculptor, apprentice design medallion.
Vin Winter, page 50, extract, VR to V/Line.
Workshops – Where Now? Part of an article by Ann DePaul for the State Transport Authority staff news.
O.E. Nilsson, extracts, The Apprentice Training System of the Victorian Railways, Conference paper, October, 1927.
Brian Knight, extracts, NCVER occasional paper, Evolution of apprenticeships and traineeships in Australia: an unfinished history.
Director, Industry skills & capability coordination; for information, please visit the PROV website (http://www.prov.vic.gov.au/contact-us) and DTP website -DPT – Freedom of Information vic.gov.au. Good luck and all the best.
Victorian historical acts, Apprentice Acts, Office of the Chief Parliamentary Counsel website
V/Line Corporate Affairs: I'm advised that unfortunately we are unable to help you access past records.

Cough…Cough again.

'I can remember being interviewed at the VRI (Victorian Railway Institute) rooms in Geelong which is still standing with very little change. At the medical, we had to strip down completely naked, ten to a group lined up against the wall while the Doc went along feeling our balls while we coughed. Didn't bother washing his hands at all. A bit different these days.'

Norm Swanwick, Apprentice 1966

Never before opportunities… read on. Well, that wasn't the start point but it was part of the eligibility process

Kilmore Free Press, (Kilmore, Vic.1870 -1974) Thursday 16 February 1950, page 2. (edited) Railway Apprentices. Never in the history of the Victorian Railways have prospects for advancement been brighter for apprentices than they are today. Within the next ten years the railways will spend £80 million pounds (todays equivalent $200 million) on a progressive rehabilitation plan that has been widely known as Operation Phoenix. The railways are to be modernised and services expanded. Wise parents these days are advising their boys not to be succumb to the temptation of a temporary job and high wages in dead end jobs.

The railway offers for the lad leaving school is an interesting career and security which enables him to plan his future. In the railway workshops he will be taught his trade by an expert tradesman. The Victorian Railways are now seeking 47 apprentices. Lads between 15 and 17 years of age with 8th grade state school standard (or 18 with an Intermediate or higher certificate) are eligible for appointment. Apprentices are given a thorough five years training with all technical school classes conducted at the Department's expense, mostly during normal working hours (day release). High performing apprentices can additionally earn scholarships for university degrees or technical diplomas and gain appointment to professional staff. During the period of training, they will be in the care of the Supervisor of Apprentices who will over-see his progress and assist in any welfare issues. The Victorian Railways offer superannuation benefits, liberal sick leave, which may be accumulated if not used, annual leave with a free rail pass and long service leave. Country lads required to live away from home will be paid a minimum of £4/2/6 ($35 equivalent) per week and granted free home travel pass at regular intervals throughout the year.

Application forms and leaflets setting out full details of vacancies may be obtained from the Secretary for Railways, room 236, Railway Offices, Spencer Street, Melbourne until February 20.

Apprentice occupations based on historical records.

Armature Winder, Blacksmith, Boilermaker, Bricklayer, Butcher, Coppersmith, Car & Wagon Builder, Carpenter, Car Painter, Engine Blacksmith, Electrical Instrument Maker, Electrical fitter, Electrical fitter (Signals) Electrical Mechanic, fitter & Turner, Gas fitter, Interlock fitter, Iron Machinist, Letterpress Machinist, Lamp .Makers, Oxy Welders, Painter & Decorator, Printer, Pattern Maker, Painter, Moulder, Motor .Mechanics, Plumber, Upholsterer, Sailmaker, Sheetmetal Workers, Spring Maker, Tinsmith, Wood Machinists, Telephone Technicians.

Railway Apprentices get the BEST TRAINING

1970 advertisement, State Library of Victoria holdings

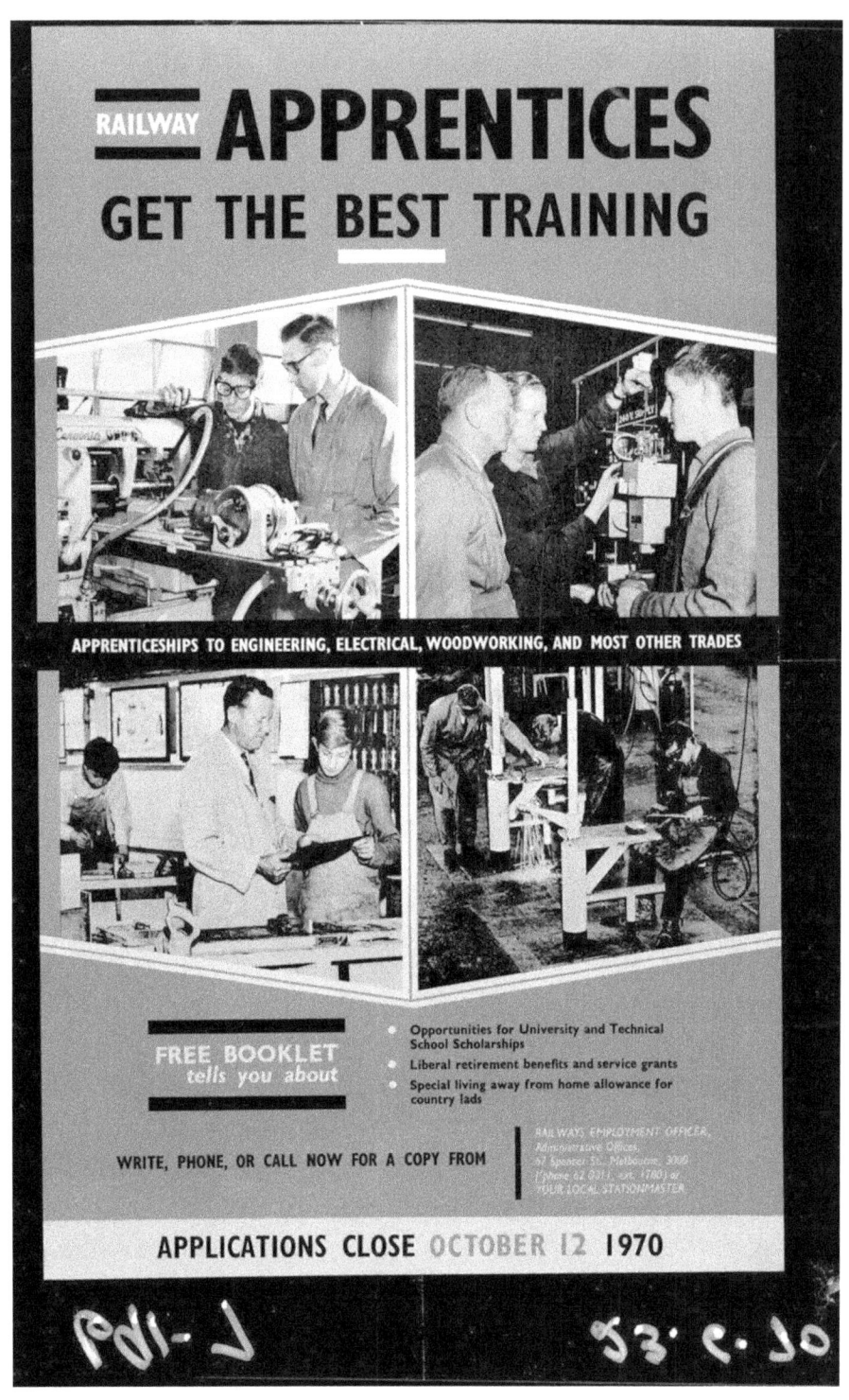

Idle Gossip!

Big advantage if they came through the technical school system

Bloody kids are stupider than ever, couldn't find his arse in a snow storm.

I was partly colour blind and couldn't pass the colour circle test, but was able to sort out bits of coloured wires.

The bloody block, that where I learnt to use a hammer with either hand.

Bit of a shock to his system when we had to scrape all that shit of the motors.

I'm sure most of the boys found it monotonous… Filing and scraping all day.

Silly little shit, I sent him for a population key and he has been missing for an hour.

There I was hanging by my overalls from a crane hook. They were all laughing.

Trouble settling in…four hours home every Friday and the same back on Sunday night.

At the boarding house…you know the day of the week by the food.

Don't be fucking lazy, wear your safety glasses when grinding.

We played one rule, the ball had to go over the top of the ring – basketball at lunch time.

Tie the bloody ladder off, before you pull the pipes into position.

Watch how they sling that load and you can do it next.

My first job was to make a small hammer. Learnt a lot about the properties of mild steel.

Jolimont was the strangest place I worked…some really odd characters.

Always place a red flag in position or disc before you go under the carriage.

That's blood…open end spanner slipped and ripped his knuckles.

It's your bloody toes, insulation tape was not invented to hold your shoes together, get some safety shoes.

Tuesday nights was practice night…member of the Victorian Railways brass band.

I remember my first pay was cash, lining up to get my pay in a little yellow envelope.

One fella only lasted a week…he was homesick.

CHAPTER 2

Welcome to the Victorian Railways

Applicants will be required to take entry tests in arithmetic, mechanical reasoning, IQ, and reading comprehension.

Dear applicant, thank you for your interest in applying for an apprenticeship with the Victorian Railways. I have enclosed an application form for completion and an apprentice information sheet. Please complete this application with your 1st and 2nd trade preference. Part of the selection process involves satisfactory completion of a series of tests. These test sessions will occupy approximately 2 hours. Please attend .... on date .... at 10am.
State Transport Authority letter example.
Application for apprenticeship form.

STATE TRANSPORT AUTHORITY
VICTORIA

Form 2800

Telephone: 619-1469
Reference:
Date:

APPRENTICESHIP APPLICATION

Dear

I am pleased to inform you that you have been selected to attend an interview for an Apprenticeship with the State Transport Authority.

AT: ON: LOCATION: Level 14, 589 Collins Street.

ON THE DAY OF THE INTERVIEW PLEASE BRING:

1. this letter
2. your original school results (not copies)
3. your birth certificate
4. if you were born overseas, bring evidence of Australian Citizenship.

You will be required to have some knowledge of what is required for and involved in your preferred trade, and explain why you want an Apprenticeship with the State Transport Authority.

Please arrive at least 10 minutes prior to the start of the interview.

Following the interview, you will be notified by mail as to whether you were successful, unsuccessful or deferred for further consideration.

Successful applicants will also be notified of a time for a medical examination to be held in Melbourne.

If you change your address or if you are unable to attend on the stated date and time, please contact me immediately on 619-1469.

Yours sincerely,

NELLA TRIGILIO
Apprenticeship Officer for
Manager, Employment Department.

Level 14, 589 Collins Street, Melbourne Victoria 3000. Telex-V/Line AA33801

WELCOME TO THE VICTORIAN RAILWAYS

Apprentice Application

Dear......., I am pleased to inform you that you have been selected to attend an interview for an apprenticeship with the Victorian Railways.
State Transport Authority letter example.

STATE TRANSPORT AUTHORITY
VICTORIA

Form 2800

PERSONNEL & EMPLOYEE RELATIONS DIVISION
Telephone: 619-1469
Reference: NT:MM
Date:

Dear Applicant,

Thank you for your interest in applying for an apprenticeship with the State Transport Authority. I have enclosed an application form for you to complete, and an information sheet outlining our expected vacancies in 1987. Please read the information sheet carefully before indicating your trade preferences on the application form. This is important as you will be considered for trades only in the order of preference you indicate.

Part of our selection process involves the satisfactory completion of a series of tests. Applicants are selected for interview on the basis of their performance in these tests. Please note that the test session takes approximately 2 hours to complete.

Your test will be conducted on **WEDNESDAY 23RD JULY, 1986** beginning at 2.00 P.M.

Location: WILSON HALL,
          MELBOURNE UNIVERSITY.

You must bring with you two good quality HB pencils, and a soft, good quality rubber. No calculators are allowed.

PLEASE TAKE NOTE OF THE FOLLOWING POINTS:

1. The application form enclosed with this letter must be completed before the test date and handed to a supervising officer at the test session.

   YOU WILL NOT BE PERMITTED TO ATTEMPT THE TESTS WITHOUT YOUR APPLICATION FORM.

2. Note the date, location and time of your selection test. Please try to arrive at least 10 minutes prior to starting time. Late comers will not be allowed to interrupt a test session, and a special arrangement will have to be made for a later date.

Yours sincerely,

NELLA TRIGILIO
Apprenticeship Officer
For Manager,
Employment Department.

Level 14, 589 Collins Street, Melbourne Victoria 3000. Telex-V/Line AA33801

APPRENTICE TO THE RAIL

1354-85

STATE TRANSPORT AUTHORITY
VICTORIA

Appendix 'D' (Part 2)
S. 149

APPLICATION FOR APPRENTICESHIP

POINTS TO NOTE

Please complete both sides of this form. Completed forms must be placed in an envelope marked "Apprenticeship" and returned to P.O. Box 4105, Melbourne, Vic. 3001, no later than 19th July, 1985.

Applicants must have satisfactorily completed the fourth form year, now, or will do so by the end of this year.

Please read the attached Apprenticeship information folder to ensure that you understand the trade(s) chosen.

You will be required to undertake preselection tests and you will be advised of the date and where to attend.

After the test results are assessed, certain applicants will be chosen for an interview. You will be advised accordingly.

TRADE PREFERENCES

First Preference..Location ....

Second Preference..Location ....

CODE NO.
(Not to be completed by applicant)

INFORMATION REGARDING APPLICANT

Given Names (BLOCK LETTERS)

Surname (BLOCK LETTERS)

Address   No. & Street

Town/Suburb (Abbreviate if necessary)   Postcode

Date of Birth ..../........./.........   Home Phone No. ....

Nearest Railway station (with Passenger Service) ....

I wish to undertake my preselection test at   ☐ Ballarat   ☐ Bendigo   ☐ Melbourne.

DETAILS OF PARENT/GUARDIAN

I live with my (Parents/Guardian)

Mr./Mrs. .... Phone

Home..................................

Work...................................

Address ....   Postcode............................

PARTICULARS OF EMPLOYMENT (IF ANY) SINCE LEAVING SCHOOL

State Transport Authority or Victorian Railways

Division employed in...Position ....Still employed ....

Other Employment

Company ....Position ....Period ....

....

....

....

WELCOME TO THE VICTORIAN RAILWAYS

You are IN…selection approved

The letter said it all arriving by the Post Master General, or from 1979 Australian Post confirming your selection as an apprentice, hopefully, your first preference. YOU had passed through all the GO/NOGO gates, of aptitude, mechanical reasoning tests and the selection panels scrutiny.

Destination big smoke.

All would remember their journey to be on time for their first day on the job that Monday morning. Many would have planned their travel, days ahead from locations on the map from the four corners of the state, unrecognisable to city boys. Some would have arrived even earlier to seek lodging with relatives or to tackle life as a boarder. Regardless of their home city or postcode their destination was Melbourne and the welcoming committee. *'The assembly point was in my case the Victorian Railway Institute (VRI) ballroom located at the western end of the Flinders Street Station building via the Elizabeth Street entrance.'* Others recalled gathering at the Victorian Railway Institute Hall at the Spencer Street station to be greeted by the Chairman of the Victorian Railway staff board. *'I surmise if my experience was similar to many young men and or much later some young women apprentices to fall somewhere between excitement and daunting. With a policy of seeking applicants from both country and metropolitan locations, many were facing both the experience of employment and the challenges of living away from home for the first time. Home cooked meals and a wake-up call if you tended to over sleep were now in the past. After the formal welcome and pep talk, the apprentices would be escorted to his/their immediate work place.'* **Dennis Denman**.

Recollections and stories.

NORM'S STORY. Norm Swanwick recalls being interviewed for an apprentice electrical fitter's position at the Victorian Railway Institute (VRI) hall building near the Geelong railway station. His application was successful and he commenced his five-year apprenticeship training with the Victorian Railways on January 17 1966.

'As I would be undertaking my first year at the Newport Railway Workshops, I decided to board away from home. Most of the apprentices from Geelong would travel back and forth each day.' 'The Victorian Railways paid a living away allowance to offset my board and many of my fellow apprentices who came from country locations'. 'There were four of us at a boarding house in Melbourne Road, Newport, two in each room. The house was fairly old and the roof leaked like a sieve. If it rained at night, we would wake up in the morning with either a wet bed or pots all around the floor to catch the drips.'

'On that first day 210 of us gathered in the VRI hall at Spencer Street Station to be welcomed.'

Assembled on this stage were the managers and individuals who were in some ways to guide our future career. An army of young men selected as apprentice had followed year on year this process but undoubtedly some in much earlier years may have followed a different path. For those of us from the middle of the nineteen fifties the pathway was directed to the ballroom and the welcoming committee. Some of these men would be recognised from aspects of the interview process that led to today. Others were soon to be confirmed as senior managers as they took their position at the top of the pecking order of welcome.

Each welcome, regardless of the time held significant words of the challenges and future possibilities. And every apprentice held to these word as they reinforced the decision of employment and acceptance. A hundred years of welcomes, and each a special message of the time, the business, its future and the opportunity to succeed beyond today.

Amid the bustle of voices and positioning chairs the faces of a legion of young men would be turned towards the raised dais at one end of the ballroom or hall. Here assembled in the suits and ties of management were our welcoming party. Over the years of 'welcome' their faces may have changed but the message remained constant.

The Railway Commissioners have always insisted on apprentices at the Newport Railways Workshops receiving a sound technical training. Extract: The *Victorian Railways magazine October 1925*.

Staying on message. Sage advice or Bullshit.

The railways are to be modernised and services expanded. The highest positions in the railways have always been open to the apprentice with initiative and the capacity to study hard. There are numerous examples of lads who started their careers as apprentices and who rose to senior jobs. The present Chief Mechanical Engineer (A.C. Allston), the Chief Electrical Engineer (H.P. Colwell) and the Manager of the Newport Workshops, the largest in the Southern Hemisphere. Extract, *Kilmore Free Press, February 1950*

If you have served your time in the Victorian Railways as an apprentice, nobody queries your training. It is in the hallmark of a craftsman's excellence. This high tribute to the railway apprenticeship system was paid by O.E Nilsson at the opening of the Victorian Railway Technical College at Newport on July 4 1960. Mr E.H. Brownbill Chairman of Commissioners, continued…We take pride in the fact that our apprenticeship training can be compared with the best in Australia.

In 1961, the welcoming committee included Commissioner E.P. Rogan with members of the Apprentice Board of Selectors, Messer's W Walker (Member of the Staff Board of Selection), K A Smith Engineer, Ways & Works, A Chambers, Rolling Stock staff selection and W. E. Elliot, General Secretary (Victorian Railway Institute, (VRI). *VR Newsletter, January 1961*. Within this assembled group were two men who were to be face of the railways in our early days and progress; the Supervisor of Apprentices and the Principal of the Victorian Railway Technical Collage. In real terms after the welcome, the blue or grey suits were immediately replaced by our immediate mentors, our first supervisor and tradesman or the manual skills instructors.

Commissioner Rogan congratulated the 219 young men on choosing a tradesman's career, because with the present technical progress their employment scope was greater than ever.

'I was one of this eager and expectant group hanging on every word as this was a role that would lead to my independence and income. Our assembly was a sea of faces but ignorant in the role and work type that was still hours away. This callow youth had somehow confused his technical subjects with electrical works that would involve single and two-way switch wiring and small a/c motors and equipment. So blissfully wrong but all unfolded on completion of our induction and my/our escort to Jolimont Workshops via Batman Avenue'. Today, the Melbourne Park Tennis Centre complex has long replaced Jolimont Workshops and the rail stabling yards with the walk from the CBD now along Princes Walk, parallel to the Yarra River and through Birrarung May Park. **Dennis Denman**.

In 1982, General Manager, Mr Bob Gallacher said the following at the apprentice awards for achievement… *'There is in the community today wide recognition that an apprenticeship is something to be sought after and prized. He told the assembled gathering of parents and young people that apprenticeships meant making a start on a specific course of training with a set objective and a prescribed standard. It was not just 'any old job', but one where there was a need to seek excellence.' 'He stressed that each individual should regard his particular job or activity as part of and not separate to the business of running a rail system.' 'We depend heavily on tradesmen for technical support, because nothing really operates until the men at work do the job they are trained and skilled to do.'*

The welcome might have included a brief history of the first apprentice intake reported as 1860 at the old Williamstown Depot, later replaced by the Newport Workshops along the expanse of Champion Road. But that didn't occur, so if history is our guide, we can divide our apprenticeship loosely into time blocks. Not the apprenticeship year, 1st, 2nd, 3rd…. etc, but time at work locations. The ground rules set by successive Commonwealth Acts that provided the framework. The period of their apprenticeship, the time of trade training and pay and conditions among the key points. The terms of apprenticeships for all skilled trades were set as five years.

First day and then the next.

NORM SWANWICK continued, *'After the Chairman's welcome we were escorted to the manual training centres located at the Newport Workshops. The manual training centre for electrical apprentices (Electrical Training Centre) was sited in half a workshop on the west side near the Melbourne Geelong railway line and referred to as the West Block.' 'The ETC was established about the same time as the new Victorian Railway Technical College in 1960.' 'We had to walk some distance to the other side of the workshops to attend the technical college nearer the North*

Williamstown station workshops entrance.' The other two manual training centres for the mechanical trades (Boiler Makers & Turner & Fitters) were located near the college.'

OWEN MURRAY commenced his apprenticeship with the Victorian Railways, Way & Works in January 1957. Although most of their employees were engaged in permanent way and track, the Way & Works Branch included sections that constructed railway buildings, installed and maintained signalling equipment, maintained and serviced infrastructure and track equipment state wide. **Owen** shares his start… *'I with three other lads were assigned to the Way & Works, Plant Division at Laurens Street, North Melbourne which was situated next to the VR Printing Works. Our first three years were spent two days per week at the Victorian Railway College near the Newport station. Also, our first year was spent (one day a week) at Newport Workshops for manual training.'*

Owen's recollection of the technical school/collage is still to be unlocked but an article in the *Rail Ways from 1980-3* nominates the first Victorian Railway College opened near the Newport station in 1923. It was demolished in 1959 enabling the construction of the Melbourne Road overpass. The demise of the original technical school progressed the new Newport Technical Collage built on six acres of leased land in Champion Road at a cost of $9 million and completed in 1960. The site is currently the home of the Railway Museum including the steam locomotive Heavy Harry at 264-tonne and a range of railway memorabilia. The college's new premises were to consolidate trade apprentice education and training that had seen steady progress from as early as 1920. In between this consolidation some trade apprentices attended the Working Men's College that post-dated the Royal Melbourne Institute of Technology. Other apprentices by trade or geography attended technical colleges that specialised in skill sets.

Specialised colleges. These include Collingwood Technical School, Footscray, Prahran and the Ballarat School of Mines and the Bendigo Technical School. Selected apprentices with high achieving exam results (award winners) could be offered scholarships to attended RMIT and other tertiary institutions for technician or diploma courses, so the relationship of some commencing a rail apprenticeship was never broken. … *'the work at the plant division was very interesting and varied, we worked on shunting tractors, mobile cranes. air compressors, pumping plants, chain saws and Casey Jones track motors. Our work also included servicing elevators (lifts) at Head Office and the laundry and baking machines at the Dining Car Depot opposite Melbourne Station. At country depots it included the mechanics of locomotive turntables, coal elevating plants, fork lifts and mobile cranes.'* Owen also had time during his apprenticeship to be a member of the Victorian Railways brass band, meeting Tuesday nights in room 52 at the Victorian Railway Institute.

Another candidate from the country commences his apprenticeship around the same time. **ANTHONY (TONY) DAVIS** arrived at the Victorian Railways Newport Workshops. *'I left Echuca technical school in 1957 and started as a fitter & turner at Newport Workshops. The first day when I arrived at Newport, I was very lucky being allocated to Vic Coulson as the Brake Shop foremen and a wonderful man Les Schroeder. Les was the fitter who took me under his wing. A steep learning curve about human relations – on one occasion just after I started in the fitting shop a fitter's assistant who had come from Malta after the war grabbed a hammer and chased another apprentice down the workshops yelling; I'll kill you; I'll kill you.*

Anthony Davis 1960, Apprentice of the year, Fitting and Turning (VR Technical College)

Fortunately, a tradesman grabbed the pair of them and removed the hammer. We were all called into the foreman's office with the explanation that not all migrants from Europe understood the terms used by Australians'. 'To be called a bastard in Malta was a very offensive expression while here in Australia it was mostly used in humour and just an expression of speech. This was what the fuss was about between the apprentice and the fitter's assistant. My first job was to use an air grinder to grind the excess weld off the metal frames for the BZ and AZ carriage seats. Then we moved them under the hydraulic press to make them level and straight. These seats could be swivelled to face the direction of travel in the air-conditioned country carriages being built at the workshops at this time. Another job on the press was to push out worn steel bushes from various components. I also had the job of going to the general store with an order for the replacement bushes. Hands on… reading drawings and learning how to use the marking out equipment. The job was to white wash a component with a scribed line so the machine operator could complete the work task, either machining or radial drilling. The marking out was done on a steel table using a surface gauge and large vertical rulers used for measurement. For a hypoid gear box, we used a dial indicator to balance the gear boxes that were mounted in the centre of axle between wheels. These gear boxes were part of the bogies under the joint owned overland air-conditioned carriages for the Victorian Railways and South Australian Railways.'

TONY CONTINUES…'*to recondition a triple valve I had to scrape the slides and seat the rings. The valves went onto a test bench and had to hold 75 psi for a certain period. The hollow cylindrical valves had to be lapped in on the air compressor before being fitted onto the 'red rattler' suburban trains. These compressors were particularly noisy when operating, - thump, thump, thump. In the Brake Shop I worked with a German named Willie Messerschmitt. He was a good teacher and told stories about the WW2. Willie was an engine fitter and worked on the Messerschmitt Me 109s fighter aircraft. He told me the German Airforce had plenty of planes but as the war progressed their loss of experienced fighter pilots could never be replaced by the inexperienced kids which became easy pickings for the allied aircrews.'*

Country carriages, Newport Workshops, (Steam rail) 2022

The big build. *'At this time the AZ and BZ air-conditioned country carriages where being built. We had the job of fitting the shit shoot, vanity basin and pan ready for the coppersmiths to measure and fit the water supply pipes. Another part of our work was to fit the overhead luggage racks. This involved drilling and tapping the structure to fix the racks. These luggage racks had been preassembled in the shop using a special jig on a heavy board that was u bolted to the rack along the top. It took a team of fitter's assistants and labourers to carry it from the Brake Shop to the carriage for positioning by set screws.' …next stop the Railmotor Shop. 'By a strange coincidence I was allocated to another fitter, also a German immigrant. He had worked at the M.A.N. engine factory and during the war was told to report to the navy for the U-boat fleet. He said to me, his greatest fear was being depth charged and water getting into the batteries and creating chlorine gas, but working on the diesel motors was ok. We reconditioned the Gardener diesel engines used in the Walker diesel railmotors and also the GM diesels used in the DERM rail cars. the engine rebuilds included valves, heads and bearings. The main challenge was getting both engines to have the same revolutions per minute (rpms) as these engines went into a common gear box assembly which was connected to the electrical generator. Unless the rpms of both engines synchronised, they would work against each other. The Paint Shop was two bays over'*

WELCOME TO THE VICTORIAN RAILWAYS

RAY CRAMPTON commenced in 1968 so falls into a period of mounting change. he shared the following. *I commenced in 1968 and after our first year in the old Brake Shop (site of the Electrical Training Centre) after which I was allocated to the Plant Shop as my first assignment in the big brave railway world.* Ray recalls being one of the apprentices assigned to the author (Denman) when he was in the Plant Shop.

At the time we were working in the 'wheel shop section' with responsibility for the electrical equipment in the fabrication shop, foundry, pattern shops and the wheel lathe and associated equipment. It was there that I first met you (Denman) and did a stint which was really good particularly working a straight shift. I was interested in your experiences (Denman) in Rail and in some ways, we ran a parallel course for some time but years apart. Ray continued, *I joined the Electrical Trade Union (ETU) and later was the ETU rep at TLD. I did the stints around Newport including the Railmotor section and the engineering office. I like all others in the Rolling Stock Branch did the rounds and ended up at TLD as my trade posting. At TLD I did the travel roster along with other aspects and basically spent my last year or two on shift in the shelter shed.* Ray resigned in 1978.

With a little arm twisting another 1968 apprentice shared some snippets of that period. **HARRY STEVENS** commenced his 1st year in the Electrical Training Centre in the West Block. Harry still remembers his token number many decades later as number 55. He readily recalls the noise that surrounded the training centre and the skills program for the metal trade apprentices. He admits that a Catholic college back ground didn't quite equip him for some aspects of the program, particularly the lathe operations and milling machines. Harry had been selected as an electrical fitter for the Electrical Engineering Branch. In his words, *'we were a pretty boisterous group of youngsters and always looking for a bit of a distraction. You sort of made fun where you found it. A group of us particularly enjoyed the occasional diversion when it came our way. One of our instructors, Ron (Doc) Little was sort of a favourite…he must have lived locally as he arrived and departed by bike. After we settled in one or other of the braver or stupid ones occasionally let the air out of his tyres and on a couple of times hid the bike for hours on end. All taken well but we were to reach greater heights for distraction. On this particular day someone had acquired the old-style detonator which was held in place by a clip to the rail. So having the 'Det' the next problem was how to get our explosive bang. A day later in the Brake shop an open top wagon was placed somewhat behind the training centre's office block. The 'Det' placed on the rail a couple of the bigger kids crowbarred the wagon on to the 'Det' with the intended result. As the instructors filed out the office, the kids disappeared to much amusement.*

During this period Ken Gennifer had become the senior instructor, Jack Lindsay took all the machine shop and lathe operations, Alf Robinson ran the electrical section and all our board works. In those days it was simple circuits of single way and two-way switching from a mini switch board to a batten holder lamp. The wiring combined split conduit and TPS cabling with switches and power outlets fixed to wooden blocks. Ron Little looked after most of the hand skills program and was exacting on our models' dimensions and finish. Then of course the legendary chipping block that combined most engineering skills, removing masses of metal before filing and scraping. Then fitting a gauge to a cross section, about ¼ inch deep that had been milled slightly oversized. To finish off we drilled and tapped 4, ½ inch BSW studs in the centre of each quadrant… One day a week during each school term we went to 'Bone Head' college for the trade theory. I didn't last long in my initial grade but soon found my way in another class. I remember one teacher who took technical drawing by the name of George Martin and surmised that they were all seconded from the railways. As the college was adjacent to North Williamstown station it was almost a direct service. Across the road from the station were the local watering holes, the Rifle Club and another pub, the Bristol that were in future years to become a school day lunch event. Naturally during our first couple of years none of us could legally buy a drink in a licensed premises. Harry at years end was transferred to his next location…the Electrical Workshops 'A' located in Spencer Street

1968 was a good year for the apprentice intake. **BRUCE NEVANDT** recalls bits and pieces of his five-year apprenticeship after being selected as an electrical fitter for the Rolling Stock Branch. He commenced in the training centre with many others who were to learn the extent of their training program. Bruce related, *I found the daily variety of bench work, learning to operate the basics and procedures of the lathes, millers and radial drills kept me busy and interested. Throw in the chipping block and that's where I learned to use a hammer either hand.* Bruce found the year progressed fairly rapidly with each day commencing with the hours plus train ride from Geelong to Newport station. *One day a week we legged it to 'Bone Head' college for our trade studies. The day-to-day grind of classroom and practical experiments lost in the highlights of the kick-to-kick football played most lunch breaks. It was robust football with packs either end and plenty of willing bodies. One I remember who stood out was Steve Pearce who launched into and above the pack. He would dominate one end.*

At years end Bruce commenced his second year, remaining at Newport at the Plant Shop. He was to remain there for around 18 months rotating through the various work locations. The Wheel Shop section. the crane maintenance section and shop electrical repairs. His merry go round or training blocks a minor adjustment from the experiences of earlier apprentices. The major rail work locations remained the business end of major overhauls and period maintenance. Bruce's next on-job location was Train Lighting Depot were his work included the servicing and maintenance of the carriages he used in his daily commute, AZ or BZ carriages included. *My next location was the Jolimont Workshops and the passenger units of the suburban system. The fleet consisting of Tait and Harris trains with the Hitachi on track.*

Harris suburban train, Belgrave line. 1970

I did stints on the 'wall section' where we mainly did unit exchanges. A brief period in the 'gallery' with coil and armature winding. The bulk of my training and work was associated with the traction motor section where we 'pulled them apart and put them back together'. Around the later period of my 4th year the option of a final posting had opened up. With a future in mind my interest was working as a diesel maintainer, and I managed a transfer to the South Dynon Locomotive Depot. Paid as an acting diesel maintainer I completed the final year of my apprenticeship in service fault finding and deep in the drop pits for traction motor exchanges. The work was varied and interesting and led to my long game of being able to transfer to the Geelong locomotive depot.

Another from the 1968 apprentice pot. ANDY BARROS was another electrical fitter who had followed his father into the industry. Andy shares his first year as part of the Electrical Training Centre located in the West Block. Repeating his experiences as similar to the rest of his year it combined much filing and scraping at his bench location to finish a high proportion of models. *After the training centre I remained at Newport at various locations, the car electricians in the East block and later the various sections of the Plant Shop. At the car electricians I worked on various country cars doing undercarriage conduits and circuit wiring. We also did the carriage compartment circuitry and lighting. This is where I got to do my first foreigner. I had to repair a bilge pump for 'Snowy Milne'. Snowy was the electrical foreman and a mad fisherman. We got on all right after our* *first meeting when he uttered; 'young Barros,' remarking he knew my father, who as one of the 'shops barbers' used to cut his hair. I was there when they bought the carriages of the Southern Aurora into Newport for storage around my second year. (1969). My next move was to the Plant Shop where I worked with various tradesmen, including you (Denman) in the Wheel Shop section on cyclic and breakdown maintenance. The section was responsible for electrical maintenance in the Wheel Shop, Erecting Shop, Roller Bearing Shop, Foundry and Pattern Making Shop. A couple of years down and I was transferred to Jolimont Workshops, firstly in the Lift shop, then a short term in the Gallery working on armature repairs. Next was the traction motor section where we stripped down each motor, before reassembly. This was piece work and we had to complete so many per day.*

On the move.

After my time at JWS I was transferred to Train Lighting Depot to complete my time. Ron Milne was now the senior foreman and initially my work was in the small workshop. Here we repaired different types of generators, battery charges and the various electrical equipment associated with country carriages. I also did some time in the battery room where the wet cell, acid batteries were dismantled and rehabilitated. This was not the place for young apprentices to work…. Leaving the confines of the workshop our main area was the various yards and stabling areas for the interstate arrivals, like the Daylight, and the Overland and carriage sets, and buffet cars from country services. In some instances, we would meet the trains at the station platforms other times we were undertaking scheduled maintenance and light repairs. Every electrical fitter apprentice in their final year at TLD was included on the travelling roster between Melbourne and Hardin (NSW). This was a fun time where we worked along with the buffet crew doing small jobs and getting to know the younger refreshment girls. This trip I was with Steve Bato and arrived in Hardin well after midnight. Steve was a great cook and character who made the interstate trips more than just learning the operation of the power van. Andy was to return to Jolimont for the bulk of his career becoming a specialist in suburban rail car maintenance and repairs including the pantograph from the red rattler to Comeng. He was part of the start-up crew at Epping Maintenance Depot where his personality and endeavour helped shape the new suburban train world before privatisation.

CHAPTER 3

Historical Overview

The apprentices to the main trades of the day, (early 20th century) were the disciplines of steam powered engines, wooden bodied carriages and state wide rail infrastructure. The trades of iron machinists, blacksmiths, boiler making, car & wagon builders and tinsmiths held sway but new trades and skill sets were needed to meet the demands of new technology for the public rail transport fleet. Training was on-the job and covered a multitude of trades to enable the construction, maintenance and servicing of the fleet and its infrastructure needs. Combine these trades with the education of apprentices and the industry skillset was in lock step. This was to remain the norm up to the mid nineteen-sixties when apprentice training for the four main trades changed to the then modern concept, specifically accelerated skill enhancement in dedicated training centres. During this period government instrumentalities, such as gas, water and electricity supply utilities along with road and rail authorities and defence were major employers of apprentices. However, in the latter period the 20th century public sector and major government utilities began to decrease its apprentice training capacity as efficiencies, multi skilling and outsourcing influenced workforce numbers. As new technologies advanced from motive power to computerised systems the skill set of some trades within the industry declined or became. redundant. The rail business was under challenge along with some trades including, type writer repairer, sailmaker (tarpaulin and wagon covers), together with iron machinist, and spring maker.

Yet opportunities remained to enable the apprentice to flourish in other trades beyond the four main trades, electrical fitting, boiler making and structural steel fabricating, turner & fitters and car & wagon builders. Years later the diesel maintainer morphed combining both mechanical and electrical skills. Some allied occupations still held sway such as, cooks, carriage painters, upholsters, plumbers, and overhead linespersons. The time lines of our experience were dictated by decisions including multiple Federal Government Acts and in-house by the Victorian Railways Apprentice Advisory Committee.

The Big Wide Umbrella - the Apprentice Training system.

The Apprenticeship Act 1928, provided the legal framework for apprenticeships and appointed the Apprenticeship Commission to manage that process.

Edited text - Part (11) Apprentice Trades

15. the Commission and every trade committee and every advisory committee shall endeavour so far as practicable to promote apprenticeship in apprenticeship trades up to the limit for each trade.

16. (1) the Commission – (a) shall exercise a general supervision over the theoretical and practical training of apprentices (b) shall ascertain the character and scope of the potential training afforded to apprentices, (c) may ascertain by practical or written or oral examination or by inspection of his work or reports furnished by the employer or otherwise the degree of proficiency of any apprentice. (d) may issue grade or progress certificates to apprentices who have attained standards of proficiency, (e) shall – when an apprentice has completed the term of his apprenticeship provided for in his indentures and has attained the standards of education and trade experience prescribed by his apprenticeship course – issue to him a final certificate.

16. (2) for the purpose of any examination or inspections; aforesaid the Commission shall have regard to results of examinations conducted and inspections made under the control of the Education Department.

Prior to and including the *Apprentice Act 1928*. **Part (11) Apprenticeship Trades**. This period of trade apprentices commenced employment with the specified branches, most with the Rolling Stock Branch to work at workshops or locations depending on trades. They learned on the job with a tradesman usually at a major workshop. Others employed to the Way & Works or Electrical Engineering Branch would start initially at their specified depot. 1900 - 1960. The term of most apprenticeships during this period were five years. Many of this group were part of the steam era and watched as the era of the diesel arrived.

The Apprentice Act 1958. 1. This Act may be cited as the *Apprentice Act 1958* and shall come into operation at a date to be …
Section 10 reads. For section 16 of the Principal Act, there shall be substituted the following section

16. 1. The Commission shall keep under review – (a) the requirements of the State for skilled tradesmen. (b) the availability of skilled tradesmen to meet those requirements. (c) the availability of young people for apprenticeships. (d) the availability of vacancies for apprentices and the extent to which employers are participating in the training of apprentices. (e) the adequacy of the training of apprentices in employers' workshops and in technical schools and measures which can be taken to improve that training. (f) the adequacy of the apprentice system as a means of training skilled tradesmen and the desirability of modifying that system or of providing other systems of training for skilled occupations.

HISTORICAL OVERVIEW

16.2. the Commission – (a) may ascertain by practical, written or oral examination or by inspection of his work or otherwise the degree of proficiency of any apprentice, and for the purposes of any such examination, shall have regard to the results of examinations conducted by the education department. *Extract selected sections.*

Next - ***Apprentice Amendment Act 1971.*** An Act to amend the *Apprenticeship Act 1958* and to repeal certain provisions of the *Employers and Employee's Act 1958*. 1.(1) this Act may be cited as *the; Apprenticeship (Amendment) Act 1971*. (2)
In this *Act* the *Apprenticeship Act 1958* is called the *Principal Act*.

2. Sub – section (1 of section 3) (a) in the interpretation of employer after the word indentures…there shall be inserted the expression, and include the Crown.

With the introduction of the *Industrial Training Act 1975* the Apprentice Commission was superseded by the Industrial Training Commission. This legislation enabled the Industrial Training Commission to be responsible for the direction and implementation of training schemes for skilled trades.

Summary - The *Industrial Training Commission* succeeded the Apprenticeship Commission on August 2, 1975 and under the provision of the Act, the apprenticeship scheme was also extended to the State Government sphere of operation and into the agricultural industry. It was empowered to issue Trade Certificates on completion of an apprenticeship and to persons who had not completed an apprenticeship, but who possessed the necessary skills subject to a trade test. Prior to 1981 the Department of Labour and Industry administered the *Apprenticeship Commission* and the **Industrial Training Commission.**

In 1981 the **Industrial Training Commission** came under the ambit of the Ministry of Employment & Training and in 1985 moved into the newly created **Department of Employment and Industrial Affairs.**

The State Training Board was established in November 1997. Its purpose to establish an authority to coordinate and administer the Government's training policies and technical and vocational training services provided by the state. The board assumed the functions of the Industrial Training Commission

The second period of VR trade apprentices started their first year at the manual trade centres located at Newport workshops. This period commenced in 1960 and concluded in the late 1990's. The **Apprentice Information folder** of the State Transport Authority (1987) details the following: Apprentices associated with the electrical, fitter & turner or structural steel trades are placed in manual training centres for the first year of training under supervision learning the basic skills of their various trades. All trades attend appropriate technical colleges in conjunction with apprentice training.

The caretakers for rail apprentice training.

In *VR–to- V/line*, Vin Winter writes, (pg.50) Apprentice Training…because the Apprenticeship Act was not binding on the Crown the railways had been free to conduct their own apprenticeship scheme and in fact had been the largest trainers of apprentices in Victoria. With the passing of the ***Apprentice Amendment Act 1971*** however, the provisions of the Act were made binding on the Crown and thereafter the intake, training and discipline of apprentices by the employer was supervised by the Apprentice Commission except for a few 'railway trades' such as Car & Wagon Builders and Car Lighting Mechanics. The Commission however, allowed the department a fair amount of freedom in the content of the course. As the timeline extended the next major reform occurred in **1987** when the Ministry of Education & Training assumed responsibility for **industrial and apprentice training.** The State Training Board established in that year under the provision of the *Post-Secondary Education Act 1978* with its primary purpose to co-ordinate and administer the technical and vocational services provided by the State.

The last period of apprentices trained up to privatisation of the Public Transport Corporation would have transferred from the workshops to the new service organisations. The direction of the *Vocational Education and Training Act 1990* would have been the swan song for rail apprentices under the orbit of the **State Training Board.**

Vocational Education and Training Act 1990. Part of:

Part 1 - Preliminary

(a) the main purposes of the act are – to establish the State Training Board and to specify its powers and functions in the promotion, planning co-ordination and administration of vocational education and training in Victoria.
(b) to provide for the establishment of TAFE colleges as self-governing institutions forming part of the post-secondary education system…
(c) to provide for the establishment or declaration of industry training boards. (d) **to provide for the regulation of apprenticeships and other work place training programs…**
(e) to provide mechanisms for the accreditation of vocational education and training courses provided by TAFE and other persons and bodies

Part 4 – Industrial Training Boards

Functions of the industry training boards

41. (1) the functions of the industry training board established under section 38 (1) (a) are:

(a) to advise the State Training Board about skill requirements for the industry it represents and the training necessary.
(b) to develop period training plans for the industry;
(c) to review and develop existing training programs to determine whether they meet the training and skill requirements of the industry;
(d) to develop and implement strategies to increase the resources that the industry is prepared to commit to training;
(c) to develop and implement strategies that the industry applies equal opportunity principles in training;
(f) to keep under review and advise the Board on preemployment and retraining programs….

CHAPTER 4

Where Did We Fit In?

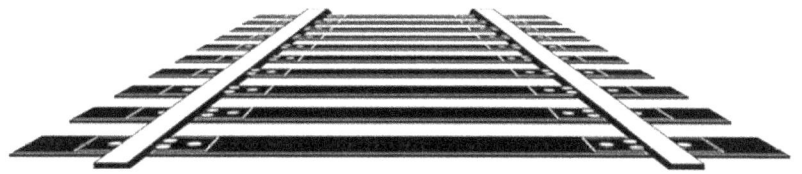

The Training for apprentices in the Victorian Railways has undertaken many changes and parallels economic, and technological changes of the rail transport industry over a hundred years. It also mirrors the social and political times which saw the structure change from a government bureaucracy to a commercial entity. **In 1962 the branches** were designated by activity and hierarchical status: Headed by the Chief Mechanical Engineer, the **Rolling Stock Branch** was responsible for design, construction, operation and maintenance of all locomotives and rolling stock, *including the major workshops and apprentice trade training*.

Electrical Engineering: Chief Electrical Engineer, to manage the suburban railway electrification system, including power supplies to stations. *Including specialist apprentice training for overhead linesmen, and the Caulfield Signal School for electrical fitters (signals).*

Way and Works: headed by Chief Civil Engineer. It constructs and maintains all fixed infrastructure such as track, bridges, stations, signalling and safeworking. *Including apprentice training for electrical fitters and fitters and turners.*

Accountancy: headed by the Controller of Accounts, to record all payments, conduct audits, prepare budgets and pay salaried and daily paid wages to employees.

Commercial: Chief Commercial Manager to set goods rates and passenger fares, solicited for new traffic to rail and prosecute by-law offenders

Refreshment Services: The Superintendent of Refreshment Services, controlled food and bookstore services at stations, managed advertisement at stations as well as the railway bakery, butchery, poultry farm and laundry. Manage the promotion and activities of the Mt Buffalo chalet.

Secretaries: headed by the Secretary of Railways to deal with policy, administration, transport regulation and legal matters.

Stores: headed by Controller of Stores, to receive all incoming stores and materials, and control the railway printing works.

Traffic: Chief Traffic Manager with responsibilities for the operation of all goods and passenger services both on rail and road.

For those who had entered the industry under the Victorian Railway Commissioners the first structural change occurred in **May 1973** with the *Railway (Amendment) Act* that passed the management to a Victorian Railways Board. The Victorian Railways was then rebranded as VicRail. The legislation provided for a seven-man Board consisting of expertise across the rail industry and commercial business. Its first appointee as chairman was A.G. Gibbs, Managing Director of General Motors – Holden Pty. Ltd.

The key branches impacting and responsible for the core trades in 1973 remained the: **Rolling Stock Branch:** responsibilities – workshops, (apprentice manual training centres) engineer of tests, superintendent of loco's, plant engineer, rolling stock engineer and car & wagon maintenance engineer.

VR Apprentice Training - Evolution to economics

Evidence or a paper trail of the overall management of rail apprentices is fleeting to date but the Commissioners always seemed to have oversight and input into the training system from inception around 1905. The then Chairman of Commissioners, Thomas Tait of the Victorian Railway Department and the Council of the Working Men's Collage established a course of technical training for railway apprentices. *(Extract: The Apprentice Training system of the Victorian Railways, O.E. Nilsson)*

Subsequent interventions included the corporatisation of the Victorian Railways with the Commissioners replaced by a Board in 1974. Beyond that restructure it seems reasonable to suggest that the main responsibility and oversight of apprentice training became the province of the Apprentice Advisory Committee. It was historically chaired by a head of branch with a number of deputy heads in support. In separate articles from the *Rail Newsletter* subsequent individuals headed this body over a period of years, including Mr L G David, Alan Firth (1968) and Bill Wilkins (1982). Notwithstanding the day-to-day management of apprentice training remained part of the Rolling Stock Branch key functions until the realignment in 1983 to the Workshops Branch under the State Transport Authority (V/Line).

Regardless of this change, both the Way & Works and Electrical Engineering Branches continued to provide specialist training after the apprentices initial 12 months in the manual skills centres. The Way & Works with turner & fitters and electrical fitters. The EE Branch for apprentice electrical mechanics and electrical fitters 'signalling' at the 'Signals School' at Caulfield and overhead linesmen

Add in the input from the Secretary Branch, later the Recruitment and Employment function of the Personnel Branch as major partners in determining the manpower needs and apprentice selection. This was to evolve again under the Workshop's management structure.

The vacancies advertise for the year 1982 indicates the changing need of the organisation as technology and business needs take on new challenges.

Apprentice country advertisement, locations Ballarat & Bendigo.

In 1982 a report prepared by Recruitment & Employment Section. Personnel Branch detailed the following. Edited extract:

The apprenticeship vacancies for the following trades include; Armature winding (Melbourne only) – Boiler maker (Ballarat & Bendigo) - Car painter (Ballarat & Bendigo) – Coppersmith (Ballarat & Bendigo) – Electrical fitter (signalling) (Melbourne Only) – Electrical fitter (workshops) (all three locations) Electrical instrument maker and /or repairer (Melbourne only) - Electrical mechanic, & fitter & turner (all three locations) – Linesman (Melbourne) – Upholsterer (Ballarat)

The lack of popular trades offered this year, such as carpenters, plumbers, motor mechanics, electrical mechanics and cooks undoubtably had a marked effect on the number of applications received. In 1979 the trades of carpenter and cook attracted 1,000 and 600 applicants respectively. In 1980 the trade of motor mechanic attracted over 650 applicants. The report also noted that other government instrumentalities had seen a decrease in responses to apprentice advertised vacancies. The State Electricity Commission reported a 5% variation in applications. The Gas & Fuel Corporation noted a 5% variation from the preceding year. The Naval dockyards reported a similar response, with the Melbourne Metropolitan Tramway Board at the time of this report neutral, as their quota for electrical fitters was still not filled.

Trade highlights: selected trades.

Armature Winder – to test, repair and overhaul all types of rotary electrical machinery.

Boiler Maker – the construction, alteration and maintenance of diesel locomotives, stainless steel suburban carriages and a variety of railway wagons and vans. Manufacture and erect structural steel railway and highway bridges, overhead and signal structures, steel framed buildings, permanent way and signal material. All types of welding and cutting use modern machinery and techniques.

Fitter & Turner – two grades cover subjects associated with general engineering.

Workshops – training on most types of machines used in the engineering field, fitting steel/stainless steel and assembly work on diesel locomotives, and the suburban and country carriage fleet including goods vans and wagons. Maintenance of equipment associated with workshops in country and metropolitan areas.

Plant – repairs and maintenance of earth moving equipment track equipment, mechanical plant, industrial tractors etc in country & metropolitan areas (apprentices in this grade undergo an additional course to motor mechanics)

Car painter – spray painting, surface preparation and treatment to interiors and exteriors of steel and wooden type of railway carriages, vans and goods wagons.

CHAPTER 5

The Real World – On the job

You may have been part of any of these locations at major workshops or depots or at state wide infrastructure.

The Workshops and other Locations.

The main locations utilised for the metal trades and support trades for on-job training included the **Jolimont Workshops**, Newport Workshops. **Train Lighting Depot**, the North Melbourne Steam Locomotive Depot, **The Rail Motor Depot**, the Victorian Railway Garage, **Electrical Workshops**, Spotswood Workshops, **North Melbourne Workshops** & Steam Locomotive Depot and the **South Dynon Diesel Depot**. Country locations include both **Ballarat** and **Bendigo** workshops and state-wide major locomotive centres. The **Way & Works depots** serviced state wide infrastructure locations. The **Electrical Engineering Branch**, maintained sub-stations, the traction supply system, overhead catenary wires and serviced the station network.

A brief overview of an on-the-job training time blocks.
1961 example – app. electrical mechanic.

Jolimont Workshops	Wall section, electrical unit exchange	Inspection Shop suburban fleet	
Train Lighting Depot	Rail motor section	Motor garage	Country/interstate fleet
Newport Workshops	50 cycle mains installations	50 cycle plant installations	General independent installations
Newport Workshops	Crane maintenance servicing	Wheel Shop/ Foundry & Fabrication Shop section	Wheel Shop/ Foundry & Fabrication Shop section
Electrical Engineering Branch	Flinders Street station section. Princes Bridge major project.	Continued.	Continued.

How do you describe the work places and locations that was the environment where we commenced our on-job training? From July 1960 to mid-1990's the core trades commenced in the manual training centres.

The time and trade dictated the start.

My lot was the Jolimont Workshops. (DENMAN 1961) *'Together with two other young men we were escorted to Jolimont Workshops walking along Batman Avenue from the city to the Workshops.'* Today there are no land marks of that morning walk and the only constant the tidal slurp of the Yarra. Jolimont workshops are long gone and demolished along with major sections of the various rail sidings as part of the state government's Jolimont Decentralisation Project.

The redevelopment of this vast area was to convert the land to public space and a partial roofing of the Flinders Yard. Additional objectives included the construction of the Federation Square, and towards the direction of Richmond a tennis precinct opposite the river.

The Rod Laver Court was completed in 1987.Over succeeding years, the Melbourne Arena Tennis Centre consolidated its primary courts before the transfer by the State Government of 5.5 hectares of the Jolimont railyards to enabled additional facilities and courts.

Back then. Trams from Wattle Park and Burwood ran directly to the City via Batman Avenue. (Today, Batman Avenue extension is linked to Exhibition Street.) The Hurst Bridge and Epping train services terminated at Princes Bridge Station directly opposite St. Pauls Cathedral.

4.1 Jolimont Workshops -The Red Brick Building.

Jolimont Workshops was part of an inner-city rail complex of multiple through running lines and off-peak stabling site for minor servicing, maintenance and cleaning. Approaching Jolimont Workshops my first impression was of a high roofed and large red brick building that dominated the skyline. This brick shed was 109 meters and 122 to 183 metres long depending on the section

Constructed in the style of early 20th century engineering building it had a predominant saw tooth roof structure encompassing the lifting shop within the main building. Adjacent to the lifting shop on the northern side was the Inspection shop, built in the same style with its high saw tooth roof enabling the flow of natural light. Further afield the paint and varnishing bay and towards the Richmond end the carriage wash dock. *My arrival was to commence a yearlong stay. My memory during this period probably needs support but along with two other apprentices, we were inducted into our workplace. After completing the paperwork and armed with my clock number we were provided with a tour of the amenities block, issued a locker and confirmation of the start and finish times. A loose exchange on the whistle sequence was lost in the overpowering works size and noise.*

Be on time and at shift's end. *Whistle one was the signal to stop work and wash up and the second whistle, was to proceed to clock off. My earlier memory was of an orderly line approaching a stampede for position. Then watch on as the workshop population dispersed east and west by either foot, tram or private vehicle.*

The Wall section. *'My start point was the 'wall' section in the lifting shop. The lifting shop and fitting bays were on the northern side of the main building. Each were 183 by 18 meters to accommodate two 25 tonne overhead cranes installed in the lifting bays and two 15 tonne electric cranes in the workshop bay.' 'Here I was introduced to a friendly rotund man in an open grey dusk coat. Don Harris was my first supervisor who quickly related that I would be working with Eric Benaim and would meet the others between breaks or when working with them. Eric explained that he was working on a M(motor) car and we would be replacing the resistance grids and cabling. Shiny in new overalls and clutching a screwdriver and pliers I was a bit taken back as we moved beneath a carriage into a pit. Like all new chums I stood out amongst a workforce who were garbed in all manners of either soiled boiler suits or bib and brace overalls with some preferring jeans and old shirts.' 'Half an hour later and I was in work mode and assisting in unfastening cabling and various clamps and connection points.*

Tait M car Newport Rail Museum, (2022)

The M car's major electrical operating components are the traction motors, compressor, the dynamotor and various grids and resistance banks, utilised as part of the motor speed control. Inside the carriage is the driver's compartment, (designated west end east end) with a feast of gauges and associated equipment including the train control selector, air pressure, and switching for head boards and lighting. Incandescent lights provide lighting in the Tait trains while the Harris trains used fluorescent lighting for commuters to light the way. Top side, on the roof the high voltage power is received via the pantograph to the car. Powered operating doors and air conditioning were years away for the suburban fleet and the commuting public.'

'This is what we did at the 'wall section'. In today's parlance …it was basically unit exchange…defective components previously detected for repair or serviced as part of a programmed 'time' maintenance. In the case of traction motors, they would be sent to the motor section for disassemble and refit. The electrical fitters and armature winders on the mezzanine floor repaired and conditioned compartment parts such as resistor grids, coils, and armatures. All around me the various trades fulfilled the function of maintenance and repair. Aspects of seat and window repair mainly done in situ as well as door replacement or repair. Air systems and piping were similarly repaired or replaced by the fitters. The suburban fleet for our attendance was the wooden body swing door (Dogboxes) converted from *steam hauled carriages built 1n the 19th century and Tait trains (Red Rattlers) similarly converted and built between 1910 -1917. From the mid nineteen fifties the steel bodied blue livery Harris trains began to enter service.'* **Dennis Denman**

Back to school.

'Somehow, I won the lottery and was told my schooling would be at RMIT. That suited me as I lived on the eastern side of the city and had little interest in the extra travel time to the Newport college. I initially attended one day a week and one evening as I had included electronics in my first year.' My subjects included;

Electricity & Magnetism old, Electric Wiring Practice, old,
Electrical Fitting 1 theory, Electrical Fitting 1 Practice, old
Electrical Wiring 1 theory old, Electrical 1 Practice, old
Trade Drawing 11, Electrical fitting 11, Theory and Electrical fitting 11, Practice

'My initial trade training as an electrical mechanic was geared to the basic principles of electrical systems and applications. It was directed to the wider industry and not specific to rail. Among the subject content included basic experiments of magnetism and its relationship to motor operation. Learning Ohms law and Faraday's experiment. The 'wow' of passing a current through a wire and sprinkling iron filings on a sheet of paper held above the wire to see the effects of magnetism. The same effect can be seen by using a magnet beneath a sheet of paper and observing the patten of iron filing around the poles. Other elementary tasks included board work circuits from a single light switch to two-way switching were an extension of electrical practice undertaken at Swinburne Junior Tech in my intermediate year. It was the period of wooden pine blocks, Bakelite switches and fittings, split conduit and rubber insulation, then pvc (polyvinyl chloride) covered wires.

Other tasks involved both T and Y joints of multiple strand copper wires. This task of intertwining wires to enable mechanical strength and electrical conductivity. The T joint involved passing the series of strands through the other wires and then wrapping each single strand around the other to form the T. After completing the joint was soldered to provide added strength and finished with insulation tape. Add in appliance fittings and three pin plugs and the gap between my school activities and rail application widened at every class. All of my peer group at RMIT were employed by private industry.' I was in some ways isolated from those apprentices who commenced in 1961, with my only contact at the work location. The reputation or otherwise of the VR college was never a part of my world.

D.Denman, Electrical Light & Power circuit, RMIT (1961)

'My time at Jolimont was divide into learning blocks in different sections. The wall section, the test section and the inspection shop. These were just the work places but the characters provided the fun.' 'First experiences remain etched in our memories and some of the characters who were our tradesmen (teachers) remain entrenched. Among the long-remembered ones was Jack Owens, the little digger. Jack who knew the trade backwards was a nice counterpoint to most of his peers. Brown as a berry with his rolling's either stuck to his lip or exhaling smoke he epitomised the Australian character from yesteryear. He along with some others were return service men and had fought behind the lines in Borneo and New Guinea. In his early forties he bought to light the real language of the land which today is sadly missed. Terms like, cobber, ridgy-didge, and mate were staples with meaning, having a fag was normal and gidday lighted every greeting.'

Others who made up the section were relatively friendly explaining the works schedule and which union represented them. Some older hands were in the Australian Railway Union while all of the electrical grades were involved with the Electrical Trade Union. As apprentices we were told to consider the ETU later in our time as the main agendas of the day was superannuation, and work conditions. Conditions that were in place for our apprenticeship and a reminder we could not go on strike. The mainstay of the workforce conversations was the government proposal of a service gratuity which amounted to about 5 pounds ($20) a fortnight. This would come at a cost for those who *accepted it as their superannuation units would reduce to 4 units, it was a distracting period for many as they weighed cash in hand against the benefits of the security and regular payments from super.*

The Gallery – where you could always place a bet.

The gallery was a mezzanine floor. It was located along the riverside of the lifting shop and above the motor section, the foreman's office and the welding bays at the Richmond end. This was the motor repair and electrical equipment rehabilitation section, accessed by stairways at each end and the stores lift that combined as the shuttle for large items for repair. Armatures could additionally be lifted to and returned between the gallery and the motor section by a pendent hoist. The talents of armature winders, coil rewinders, electrical fitters and labourers combined at its production centre. Armatures rewound and banded, commutators tested and undercut and balanced. Stator field coils rewound and replaced, brush gear repaired or replaced and tested and assembled. The smell of industry, and the lacquer bath was a distinctive reminder of every visit. The gallery was also the pathway to 'Snowy' the bookmaker who would accept any bet from a shilling (10cents) to a pound ($2). The racing paper ever in view. Snowy was also the short-term money lender for those always short from payday to payday. As the industry was paid fortnightly the lesson of money management was there to see. Another lesson, among the many presented to the new boys. The regulars who were at his door were the ones who might ask for; a couple of bobs (50 cents) till payday, or always botting smokes from their workmates. The 'shops' were as much about its workforce pecking order and the dynamics of each group as it was about the trade.

OWEN WALDIE was to commence his electrical fitting apprenticeship at the 'gallery' after working for a few months as lad trainee. *Owen related that after being accepted as an apprentice in December his mother contacted the 'rail' about some early employment.* Their solution, a couple of months as a lad trainee before commencing his apprenticeship in the coming January. 'I started in the inspection shop pits cleaning the brake dust and grime off insulators under the tail car motors.' It was a shitty job and covered in brake dust most of the time.' Owen was part of the 1961 ball room induction before making his way independently to Jolimont. New day, new role and a change of scenery as he reported to the gallery. The challenges commenced almost immediately as the tradesman he was allocated to barked…take this piece of steel and make a small hammer out of it. It could be filed, ground, cold bent, and drilled. Job done, he explained, *it took a couple of days to make the hammer and taught me lots about steel and its properties. The next period saw endless activities from copper contacts being shaped and fitted to the multiple roles involved in motor component repair, coil and armature winding. The special job for an apprentice was undercutting the commutator segments after a commutator had been cleaned up in the turnery. It involved using a half-length of a hacksaw blade, with one end shaped to a smallish hook to score between each segment.* Yet there was also time for a job for the boss. Owen described, 'my supervisor was a top bloke and this day he asked me to make a camp stretcher out of 1" (25mm) conduit.' 'The design required it to be assembled and disassembled by screwing/unscrewing the sections, portable and naturally, to fit in a car boot. It was a relatively easy job and opened my eyes to the other world of the workshops.' Owen was to follow the block time period for electrical fitter apprentices within Jolimont including the motor and electrical test sections. At this time Freddie Corn was the test electrician responsible for testing all train electrical equipment and components. Owen described the test area. *The set up was a long bench with outlets and test equipment to cater for various low and high voltages. His special toy was a portable set up (trolly) that enabled him to work throughout the shop. Among his tricks for a new apprentice was to have the 'new kid' hold a section of cable and bend it at 180 degrees. This cable was the supply to an incandescent light to which he (Freddie) had a secondary on/off switch. As the apprentice folded the cable in and out Fred would operate his secondary switch out of sight. Lamp on – lamp off. Having previously implied that electricity is similar to water and like a hose bending the cable shut off the power, releasing it enabled electricity to flow. Harmless and other episodes lay in wait.'* Owen remembers his time blocks as an electrical fitter, firstly at Jolimont and later Newport and TLD. He remained at JWS for the first two years with his time divided between the gallery, wall section, motor section and a period in the inspection shop.

A brief overview of an on-the-job training time blocks.
1961 example – app. electrical fitter.

Jolimont Workshops	Gallery section	Gallery section	Electrical testing Wall section, electrical unit exchange
Jolimont Workshops	Traction motor section	Inspection Shop suburban fleet	Inspection Shop suburban fleet
Newport Workshops	Plant Shop	Wheel Shop/ Foundry & Fabrication shop section	Car electricians/ Harris trains
Newport Workshops	Turnery section	Turnery section	Drawing office
Train Lighting Depot	Shop maintenance	Country/interstate fleet	Country/interstate fleet

In the gallery section learning all aspects of repairing traction motor components. He described the motorised hoist delivery system that enabled an armature secured in a purpose-built cradle. Alternatively, the stores lift enabled movement between floors. In the motor section he assisted a tradesman in stripping out component parts after testing. Armatures for the lift to the gallery where the cycle of repair would commence. Banding cut and removed, armature commutators skimmed and undercut, wedges replaced in positioning coils and leads resoldered. His skill set increasing at every stage.

The Inspection Shop - Getting my hands dirty

DENMAN. *A half year into my time and the Inspection shop and the rail yards became my play yard. Recalled with a smile it was about a different type of freedom within the work day. The inspection shop was mainly about periodic set exams and minor maintenance. The reported inspection frequency of the suburban units generally was; Tait trains every 5600 kilometres and Harris units 15000 kilometres. General checks in the yard during off peak periods should be at intervals of every 2 days for the Tait trains and every 4 days for the Harris trains. This was my learning curve about the industry and train operations and where our work matched the 'service' needs.*

The minutiae of train maintenance swung between same, same and different, from pantograph pan replacement to traction motor commutator cleaning and brushes to be checked or replaced. Ideal work for an apprentice, me, squatting in a grubby pit to hold an emery stick over a turning commutator. Seating new brushes required a dab hand ignoring the dust and carbon residue. Welcome to respirators and safety goggles.

Approach to the Lift Shop, Jolimont Workshops (O.Waldie collection)

Playing trains, peak and off peak.

In layman's terms the suburban rail operations of the day operate around two peak periods, the morning peak and the evening peak. One peak brings the population into the city and beyond on linking lines. The other, the evening peak is the reverse with the population for their return journey. But it is in the off-peak period and layover of the fleet that is the window for repairs, maintenance and cleaning. Repairs in situ and programmed maintenance in the inspection shop. And the inner-city yards at the time combined designated locations for the off-peak stabling of trains from the Epping and Hurst Bridge lines, other lines for the Jolimont yards and the Flinders Street yards. This great swathe of land comprising some 33 hectares was situated between the eastern section of the CBD and the Yarra River. Bounded by Wellington Parade, Jolimont Road South, Swan Street, and Batman Avenue. This location and all its surrounding rail yard were the major hub of suburban rial operations working. The yards were about adventure and 'finds' for that part of the workforce who undertook the response to the drivers and guards' reports left in each cab. The yard approaching the period of the off peak was a steady stream of both trains and personnel. Drivers and guards completing their stabling protocols and returning to the nearby Electric Running Depot. (ERD). And a steady stream of maintenance and cleaning staff accessing the units. This environment was part of the on-job-training.

Don't do that...

Ignorant in the ways of men but more to the point my attempted assistance to an equally young car & wagon builder. Who would have guessed that the head of a screw had meaning other than to lock a fitting and for its release? Under the 'shops' agreement a 'Phillips' head screw was the domain of a C&W builder or upholsterer and a single slot head the domain of electrical & fitting staff. Years later I was to learn about another 'shops agreement' of a maximum number of refits/rebuilds of traction motors for a shift. A quota system apparently fixed by a management/union agreement in some distant past. For the electrical fitter apprentices doing 'time' in the motor section; a fleeting example of culture or 'how we do thing here.'

Seek and Find - A workforce of scavengers

I quickly learned why the morning peak was so anticipated: it was a race to find the booty left behind. Competitiveness between the drivers and various trades were good-hearted and shared. The morning papers first – the Argus, the Age and the Herald or Sun – followed by the commuter's memory losses on a wide range including, umbrellas, bags of all sorts, books, and sunglasses. Items that may have been located by station staff and sent to lost property.

Time lined by some years and after completing his twelve months at the training centre, **NORM SWANWICK** was appointed to the Rolling Stock Branch and followed the pathway to the Jolimont Workshops. This was Norm's on-job-training introduction to suburban train maintenance and where he remained for the next 12 – 18 months.

Employee, time clock at workshop locations (Newport Rail Museum)

NORM SWANWICK, *I remember the sign on clock which had a large rotating arm with holes around the circumference. You lined the arm up with the hole indicating your staff number and punched it. There was a character who would come in and punch a whole stack of numbers no matter if they were in or not. At shift end the workforce lined up to use the same time clocks (2 in number) much like a sheep run, the image of the jostling and rush to depart the premises at day's end remains a distant but clear memory. (A similar timeclock is held as part of exhibits at the Newport Railway Museum at North Williamstown) I can remember working in the lift shop where, in the morning we would climb into the pits below the carriages to carry out maintenance on the various relays and electrical equipment. In the afternoons we would all climb up into the carriages for an afternoon nap or play cards. The foreman was aware of the practice and on occasion join us.*

Later groups that followed to Jolimont Workshops would have little or no memory of the 'red rattlers' and Tait trains.

Tait train shuttle, St. Kilda Line, circa 1968

Depending on the timeline of their apprenticeship work placement they would see the Harris trains being taken from the suburban system and replaced first by the Hitachi stainless steel trains over the period from 1972 to 1981 to be followed by the Comeng trains for the next two decades

Twenty years later 1981.

Coined over the years as an eyesore on the city the Jolimont railyards had been the focus of succeeding governments. In 1981 a report commissioned by the Railway Board was submitted. Undertaken by Transmark, a Transport Systems & Market Research Limited, London. *(Source Victorian State Library)*

The report recommended a four-year timetable to decentralise the inner-city stabling yards and maintenance facilities to outer locations. The freeing up of significant lands in this location would enable both commercial opportunities and land for public use. They concluded the most cost-effective outcome were to replace facilities elsewhere for stabling and maintenance and to realign the running tracks through the centre into a group of four. The locations recommended initially for maintenance depots include Epping, Newport and McCauley.

A new name for an essential service. (*VicRail News Aug. 1982*) **The Metropolitan Train Maintenance Depot at Jolimont**, formally the electric suburban train depot has 150 passenger trains in its care. 600 employees in six areas of operation – inspection, lifting, car & paint shops, the washing plant and the yard. The consist is 7 Comeng, 61 Hitachi, 55 Harris and 31 Tait trains.

Epping Depot was opened in 1990 as a replacement for Jolimont workshops as other depot locations were selected to support eastern and south eastern corridors. The Epping depot was designed with a main workshop building, four elevated tracks, two lifting tracks and a train wash to accommodate 31 trains. The depot and rail sidings cover an area of 10.8 hectares to accommodate the northern rail group. Over an extended period of relocation, the workshops (JWS) finally closed in April 1993. Track and overhead were removed by late 1993 with the workshop demolition approved the following year (May 1994) and the Inspection and Paint Shops by August.

5.2 Train Lighting Deport – The Large Tin Shed.

Described by others as next door to the Shelter Shed at West Melbourne

In an earlier article in the *Feb. 1949 News Letter*. TLD staff, electrical and gas fitters replace globes and mantles maintain wiring and conduits in good order, replace belts and repair generators, keep batteries charged and replace gas cylinders, buffet car refrigeration checked and topped up. Putting a light in a carriage is simple – apply a torch to the mantle or through a switch. Batteries are changed out every 2 years, stripped renovated, filled with fresh acid and charged.

D DENMAN recollects. *Year two commenced with my transfer to TLD the new designate for the West Melbourne Car shed. At the time under the management of the Train Lighting Inspector and a staff of electrical mechanics, electrical fitters, gas fitters and undergear repairers, battery repairers and cleaners. It was the service and maintenance location for the interstate and country carriages between rail operations. The depots layout was the offices/administration and a small equipment repair workshop and an adjacent battery room where all sorts of activities occurred at each shift. Initially I was supporting the electrical maintenance of the railmotors that were part of a satellite depot stationed at Spencer Street. This was the service and fuelling centre for the Walker Rail Motors or Diesel Electric Rail Motors (DERM) bought to fulfil the Bolte Government decision to upgrade the service for commuters on country branch lines. Purchased from England in 1948 with additions over the period to 1965. The car bodies were built locally by Martin & Kings and assembled at the Newport Workshops. My recall for the period was changing defective lamps and small wiring replacement work with regular checks on the 24-volt battery units and belt driven generators. Away in the distance was the North Melbourne Steam Locomotive depot with the now diminishing fleet of engines. Within a few short years that depot would be demolished and the steam engine and all its support trades would disappear from sight.*

Within the shed. *The best way to describe the work environment of the carriage roofed section at TLDs (circa 1960) is to imagine a large tin shed open at one end with a series of dedicated tracks from the Spencer Street yard ending at the point of Adderley Street along Dudley Street. Facing the station, possibly 10 roads were roofed with corrugated iron with clear sections at intervals for natural light. Each road had wooden plank decking with access to airlines, water and electrical power services. The floor level was at door height of a carriage or train when docked with access to undergear, electrical equipment and power jumper cables between carriages. The shed was not only aged but years of pigeon shit graced every rafter and the smell of excrement and grime was part of every road. Long before the use of sullage tanks most country train toilets vented to the track. Although regularly cleaned this was long before the introduction of the Health & Safety Act. My time was linked in learning the regular carriage exam requirements and associated electrical equipment of this new world of intestate and country carriage sets.*

Train Lighting Depot, inside the Carriage Depot, circa 1950

Usually, we would meet the interstate trains at either platform 1 or 2 depending on its arrival from either Sydney or Adelaide. In shunting mode, we would ride the Adelaide (as an example) back to depot for an early sight of the conductor's report or fault report. Compartment lights were an easy fix, so to an urn which would be a unit exchange with repairs done at the depot. The testing of thermostats for the heating and cooling of the carriages were the bane of the electrical staff life. It was during this period that I began to observe the odd pressure of business and coping mechanisms. Always an exception, but this group were diligent in completing the exams and other cyclic work. An "A" exam would detail a full inspection and test operation sequence, plus cleaning all copper contacts, check and relace copper braids and all fuses. Most were conscientious but a couple would regularly do little more than a cursory check and close the panel. The comment, 'it's working now why cause problem's'. Around us the depot yards were a scene of continuous movement as country trains were positioned for cleaning and servicing and others prepared for departure. Mostly the AE and BE wooden body country car categories that were all powered/lighted by batteries. Similar to a motor car's electrical system of a battery linked generator or alternator. The AE, BE carriages were supplied from a battery system supported by a belt driven generator from the wheel axle. Replacing belts were a daily event. Also, part of the fleet was steel bodied AZ and BZ carriages with different configuration including air-conditioning. Rail safety was learned by rote, a disc staked at the end of a road and a red flag clearly visible on the leading carriage indicated work in progress. Frequent stories of staff working under a carriage would jump as a nudge on the carriage and moments later the air system surging. Shunters had removed the disc and flag and coupled the engine before checking - all was clear.

So, the saying went - Just like a welder, a shunter was an electrician with his brains kicked out.

H cars utilised on country services, TLD. (O.Waldie collection)

Not all about trains. TLD (1962)

The overall manager by memory was Mr. J Deacon, but a more memorable character had taken me under his wing. His name was Neil McMillian and he was one of the electrical supervisors. Gowned in the garb of most supervisors, the traditional grey dustcoat belted at the waist. Neil was of middle height, in his early forties with mischievous eyes. Combining both a wry sense of humour and electrical nous, I was to learn a lot about this part of the industry and other life lessons he felt necessary as part of my training. Electrical fault finding was Mac's forte.

Working with different tradesmen, Neil over saw a variety of my work experiences and watched as the temptations for my age group progressed. As may be inferred by the time the number of the fairer sex visible in the industry was minimal, or not in the workshops other than canteen workers and the nurse. Certainly, women were employed in the typing pools at Head Office and a few station staff but beyond that invisible. Not so at the depot, or adjacent to – female refreshment staff were on most buffet cars on most country services. It was here on the Taggerty normally part of the 12 noon Melbourne - Bendigo service that Neil put me to the sword. Beneath a veil of his pipe smoke, he introduced me to all the female buffet staff with the promise, that I was available; if they had any needs.

Red was the colour of my ears and else ware as I was assuredly out of my depth. Fast tracked to the meal room and over cards would be the stories of both country and interstate travel experiences. Here amid the food of choice the stories unfolded between the travelling electrical and depot staff. If there was a hierarchy of sorts it was only about take-home pay. The travelling show had the bonus of shift and travelling allowances that made for a healthy income and appreciably more than the depot supervisors. Add in any late running and cream was added to the cake. Stories abound on the produce returning from these layover country locations from fresh eggs to ham on the bone and even a live piglet. The Victorian train crew stayed at Junee locomotive depot, while the travelling electrician rode further into NSW at Harden. This was the produce centre and another insight into the business of transport and variations.

The other pea position was the travelling staff for the commissioners or state car used for regular tours or ceremonial visits. The State Governor at this time was Sir Dallas Brooks followed by Sir Rohan Delacombe from May 1963. The key positions of commissioners' driver, guard, conductor and electrician elevated these individuals above the masses and a degree of recognition. The state car was old world opulence with a combination of high white ornate ceilings, richly timbered surfaces and warn leather upholstered seating, add to the décor, Queen Anne chairs and plush velvet curtains which complimented both status and comfort. Modern electrical services were also available from constant upgrades. Whether true or a mischievous snippet provided high mirth at our meal table. An apparent complaint was that the toilet rolls had been placed incorrectly. 'Dear boy' someone mimicked, 'everyone knows you roll from the top; not the bottom.'

Unrelated to his time as an apprentice, decades later **OWEN WALDIE** in his role as Train Lighting Inspector (management role) suppressed a grin as he followed up our chat…diverging from the State car electrical circuitry to toilet rolls. *He recalls that on a past royal visit, (Charles & Diana) according to rumour, an unknown assailant had written some uncomplimentary commentary on the royal roll. As relayed to Owen this blaggard had hidden his message well within the sheets. Years later on*

Owen's watch, Elizabeth 11 again graced Victoria. Prior to departure from the then Spencer Street station, he was under a 'head office' directive to have a supervisor stand guard and have the 'roll' inserted just prior to their arrival.
(State car 5) **Another State secret at last revealed.**

Owen's time block at TLD was initially in the depot workshops were all of the minor country car repairs were undertaken. This includes repairs to electrical equipment on the contactor boards and underfloor generators. Belt driven from a wheel drive they were a constant source of work. The depot had a small works inventory from kitchen equipment from the buffet cars and urns and lighting units from the *Overland* carriages. His memory includes the layout of the depot and surrounds that included the adjacent battery repair workshops where the lead acid batteries were stripped and disassembled for repair. The roofed section of this tin shed was the stabling section for the *Overland* and some country services. The roads facing the depot were open to the elements and never lost the smell of shit. The other key services included the laundry nestled beside the *Overland* stabling. Towards West Melbourne along the line of Dudley Street were the bakery and butchery. It was the nerve centre of the interstate and country rail services.

Owen was possibly the last of the 'old school' electrical fitter apprentices who did not attend the manual training centre full time. He was to attend the VR college, one day a week for the first three years of his apprentices. He revealed his skill sessions on the 'block' was one half day a week for half a year at the fitting shop.

Others followed with some variation on their 'time based' adventure.

NORM SWANWICK was now in the third year of his electrical fitting apprenticeship. He continued *'During the past two years of on-job-training we would periodically return to both the technical college and the manual training centre to further our knowledge and skills.' 'At some stage during my training, I was located at TLD in Dudley Street, West Melbourne. Four of us, all railway apprentices (Brian, Keith, Ian and myself) decided to share a flat. At the train lighting depot, we would undertake maintenance work on the VR passenger rolling stock. Part of our duties was to accompany a tradesman on the Spirit of Progress and the Inter-capital daylight express as train electricians. We would travel from Melbourne to Harden and back monitoring the power van, air conditioning and if we wanted free eats, helping the dining car crew by washing dishes and emptying the bins etc. The dining car crew would change at Junee and we would continue to Harden arriving about 3.30 pm where an NSW electrician would take over. There was a large railway barracks at Harden where we would get some sleep and be up at 2.00 am to catch the 'Spirit' back to Melbourne.'*

This was the real world of rail operations rather than the static repairs, refits and overhaul of units.

Pre, 1962 – Board gauge.

The two Sydney – Melbourne inter-capital trains were flagships for the rail industry and their respective communities. The *Inter-capital daylight* was a day service between the cities commencing in 1956 and completed its last service in 1991. As a shared service of the NSW and Victorian rail systems terminating at Albury. The Victorian train consist was air-conditioned S and Z cars, including a buffet car and hauled by a B class locomotive.

The NSW train consist air-conditioned RUB carriage sets hauled by a 42-class locomotive. During the seventies the NSW 422 class and the Victorian X and S class shared the workload.

The *Spirit of Progress* was the vanguard of rail services between the two State capitals, Melbourne – Sydney. Commencing in 1937 the 'Spirit' provided the service between Melbourne and Albury where commuters changed for the Sydney link on the Melbourne Limited Express.

Design and innovation-source, *(extract of Wikipedia)*. The train featured many innovations new or recently introduced to Australian railways. Stream lining, full air-conditioning and all steel carriages. Its interior featured art-deco style and internal fittings such as stainless steel and Australian blackwood veneers. It also provided a dining car with a modern kitchen and parlour/observation car. Hauled by a stream lined S class steam locomotive it had an enviable reputation for speed and comfort. The innovation detailed additionally provides a snapshot of the support trades and their apprentices into the skill base in different and newer technologies and materials. Coal burning steam locomotives were not part of the future.

Post 1962 - Standard gauge between the capitals

In a new age for inter-capital travel the *Southern Aurora* became the principal passenger service between Sydney and Melbourne providing a nightly sleeper service in each direction. The 'Aurora' commenced in April 1962 with a consist of stainless-steel carriages jointly purchased by the NSW and Victorian government railways. Though spectacular its life span was relatively short and due to declining patronage, it was combined with the Spirit of Progress and the Southern Aurora into one service around late 1986 – the *Sydney – Melbourne Express*. By 1993 the *XPT* was the only main line train between these capitals.

5.3 Ballarat North Workshops.

Ballarat the location renowned along with the City of Bendigo as part of Victoria's golden age and the site of Eureka uprising. Preceding the Bendigo workshops by a few months, the Ballarat workshops undertook work that paralleled the work undertaken by Bendigo. Its main work during the steam period would have included the repairs and maintenance of wagons and locomotives. It was to mirror the steam locomotive construction program of Bendigo pre-ceding the 1919 – 1922 period. It was the time of high grain harvest movement and goods and freight haulage that was to continue into the late seventies.

Ballarat North Workshops, circa 1950

During this timeline as the ratio of employees to work declined so to the employment of apprentices. Previous periods had seen Victorian Railway apprentices undertaking their schooling locally at the Ballarat Junior Technical school, this included blacksmiths, coppersmiths, car painting, electrical fitting, boiler making, and spring making. (*Victorian collection.net.au. Federation University archives*) As late as 1981 the following intake of apprentices were advertised in the Ballarat Courier and the Bendigo Advertiser. Vacancies in boiler maker, electrical fitters and fitters and turners, a lesser number is available in the following trades, electrical mechanics, car painters, (Bendigo and Ballarat only) upholsterers (Ballarat only) and coppersmiths. **New challenges**. The Workshops Board Meeting in February 1986 confirmed the Workshops Division is undertaking substantial change in its organisation to become an autonomous commercial and modern engineering organisation supplying V/Line & Metrail as well as tendering in the open market.

The Ballarat Nth. Workshops primary roles will be the overhaul of V/lines carriages, steel fabrication, wagon construction and general engineering for TOD, the MET and Workshops. The *STA Journal October 1986* records The Rolling Stock assembly line is geared up for a 200-wagon production run costing $15M, all designed by V/line. The workshops at Ballarat are turning out, 56 tonne bogie bottom discharge wagons every other day. The labour force of fabricators & boilermakers, fitters, blacksmiths, coppersmiths & other trades have been essential to this success. Economics and service delivery contracts became the final factors of outsourcing the rail fleet maintenance and privatisation.

5.4   Bendigo Workshops.

Bendigo workshops was another integral part of the rail fleets construction and servicing. Initially a 10.3-hectare site with 31 buildings with its centre piece a 10,000 square Workshops building. History recalls that its main work was repairs and maintenance to existing wagons and locomotives, including building thirteen new steam locomotives in the 1919 – 1922 period. With the entry of diesel from the mid 1950's the workshops undertook a program of scrapping and cutting up redundant steam locomotives. Its activities were to fluctuate as political and business needs clashed as work passes to VLX louvered van construction and supply chain items including spring manufacture, construction of stainless steel footwarmers and electric train pantograph assembly. With the 1980 restructure the workshops passed to the State Transport Authority and consequently the Workshops Division. **Bendigo Workshops** activities will be wagon and diesel railcar maintenance with some capacity for electrical and commercial work. The engineering report to the Workshops Board Meeting in June 1992 detailed in part, the high pressure VPCX walkway modifications has been accelerated with 36 completed. The Sprinter car bogies for Goninan's have scheduling completed, material received at 90% and 80% of jigging completed. Its years of local employment including the training of apprentice continued to decline through the decades of the seventies and into the nineties until privatisation.

5.5   Electrical Workshops Spencer Street.

Specialising in major maintenance and repair the Electrical Workshops 'A' occupied a major area of Spencer Street, north of the station complex. A multi-level building it shared space with an annex occupied by workshops 'B' for the Way & Works. Workshops 'B' housed the major repair centre, ranging from electric signals and points equipment to the locksmiths. Workshops 'A' was utilised for the repair and maintenance of the substation generators and ancillary equipment including signalling infrastructure.

This was to become the next 'home' for second year electrical fitter **HARRY STEVENS** after his first year at the Newport training centre. **Harry** voiced his settling in period and on job work types.

Initially I did small jobs which included dismantling small electric motors to repair and in some cases to rewind armatures. The larger rotary convertors and traction motors for the diesel electric locomotives (B & S class) on failure were sent over from South Dynon and dismantled on the lower floor and the armatures lifted to the upper floor for repair. In some ways the work was a little repetitive and the occasions when we serviced the lifts at Head Office at 67 Spencer Street was a great distraction. I had always wanted to be an engine driver but my eyesight was not up to scratch. The next best was diesel maintainer and that's where I saw my future. I spent the rest of my apprenticeship at workshops 'A' with periods of freedom doing onsite maintenance at various distribution sub stations located along the rail network. The major electric traction substation was on the Richmond side of the Jolimont Workshops.

It was possibly a 2250 kW British Westinghouse rotary converter and transformer. I was to see the last of the mercury arc rectifiers before the introduction of the first semiconductor rectifier years before his transfer. Harry related that this transfer was another 'rail' story. *A year after I had completed my apprenticeship, I had on numerous times requested a transfer to the South Dynon Locomotive Depot as a diesel maintainer. The sequence of responses in the negative was on-going until I found a vacancy for the position, duel advertised in the Weekly Notice and the Melbourne Age. Applying via this media enabled an interview to state my case. Whether by perseverance or my skill set, one of the few inter branch transfer came through. I was to settle in and continue my career as a diesel maintainer till retirement. A dirty job but with ample overtime, lots of clean money.* The Electrical Workshops were later relocated to Spotswood as part of the Spencer Street station services upgrades.

5.5.1 Electrical Engineering/Overhead Depot & Power Operation room – Batman Avenue. 1964.

The E.E. Branch depot and POE room were located on the second floor building overlooking Batman Avenue at the city end. Positioned between the Electric Running depot for drivers and guards it was also the supervisory centre for the metropolitan electrical maintenance work force. The POE room controlled the 20,000-volt SEC supply and 1500-volt dc traction system sub stations and signalling supply. In 1981, this site was utilised for Metol as part of the train control upgrade with the opening of the Melbourne underground loop. All these facilities were later relocated to Transport House in 1993 to enable the construction of Flinders Street Square and the JDP decentralisation project. Electrical mechanics and overhead linesmen were key personnel in maintaining High voltage train and 240-volt station supply systems. In *Aug.1981 the VicRail News* reported the completion of a new linesmen school at Port Melbourne. An apprentice linesman spends the first two years of their work experience with the Light & Power division and the final two of their 4-year apprenticeship with the Overhead division. They learn, safe maintenance procedures of high-tension 1500-volt power. They additionally attend the State Electrical Commission's high voltage training school at Chadstone.

5.6 South Dynon Diesel Maintenance Locomotive Depot.

Purpose built for the servicing of diesel and electric locomotives the depot was opened in July 1961. Set in the area west of the 'salty creek' the new depot is adjacent the South Dynon Carriage Shed that serviced the standard gauge interstate trains of the day. The inner workings include drop pits to facilitate bogie and traction motor repairs. The depot has the capacity to perform all major repairs and maintenance for the fleet. *Wikipedia* lists the following diesel /electric locomotives for broad gauge running; B class (1952 -1982) C class (1977 -1995) F class (1951 – 1987) H class (1968 – (1999). The format of rail working saw two major turn tables and feeder lines between through running and the depot. Outside the western end (Footscray Road) was the fuel point and annex housing the fitter foremen and running shed supervisor who collectively deal with arriving engines for fuelling and repairs. The depot maintained and serviced the motive fleet as the impact of operational practices impacted freight and passenger trains. The complex was later acquired by Freight Victoria in May 1999 with the sale of V/line Freight, but remained a VicTrack asset. Further commercial acquisitions were to occur.

VicRail "B" class loco, Intercity service, circa 1981

5.7 Spotswood Workshops.

Spotswood Workshops, built on a triangle of land squeezed between the Williamstown Beach line and Williamstown Road was an important cog in rail maintenance. This acreage also contained the main store's location and the material reclamation area. Historically the Way & Works branch workshops were an amalgamation of the shops at Spencer Street and Arden Street. A dividing road separates the workshops into the woodworking shops and the mechanical or metal working. In distant years the spread of manufacturing from the woodworking section ranged from building furniture to buffet stops. Items like, gang boards, hand trucks, wheel barrows, ticket cabinets and office furniture. The mechanical section function was to repair everything in metal work which Newport workshops does not make. From the section comes heavy duty equipment such as; locomotive turntables, water cranes, bridge girders, signal masts and fish plates. Smaller but equally essential repairs and re-conditioning of picks, shovels, dog lifters automatic staff interlocking machines. Electrical repair includes switch boards to electro-mechanical signalling apparatus. (*Extract: Jack of all trades at Spotswood Shops, pg. 40*)

Another story submitted for **KEITH SMITH** and found online is a selection of memories and stories working at the Spotswood Railway Workshops.

1944. **KEITH** commences with: *My story starts in Sale, Gippsland at the Sale technical school. The second world war was still ongoing and there was no work in Sale so on the woodwork teacher's advice I applied to the Victorian Railways to be a 'wood work apprentice' based at Spotswood workshops. It was difficult decision for me to apply for the position as I would have to find accommodation in the Williamstown area and leave my home town of Sale. They wanted 113 apprentices that year of various trades, only three positions were offered in woodwork, as the standard of applicants was so high, they actually selected five and I was one of them. Starting real work was a shock to the system, meeting so many people was quite a change from school life in Sale. It was very demanding, long days at work and study as well. Working hours were from 07.20 to 5.08 daily. I had just turned 16 and Melbourne was a strange place for me to find myself, so different from my country hometown. I thought school work was finished, but soon found out it was just starting, one afternoon per week at Newport college and two evenings per week at Melbourne Technical College. This went on for two years and if you failed a subject at Newport College you had to do a repeat course at Melbourne Tech. in the following year at your own expense.*

The problem *with the woodwork course was the apprentice carpenters and joiners had to be their own tools. Due to WW2, they were very hard to find and expensive to buy. The training was intensive and well rounded, three months cycling through the following four areas, saw doctor, front office with an architect and head office at spencer street. I believe we were the best tradesmen around. Of the starting 113 apprentices, 16 moved into teaching at technical schools. My first-year salary was 17/6 (shillings and pence) per week and we were given a living away from home allowance taking a total weekly pay to 40 shillings or 4 pounds. Equivalent estimate $50. Accommodation (including meals) in Williamstown cost 35 shillings per week, so I was left with little spending money.*

In an article titled *'Tradesmen of the Future,'* from the *Victorian Railways News* in November 1949. An edited extract of apprentices and their work locations: the first two years of an apprentice's course is the testing time. By his third year he has settled down as his trade skills unfold. On a visit to the electrical shop at Spotswood we meet **GEORGE SAYER**, 17, a 2nd -year apprentice. He is convinced he could not find a better place to learn his trade. In the same shop **DON MCKENZIE**, a 1st year electrical fitter apprentice following in his dad's footsteps. His father is the fitter in charge. Along with other lads the two boys learning to be electrical fitters are set mechanical exercises as part of their work. They are taught telephone work, signal and safeworking instruments, locking devices and low voltage circuits. They are also shown how to detect wiring faults and to operate lathe, grinding and drilling machines.

Three down, two to go. In his third year of the course the apprentices are given outside experience with time in the drawing office at the Spencer Street Head Office. With continued varied equipment exposure to rail maintenance on completion of their time they are fully fledged electrical fitters. At the Newport Workshops **HARRY HEARSE**, 17 is a 1st year apprentice boiler maker commencing his apprenticeship at the Boiler Shop. Harry has found plenty of interest in the boiler shop where the range of work extends from the smallest bracket to the biggest bridges and water tanks. He is assisting in the building of the overhead structures for the electrification schemes. Most of the trades are represented at Newport which absorbs three-fifths of the yearly intake. A high light of the training scheme is one day a week release for three or four months for manual trade skills. It is claimed the development of hand skill is accelerated with the benefits to the apprentice and the industry. In the various shops in which apprentices are being trained at Newport and Spotswood efficiency is a by-word.

SCOTT GOULD started his apprenticeship in 1988 as an electrical fitter, signals and maintenance and after his twelve months in the manual training centre recalls his time at the Caulfield Signal School. *Here I worked and learned signal specific equipment and fault-finding operations. My workplace time blocks included periods at the Adderley Street workshops fitting two-way radios to M cars and overhauling 1500-volt DC circuit breakers and signalling relays. At Spotswood workshops my training included armature winding, motor overhaul and making up locomotive jumper cables.* He recalls, *at 'Spotty' a period when the tradies were on strike, but the labourers were still there and a couple of them thought it would be great fun to put the crane hook through the back of my overalls and hoist me up.* Scott was awarded a first and third place in the apprentice of the year competition for signals maintenance…the highly valued jig-saw puzzle medallions for the Victorian Railways.

The closure of Spotswood Workshops became the result of the rail workshops rationalisation and privatisation.

5.8   Newport Workshops – A City Within a City.

> *'Newport Workshops was a melting pot of humanity, politics and religion or race bigots, money lenders and nut cases complimenting great blokes and personalities for the trade and life'.* **TONY DAVIS 1960**

Foreigners Of All Kinds. The location where a foreigner was not about race or emigrants but a huge resource to make or repair anything from shaping the heads of a car engine to a 21st key. **If you were in the know, how to get a 21st key;** find a contact to pass you along the line. Have a **key** cast in brass at the foundry, then filed and cleaned before chrome plated at the plating shop. The key was then buffed and polished and finally finished in a stained timber plaque or box, preferably made in the pattern shop.

THE REAL WORLD – ON THE JOB

Let's walk in the shoes of two young men and see the Victorian Railways through the smoke and residue of the mainly coal fired steam engine locations. **RON LITTLE**, born 1922, App. Fitter & Turner and **DONALD CAMERON**, Apprentice Boilermaker born the same year. For our insight into the workshops, Ron and Donald's most probable destination was Newport workshops located in the wedge of land that resembled a triangle from Newport station and bordered on the western side by the Werribee/Geelong rail corridor and on the eastern side by the Williamstown Beach line. This triangle of land had its base as Champion Road from the North Williamstown Station to the western rail crossing. Arriving on the 'shops train' at the workshops platform they would have immediately been confronted by the towering clock tower and the administration centre of the largest rail workshops in the Southern Hemisphere. The spill of the 'shops' throng as they bustled to the layout of their particular workplace. The greeting of workmates and the rush from the platform as they cleared the space to let those in the trailing carriages emerge. Ron may have been directed to either the Turnery or Plant shop and Donald most probably to the Fabrication or Boiler shop.

Clocktower & Administration NWS, circa 2022

At either location they would have been confronted with the noise and theatre of industry. Within their eyeline would be the industry of steam locomotives, wooden body carriages and mainly open body wagons. This period was pre-WW2 and by their apprenticeship end would have seen the workshops undertake munitions and hardware manufacture. Let's start apprentice Ron Little in the turnery. Newport was a combination of sensory extremes as the rail industry began each day. From the West Block could be heard the steady rhythm of the drop hammers as they forged axles. Entry to the turnery would see rows of lathes in all manner of cutting and turning jobs as spirals of steel fell to a steady flow of cutting compound. Beneath their feet as in most shops were the original teak blocks, a testament to past years. White painted lines defined the walkways and work areas. Beyond the East Block the heat and smell of the foundry could be felt from its doorway. The production of brake blocks a daily production run. Nearer to the Williamstown Beach line, the business of the Erecting and Fabrication shop, including wagon builds to bridge construction. This was a world of welding flashes and deafening air purpose rivet guns demanded ear and eye protections. In other main shops the world of locomotive repair and heavy maintenance were primary activities. Designated by their work type, every shop supported every aspect of carriage builds and refits from updates of external paint to seat upholstered replacement. The builds of C class and K class steam locomotives to the modified N class 2-8-2 and later the X class design bringing the rapid changes that bought the rolling stock into currency of similar major railways

Newport Workshops, outline and workshops – 1985 layout.
Where every location is on the map.

1 – Blacksmith's extension
2 – Spring shop
3 – Blacksmith's shop
4 – Diesel engine rebuilds
5 – Fitting shop
6 – Copper shop
7 – Tool room
8 – Vehicle maintenance shop
9 – Machine shop
10 – Machine shop extension
11 – Motor garage
12 – Plant shop
13 – Stores
14 – Management/Office (clock tower)
15 – Weighbridge
16 – Turntable
17 – Store
18 – Bulk store
19 – Loco load test
20 – Casualty room
21 – Garden
22 – Paint shop
23 – Upholsterers
24 – Spray paint shop
25 – Under floor wheel lathe
26 – Car & wagon shop
27 – Car shop
28 – Store
29 – Saw mill
30 – Transport office
31 – Timber store
32 – Timber shed
33 – Car fitting shop
34 – Plating shop
35 – Canteen
36 – Laboratory
37
38 – Radioactive store
39 – Way & Works branch
40 – Pattern shop
41 – Foundry
42 - Fitters & Welders
43 – Amenities
44 – Bearing wash
45 – Wheel shop
46 – Locomotive shop
47 – Roller bearing shop
48 – Stores gantry
49 – Canteen
50 – Mech apprentice training centre
51 – Elec, training centre
52 - Boilermakers training centre
53 – Administration office
54 – Structural fabrication shop
55 – ARHS railway museum
56 - Tarpaulin shop
57 – Canteen.

Newport Workshops from – North Williamstown Station

| Wheel shop | Boiler/fabrication shop |

East Block

Saw mill	Car fitting shop
Car & Wagon shop	Car shop store
Tarp shop	Car shop
	Upholsterers
Paint shop – 2 roads	

| Clock tower
Administration – Drawing Office | General stores | Plant shop |

West Block.

Machine shop	Machine shop extension	Motor garage
Vehicle maintenance shop	Tool Room	Copper shop
Diesel engine rebuild shop Blacksmith shop	Fitting shop	
Spring shop	Blacksmith extension Drop hammer & Forge	

Others eyes described the workshops. **JOHN MONKS,** October 1936, 16 years old writes about his impressions in a section of *Eddie Butler- Brown's – In the Service. A History of Victorian Railway Workers and their Unions. (State Library of Victoria collection).* Newport workshops – It had two passenger stations for its employers. It had at least four trains in and out each day. There were car shops for building carriages, a truck shop for wagons, a bush mill to cut whole logs into usable billets of timber. Billets were transferred to large drying and seasoning sheds or sent to the sawmill to be cut down. Newport also had a Paint Shop for painting carriages *and wagons etc…the Erecting shop was where steam locomotives were built and repaired, a Boiler shop for boilers and locomotive construction. Nearer Champion Road was the foundry for casting engine parts to brake blocks and the Tarpaulin shop where sailmakers used rows of heavy sowing machines to shape tarps for the open wagon fleet. A Bolt shop for the manufacture of dog's spikes alongside the Blacksmiths and Spring shop, the home of the large drop hammers and stamping hammers. Outside in all-weather the shunting engines and tractors pulled or pushed completed or partially finished rolling stock between shops for either the next phase or completion.*

RON LITTLE AND DONALD CAMERON, on selection for an apprenticeship would follow the pathway of welcome and induction. They have been told about the apprentice's school and where to report for their first day on the job. Consider the average age for acceptance was about 15 then these young men may have commenced their apprenticeship in the years of 1936/37. Surmising that they lived in Melbourne's suburbs they would freely associate with the wooden bodied red rattlers on the suburban rail system. If they had arrived from the 'bush' they would have arrived at Spencer Street station by a steam locomotive hauled engine in the comfort of either ABE or BVE sitting carriages

Ron & Don's story continued. Rail lines leading to nearly every workshop, Newport was a flurry of activity as builds, next generation updates and refits continued on plan. The original site extended to 160 acres (approximately, 65 hectares) and was slowly reduced in later years by economic drivers and rail transport needs. Yet at the time of our two nominees' arrival the layout was entrenched. The site was set out along the line of a military camp. If you take a mid-point of champion road between Nth Williamstown Station and the Werribee/Geelong line crossing the facing buildings have been separated into the East Block and West Block. North of the West block towards Newport is the tarpaulin shop and the additional 'shops' platform. All the main buildings are cavernous structures with high saw tooth roof construction that enables natural light to fill the buildings. This design is repeated to the other core buildings including the wheel shop, boiler/fabricating shop, the foundry and pattern making shops. But we are not quite done as the precinct also includes a garage, wash dock, stabling yards, canteen/cafeteria and the railway testing laboratory. Under the control of the Engineer of Tests this laboratory was fully equipped with testing apparatus for chemical, metallurgical and physical examination. These two young men as they approach the administration centre may be momentarily lost in a workforce of approximately 3000. Whether their day one was in the Turnery or the Plant shop or the Fabrication shop is conjecture.

Many trades and the past by record.

The ground rules set by Commonwealth Acts provided the framework for those earlier apprentices in their indentures, trade training and pay and conditions among the key points. **The Apprenticeship Act 1928.** Both Ron and Don would have seen the workshops move into war production during their time.

APPRENTICE TO THE RAIL

WW2. Railway at war, source *VR Newsletter September 1954*, listed some of the Newport workshop's contribution to the war effort…it was considerable ranging from surgical equipment to armament. 400, 000 designed, forged and production tooling of forceps, scissors to needle holders and mouth gags

Seven hundred (700) complete fuselages for Beauford bombers, eight ocean going tug boats, dimensions 73 feet long, (22.2 metres) 18 feet wide (5.68 metres) and 17 feet (5.18metres) keel to deck beam. Munitions, nearly 1Million, 3.7-inch anti-aircraft shells. 25,000 vehicle covers, 2087 tents and 279 large marquees,

For many, that period can only be viewed as a historic period of national and international tragedy. The work of the rail industry and its workshops workforce continued supporting the war. Apprentices included.

Add some years and the pathway continues. 1946 and apprentice fitter and turner, **NEIL HARRIS** recalls in a segment of Nick Anchen's, *'Life on the Victorian Railways'. After graduating from Melbourne's Newport Workshops, he transferred to the busy Seymour Depot, where he spent the remainder of his twenty-year railway career. "I joined the Victorian Railways in 1946 at Newport workshops, and commenced a five-year apprenticeship as a fitter and turner. It was a very thorough apprenticeship and upon competition you were expected to be able to think for yourself. This was further accentuated in the country depots, as things often came up that were out of the ordinary." His story at Seymour enables us to share brief aspects of the industry and the relationship between the maintainer and operations. Post apprenticeship and his first job was… "On my first day at Seymour, the foremen, Arthur Eaton, said to me 'Neil there's a centre piston on the 'S' class wants a new set of rings, off you go'. "So, I went underneath and pulled it to bits and fitted the rings, which was very awkward. You had to knock out a gudgeon pin and move the piston forward, then reach over the sway beam to access the piston. What a bastard of a job! We had to look after the four S class locos, as well as 49 other locos, all with just twelve fitters – we never lifted our heads. The locos we had in 1951 included D's, K's, N's and later J's and Rs arrived."*

JOE SIBBERAS *in the…ARU Gazette. I went straight from school to the railways in 1948, starting as a lad labourer at North Melbourne before getting an apprenticeship. Within the workshops there was a real hierarchy and we were all terrified of the foremen; they had unlimited power. Next were the leading hand and then the tradesmen, trade assistants, labourers and right at the bottom…the apprentice.*

A.J CLARKE *in an article for the Australian Railway Historical Bulletin, Feb 1996, writes of his Reminiscences of An Apprentice at the Victorian Railways' Newport Workshops 1959-1963*

In part…*I applied for and after fronting an interview panel was accepted as an apprentice fitter and turner being one of 221 appointed to the various trades out of nearly 650 applicants. These workshops, when I joined, still employed about 3,000 people but the sad decline of the establishment was evident. I was assigned to the fitting shop behind the west block under two men who had regularly repaired and maintained X class (2-8-2) steam locomotives. The Newport Workshops gave me an impression of size and age. Most shops had wooden floors. The Fitting Shop was laid like sleepers, whilst others used blocks or cobbles. My training continues…I spent three or four months in the*

Fitting Shop. one job that seemed endless was tapping out turn buckles after they had been zinc platted. Another task was pushing case hardening bushes into diverse plates and links. Sometimes before doing this, the holes may have to be broached (cleared or enlarged) to enable the bush to fit snugly…to the east, the shop next door was the Copper Shop where the coppersmiths and sheet metal workers plied their trade. The next bay west of us was the Oxy Shop where the boilermakers cut steel out for components for the adjacent Preparations Shop who were preparing parts for the converted wagons being assembled in the nearby Steel Construction Shop. Towards the middle of 1959, I received my orders to commence the next stage of my training in the Erecting Shop.

West Block overhead of Steam Rail fleet, circa unknown.

An on-the-job training time blocks. 1958, example – app. turner & fitter.

Newport Workshops	Brake Shop	Turnery
Newport Workshops	Erecting Shop	Erecting Shop
Newport Workshops	Boiler Shop	Drawing office
Newport Workshops	Roller bearing Shop	Railmotor Shop
Newport Workshops	Turnery	Tool room

TONY DAVIS - Newport Workshops. *Every day when we arrived, we went to the token board. This board had individual round numbered discs that was the indicator to the office that we were on the job. Each employee removed his token from the board and would replace it at shifts end. Larger than a penny and twice as heavy it became the employee identifier for all the daily paid workforce at Newport. If you were late or forgot to pick it up you had to go to the pay office. Three times in a month and you would receive a note warning of a fine. Like every location lining up to replace your token at night was a mad rush and jostle to get a seat on the first departing shops train. Another version of time keeping (Jolimont punch clock) with a weekly time card to be handed to your supervisor. Each work allocation in theory had a job number that working hours were booked against.*

Paydays were paid fortnightly and long before direct debit to personal accounts. We lined up outside the foremen's office to receive a small metal tin with your pay (cash in notes and coins) in it. You had to count and confirm the correct amount against your pay slip in front of a supervisor before handing back the tin.

Employee token system, Newport Workshops.

Merry Go Round, apprentice fitter & turner style.

TONY now finds himself at the **Erecting Shop.** *I suppose the 'Sheep trucks' became the business at hand. We were doing brake repairs, triple valve replacement, hoses, piston repairs/greasing and checking for the sliding door ease of movement. We were working outside on the tracks leading to the shop beside the shunting yard. Out in the cold during winter weather with a small humpy to shelter in if it rained. Here we kept our basic fitting tools and oxy-acetylene plant. Part of a team, occasionally we had to wait for the coppersmiths to move the branch pipe from the train line to the triple valve to enable the brake system to be tested for leaks. It was an experience with slip shunting occurring in the adjacent goods yard with reputedly a constant stream of complaints by the nearest locals over the crashing of trucks and the exhaust made by the T class locomotives. The down side working under sheep trucks is you got covered in dried sheep shit. Upside if any; was the payment of a 'dirty work allowance.' Other works included the GY and RY wagons, scraping white metal axle bearings, checking and repairing brakers, latches, tarp poles and W beam guardrails.*

Blue trains program. *My timing was good as the new blue suburban train carriages were being built. The underframe, sides and ends were manufactured in the UK by the Glostershire Railway Carriage and Wagon Company and later Martin & Kings. Transported to the workshops in large wooden boxes on flat trucks. A large group of labourers used flogging hammers to break the boxes open. In the process large amounts of asbestos dust flew into the air. No personal protection was given and years later I was tested for signs of ingestion. After unboxing the steel sections were positioned on jigs to enable assembly. Boiler makers welded the sections together. Our fitter's work* was to drill and tap various parts that had to be bolted to the frames and position air lines and ancillary systems. These Harris units were major works of the shops. Tony recalls; some other 'funny goings on' including the day the boilermaker supervisor was standing beside the workshops manager when a wag snuck up behind him and painted his boots with white marking out paint. How much did he win for his bet was never known.

Note: 1962 saw the first 5 trains of a second group of blue trains completed at Newport and in service. Thirty additional Harris trains entered service between 1961 and 1971.

TONY'S next location was the **Boiler Shop.** 'My work on various wagons was varied from general repairs to fuel tank wagons that belonged to the oil companies. These wagons had to steam cleaned inside the tank before positioned into the shops.' Another dirty job. 'The bulk cement wagons were brought into the workshop because of problems with the aeration mechanism at the base of the hopper. This mechanism had four segments of cone shaped bronze plates that formed the enclosed cone. This cone had small holes in them to enable the 75-psi air pressure to force the cement to be discharged. Where excess moisture got into the cement it reacted to block the discharge mechanism. Our work was to clear and clean the bronze plates mechanism. It was a messy job. Spillage was fair game, some of it left the premises in a few blokes' kitbags.'

Now at another on-job work location, the **Roller Bearing Shop.** 'This was the best place to work as the building was heated when I completed my next stint during the winter months. It was very clean and I enjoyed the blokes I worked with. The fitter I worked with was a good bloke and teacher. Helpful when we fitted SKF spherical bearings onto axles. He had also been a home guard in the UK during WW2. The team included a fitter's assistant who related he had a bottle of stout and a bag of cashew nuts after every evening meal. They were great characters.'

A moment of excitement – on this occasion the fitter that Tony was working with had scraped some white metal bearings for a DERM axle boxes. On fitting the DERM was to complete a test run before going into service. This 'run' was normally on the Altona line and they decided to take in some different scenery. 'It was an opportunity for a joy ride. Much to our embarrassment after half an hour we had a 'hot box' on one of our bearings, returning to the shops long after knock off time'. The following day the shit hit the fan but other than a verbal caution it was soon forgotten.

DENMAN 1963. 'Locations for my on-job training could roll of my tongue as I handed my papers to the office clerk. Like the army of apprentices before and others to follow the pathway for apprentices was seemingly known to a few but not the apprentice. A view possibly clouded by time, but movement between depots or locations came by a memo of transfer. Certainly, in my case I have no recollection of any individual mapping out my program as an apprentice electrical mechanic or the reasons of this 'time-based location' against another, hence the merry go round. Others including Tony Davis (Fitter & Turner) clearly had a program in various shops. My objective from day one, though not at times understood by the 'hierarchy' was to qualify for the 'A; grade licence issued by the State Electricity Commission. Only speculation on my part but other electrical mechanics in the Rolling Stock Branch may have similar experiences.'

If so, get in line. O.E Nilsson in his 1927 conference paper detailed the following. **Practical training in the workshops** – the details of the method adopted for the practical training of apprentices in the various workshops <u>does not fall within the scope of this paper</u>, but it may be stated that the lads are given opportunity to obtain a wide experience and to learn their trade thoroughly. In the case of Newport Workshops all apprentice fitters and turners come under the special care of the assistant workshops manager who keeps a record of the location of each lad and it is his duty to see that each apprentice is moved around the various departments throughout the term of his apprenticeship. He also selects lads who receive good reports from college and shows ability for special work in the tool room, maintenance department and local drawing offices. The foreman in charge of a department is responsible for the training of apprentices in the work connected to a particular shop. He generally puts a lad in charge of a competent leading hand to supervise his work. In the case of apprentice fitters & turners the recommended time in each shop – Engine Construction Shop, 6 months; Engine Repair Shop, 6 months; motion benches, 3 months; axle boxes and wheels, 3 months; Brake Shop, 6 months; Lock Shop, 3 months; Car and Wagon Shop, 3 months; Machine Shop (milling, turning, slotting, shaping), 30 months. Total time – 5 years.

DENMAN *The merry go round moved me around. Jolimont Workshops, the Railway garage, in Batman Avenue (before relocation), the North Melbourne Steam Locomotive Depot, the Rail Motor Depot in the Spencer Street yard and the Train Lighting Depot. (Previously the West Melbourne car shed)*

Two years down and three to go.

The Plant repair shop was at the southern end of the large building that enclosed the two levels of the main store area. Unique to my recent work places was the absence of rail lines converging into this building. Not a carriage or wheel in sight. This large rectangular area was divided by a central wall of lockers, providing the working areas for the mechanical fitting and electrical staff. The hierarchy for electrical staff was Senior Forman James Riley and Ron Feigan. The two fitter foremen were George Smith and Len Smith (no relation) reporting to the Plant Manager or Engineer. My work for the period of the next 24 month included stints in the progression of the 50-cycle electrical replacement program.

Ongoing for some years, the steady progression of mains and sub-switchboards first and then replacing the overhead lighting with now gas -discharged halogen lamps. Followed item by item of plant from a machine lathe to a wood planing machine. Progress from shop to shop of these conversions enabled the wider view of this other city. The Turnery, Paint Shop roads, the Upholsterers, the Tarp Shop as the program extended to all parts of the workshops

That year passed relatively quickly *with the 50-cycle conversion program the major experience. The shop workforce was a wide group of nationalities with my peer group mostly Australian and the labourers and trade assistants mostly southern European. The mix was soon to change. Once more new work types and experiences confronted me as I was used through different roles suitable for a 3rd and 4th year apprentices. From the early* *period when you have limited skills and know how you build your knowledge through a combination of repetitive work and the explanation of those about you. Theory merges in job applications with anyone from a supervisor to a trade's assistant, many who had mastered the job from observation and repetition. Soon paired with Alfred Pugh we continued the rewiring and installation of main and secondary circuits. Alf or 'Gramps' as I called him was a warm friendly personality, below medium height with thinning hair and for his size strong as a bull. His favourite lunch time or gone-missing activity was sun bathing which was a bolt hole on the West Block roof above the garage.*

Working on heavy installations my pathway involved new skills in managing heights, ladder use, and handling 4-inch (100mm) water pipe. They were convinced I needed building some muscle. On-going for some years our work moved between the shops as the conversion program anticipating the 25-cycle closure. In the timber dressing shop, mains and switchboards first and then relacing the overhead lighting. Every light point required a new circuit. Industry circuits of the day were enclosed in steel conduit and most lengths had to be cut and threaded by hand. Swinging a pipe threader soon added the muscle they continually reminded me I lacked. The physical aspects of installations were demanding with circuits at roof height demanding grunt and smarts. The mains water pipe (cable protection) was lifted into position manually from ground to roof level and often using block and tackles or chain blocks. From the turnery to the timber shop the program rolled out. In the timber shop every machine prior to the 50-cycle conversion had been driven by a discrete belt system located below floor level powered by a number of large 25-cycle motors. Unlike any previous experience I seemed to have strayed back in time forgetting I had replaced minor circuits and lamps on a steam locomotive.

Team Work

The team work between the fitters and electrical staff in relocating planers, saws and every type of wood machining equipment was apparent even with the odd disparaging remarks. Sawdust exhaust systems included. Every machine now positioned to best impact production or work flows – change was ever present.

The VR Newsletter July, 1964 detailed

Good progress has been made in the conversion of the departments power supply system from 25 – to 50 cycle frequency. To date, more than half the obsolete 25-cycle substation plant has been replaced and augmented by modern 50-cycle plant. So far, the savings made by the conversion amount to 88,000 pounds (estimated $250,000) a year.

A similar program followed in the turnery as once more the 50-cycle mains proceeded the machine shop requirements as individual lathes, drilling machines and milling machines were changed over with minimal production loss. Ladders and heights were to become second nature. Our next location the Tarp Shop to commence the overhead lighting and sowing machine change over. Tarpaulins for open wagons were still a major part of goods and freight. Security lighting was another variation to these activities located external to the buildings. The latter circuitry was undertaken at the ladders end. I was now proficient at ladder carrying and handling. The balance point of an eight-foot extension took a little practice but could be added to the list.

Settling in over this long year had seen the odd pranks and disagreements between others usually about the pay packet. Overtime was available to a core group who carried the load. Some aspects of major installations and maintenance could only be done outside of production times. Saturdays at time and a half or double time was to be fought over. No issues here as apprentices in the first four years were not in the race. My time was to continue with periods in the wheel shop maintenance and the crane section before independent work in both minor lighting and machine installations to fault finding. During this period, I completed my apprentice course requirements at RMIT and commenced other courses of interest.

Something new - Cyclic Maintenance

Most of the following year I had stints in maintenance by working with teams dedicated to cyclic maintenance and breakdowns. With Alex Kelso on overhead and gantry crane maintenance and John Richards (Nigger) in the wheel shop section, the learning curve continued. Cyclic maintenance enabled working through the operator's lunch break as a straight shift so was highly desirable. Our responsibilities combined pendent operated cranes to driver operated in various shops or gantries utilised for steel and stores supply in all-weather environments. The team was one tradesman, Alex, an apprentice me, and a fitter's mate. This period combined aspects of monkey scaling (steel rung access ladders) to the overhead crane's cab and surfaces and the use of a chain lift when a motor was replaced on failure. It was a team effort between us and the fitters. It was the period when trade demarcation ruled on paper but give and take on the floor. Working on break downs usually combined a dedicated fitter and electrical staff for the key components of production.

Lifting crane NWS (Steam Rail 2022)

The wheel lathe, the foundry and the boiler and fabrication shop. each important in their role. I soon had an appreciating of the impact of down time. The failure of a skip hoist in the foundry could lead to loss of metal in a pour. The foundry's key role was the manufacture of brake blocks and other cast iron job fittings. Our two priorities were the magnetic lifting crane and the skip hoists. Attending the skip in summer was a journey into hell with the combined heat from the foundry maxing the ambient temperature. Beyond the foundry and pattern shop was the boiler shop. My first experience at the door of the Boiler/Erecting shop was an assault on the senses, the noise of rattle guns, the smell of burning coke and red-hot rivets being tossed, add arc flashes and it was welcome to heavy industry. At this time major bridge spans were under construction.

Independent work. *This was the next learning phase when teamed with another apprentice. My partner was Len Hanrahan. We were easily discernible by size and physique. Len a bantam weight to my light middle weight, we soon found common factors both Ballarat born and both with quirky senses of humour. Len was an a-typical country apprentice who boarded in town and returned to Ballarat to his beloved MG, TC model. Len who had attained his licence immediately at age 18 was driving a 1948 Peugeot 203 for his daily and weekend commutes. His interest and spare time totally devoted to rebuilding and enhancing his sports MG. My licence and car ownership were still years away. At lighter moments he could when prompted state the sequence of meals that were provided each night* *and never varied. Each team or tradesmen involved in circuit installation was allocated a portable bench. Len and I were to share our unit. Think the size of a student desk on wheels, reinforce the top surface and at one end fit a pipe vice and at its side about centre a four-inch (100 mm) jaw bench vice. Add a secure drawer and this was the base for our portable modus operandi. The other material/personal mode of transport was the battery truck; used mostly for material movement but at times for exhilarating racing.*

Transportation, Newport Workshops style, circa 1947

These battery trucks resembled a modern golf buggy with a flatbed tray. These units enabled heavy items and motors to be moved easily and quickly to every shop. Easy to drive with a central arm replacing a steering wheel and foot-controlled power, they provide as much entertainment as transport. Our early roles were all basic light and power 240-volt circuits in offices and lighting in various settings. Memorable among them was replacing incandescence lamps with fluorescent lighting in sections of the canteen and adjacent storage areas. We worked well together and had completed the circuitry running and clipping the relatively new TPS cable. Although relatively hot in the ceiling recess, Len was in the ceiling and about to feed cable down for connection. I was standing on a set of steps having secured the fitting in place. Our drama commenced with a sort of cry of disbelief as Len's foot suddenly appeared through the plaster. He hung on for dear life as we secured the situation and rescue. Overbalancing he had lost his footing on the bearers and ceiling supports. A day later with the ceiling repaired we lighted up our first independent circuit in the glare of the fluorescence. We were a good team and more adventures where to unfold.

Not on my play list.

I readily accepted the local frivolity, such as sending a lad for a population key and the occasional smaller sized apprentice being locked in his locker. The act of light-hearted buggery, or as they referred to it; a daisy chain or simulated doggy-style sex amusement was not on my playlist. Woe beholds the innocent inadvertently bent over a workbench or similar. In a twinkling a few smirking men were nose to tail, grinning and laughing in this choreographed dance. It seemed to be a Plant Shop thing and out of sight or ignored by the office. My one experience of someone's indiscretion concluded with my swinging hammer missing his head before taking out a door window pane as he ran for his pride. It was a simple message for personal space and privacy. Many years before workplace policies were enforced

An embarrassing moment, one among many.

Ladders were to bring about another self-inflicted minor disaster. Ladders were a normal part of our working life and I had mastered carrying and operating a 13 ft extension ladder about 8 feet before extension. At the time ladders used for electrical work were made of timber without a metal strengthening wire along its length. On this particular day the team of apprentices Denman and Hanrahan were installing a watchman's security light on the side of the famed water tower near the Champion Road main exit/entrance. Rising above the line of the distant clock tower the water tower is circular and sits above the several storeys of a store section. the lower section to about 10 metres is a brick outer-casing with the steel water tank atop. To fix the aerial connection I had positioned a ladder on the rounded surface of the tower and after drilling the fixing holes bounced the top of the ladder to another position. Obviously because of the surface I could not tie the ladder off and Len had momentarily moved from 'footing' the ladder. Gravity and other factors came together as the ladder slipped out at the feet and I rode the 'horse' to the ground. Totally out of control as to have both hands free, I had interlocked one leg through the rungs while standing on the next but two rung. Fortunately, I survived without any personal damage, so too Len and the ladder and associate equipment. (**Denman**)

OWEN WALDIE. His Newport time block commenced at the Plant shop before moving between the Car Electricians' section to the Turnery and the Drawing Office. His work in the Plant shop included AC motor repair and the cycle of the various maintenance sections. At the car electricians the Harris car wiring program was in full swing. He quickly learnt to read a print and schematic diagrams as the program completed both motor and the passenger carriage units. PVC cables of every size and voltage rating were part of this complex operation. He recalled Ron Milne as the supervisor and his day-to-day energy.

The Turnery was different in every way with his skills now returned to production work. With set pieces of machine operation including lathe and milling his work involved turning and shaping white metal bearings. *Owen related…I had the opportunity to work afternoon shifts and appreciated the extra allowances and take-home pay.*

Radial drill Newport Workshops Turnery, circa 1950

TONY DAVIS ... *when I went into the Machine Shop on my first rotation, I was told to look for the big spider in the saw tooth roof. For the innocent apprentice it could be seen as a spider but it could also be interpreted as a naked female lying on her back with her knees drawn up with legs apart. Her breasts were the spider's eyes. This image had been drawn by the gantry crane operator. Highly skilled they would manoeuvrer heavy machine parts and axles into position to enable the different work functions to be completed. It was a great experience to learn the different machine and lathe operations on large components of the industry.*

Tool room...my time in the tool room coincided with the introduction of the metric system. one job was the making a number of 12mm socket heads cap screws. This involved machining the blanks from stock round by turning the shank, cap and the hexagon recess for the hexagon punch. With interesting work around, I was fascinated by the 'old timer' who designed the dies for the press. All he received from the Drawing Office was a rough sketch of the component and the dimensions. That was enough for him to make a model on sheet metal in the shape of the die before the finished product. He was extremely talented and willing to share and show each apprentice – the process.

THE REAL WORLD – ON THE JOB

White-collar time.

OWEN WALDIE shared his memory of his time in the Newport drawing office. *He recalled, my main role was to visit all the various offices and check off the date of all production drawing.* He related that every item for manufacture from a bolt and nut pairing to the component parts of a bogie had been drawn and registered. Additionally, every carriage and locomotive had detailed schematic and layout prints of electrical circuitry, and mechanical and air systems. In Owen's period, blue prints were a fact. This involved using a cyanotype process involving a light sensitive chemical reaction that produced a negative image on paper. *One of my first jobs was to draw a mechanical part. It was a reversing arm from a 'W' class diesel/hydraulic shunting locomotive. I had to freehand the part and then provide a detailed plan and elevation including all relevant measurements. It was a foundation moment and taught me the skills of perspective and form. It was an easy job after the grime of the workplace and was the beginning of my understanding the importance of accurate drawings and circuitry prints.*

Some years earlier the tasks associated with the Drawing Office was part of the memories of another apprentice. **TONY DAVIS** continues. *Situated in the Clock Tower the Drawing Office had an extensive range of blueprints and drawings going back to the 1800's. I remember sorting through a stack of these to find drawing to enable some specific parts to be manufactured in the workshops. Once I found what I was looking for I had to make an A4 tracing paper copy to be forwarded to the shop. we had occasional visits from the workshop mechanical engineer. His use of foul language always created a topic of conversation among the staff. Another occasional visitor was the workshops manager (Mr R. Roach) seeking the progress of drawings required for major builds. This was an enjoyable period and I learnt a lot about the link of essential drawings to manufacture and the need of updates and amendments to accommodate the process of production. All to be noted above the main title block for reference.*

Back to the Machine shop. *In 1962 before I finished my time, I was doing general centre lathe work and was offered a position as a diesel fitter at the Dynon Workshops…I declined. Some week later, I accepted an offer to work in the* **Tool Room**. *It was the type of work that I was interested in and my old boss was the supervisor. The work in the tool room also fitted my night school studies at Caulfield tech, including subjects in metallurgy, engineering and machine tool operation. The tool room provided a lot of interesting work for hand and machine skills, such as; scrapping the surface of 18-inch (300mm) cast iron surface plates against a master plate and straight edges, to cleaning and adjusting micrometre callipers to read zero on the graduations. Another operation was operating a Bridgeport horizontal milling machine. This was to gang mill the serrations on a crankshaft main bearing caps for the GM diesel engines. I was to work on one of the first Sheraton centre lathes. It had a direct gear drive from the motor to the headstock gear box and was exceedingly noisy.my work here was turning high steel carbon steel studs used in the gear box of the M class hydraulic shunter locomotives. I completed my time in. the tool room and after a 10-year period, with stints as a supervisor in the Boiler Shop resigned to join the Education Department.* Tony resigned in 1978

NORM SWANWICK *after his allocated time at Jolimont continues – it was back to Newport. During this period, I decided to move back home and travelled each day from Geelong. We only paid quarter fare for our train travel and on holidays we were given free travel. At Newport I moved around between the various workshops spending a few* *months in each. I especially remember working in the east block wheel shop where the electric diesels were maintained. The cabs would be partly lifted above the bogies and we would have to crawl between the two to disconnect the bogie motors from the main body of the engine. It was dirty work, for which we paid a dirt allowance and claustrophobic to boot. The tradesman I worked with we called Mama Cass. He was a big Slavic guy who grunted and growled at you. You kept hoping that the drivers cab would not slip and crush you under it. I was glad the day came when I moved on to my next section. Some of the other shops I worked in included the Plant Shop carrying out routine electrical maintenance and the Drawing Office where I spent most of the day wandering around the various shops looking for drawings long lost and never to be found.* **Final year as an apprenticeship.** *After the Train Lighting Depot, I then returned to Newport Workshops and in 1969. I was selected as the outstanding apprentice in the Victorian Railways for 1968. At the apprentice week awards night, I received a medallion from the Governor of Victoria. I completed my apprenticeship in January 1971 and was transferred back to TLD and a month later left to commence an electronic engineering traineeship with the Department of Defence. Some great friendships and fond memories of the best years of my working life.* Norm resigned in February 1971.

Outstanding Apprentice Award (VR electrical fitter) Norm Swanwick, 1968

Times dictate the view. It is difficult to underscore particular functions as of greater value than others but within Newport's Shops some specific functions and machines were standouts, once more the times dictate the view. The conversion of the 25 to 50 cycle programs as an essential supply in the modernisation of all electrical machinery and equipment. The foundry with production of brake blocks (long before disc braking systems) the wheel shop and the wheel lathe, gantry cranes and overhead lift cranes essential for the positioning of steel, to carriage and locomotive refits and repairs. In 1984 the following report detailed … a major upgrade of the foundry operation recommends the replacement of the coke fired furnaces with electric induction furnaces. The primary function remains the production of iron brake blocks – freight wagons and locomotives. Further upgrades include the replacement of hand operated moulding machines to automatic systems enabling a reduction of foundry employees from 70 to near 40. Other initiatives of V/Line commenced with a $110M locomotive build and refurbishing program. The business was rapidly changing and different and newer skills demanded.

THE REAL WORLD – ON THE JOB

Headlined as – Workshops – Where now.? Extract from an article by *Ann DePaul for the State Transport Authority Staff Newsletter*

V/Lines workshop strategy was born in 1986 – a vital step in the Authority's development and the future of Victoria's rail transport – it's a fact of life that greater efficiency and modern methods reduce costs. To exist as a viable operator competing with other organisations, V/Line must streamline its operations and adapt to the changing needs of its customers. Changes must be made to the way the workshops operate as the government could no longer sustain the losses incurred over the past years. The changes will see a replacement of the wooden bodied non-airconditioned carriages with a smaller fleet of cool steel bodied cars. The wagon fleet has reduced from 20,000 mostly 4 -wheel vehicles to 5,000 bogie vehicles. Larger main -line locomotive numbers will be reduced for smaller types to enable greater usage and flexibility of the fleet. The 130-page report looked at the future fleet size and the projected workshops role as primarily heavy overhauls, such as component reconditioning and manufacturing. The Workshops Business Plan forecast up to 5 years recommended a capital investment of $15m and progressive reduction in labour costs. Manpower to be reduced from 2190 in July,1987 to 1473 over this period. The Newport workshops will be rationalised and concentrate activities on the eastern side of the site. Work undertaken there will include steel fabrication, the foundry, rolling stock wheel and axle reconditioning including rail carriages bogie overalls and collision damage and repairs for the MTA.

STUART SMITHWICK commenced his apprenticeship in 1985 as a Turner & Fitter with V/line at Newport and continued employment with Clyde/Downer Group after privatisation.

The final stage was the privatisation program that contracted the key component of rail maintenance and repair to Evans Deakin Industries EDI. (2000). EDI was later purchased by the Downer Engineering group.

Report of the National Trust of Australia – Newport Workshops site. (Douglas Hill 1993) extract. The historic Newport railway buildings are unsuited to current operational needs of the PTC. In recent years they have been progressively phased out. The fronting to Power Street has been passed to the Urban Development Authority for housing development. The recommendation that the East block be allocated to the railway museum and the west block provided for the railway preservation group such as Steam Rail.

DENMAN. *After completing the third and fourth year of my apprenticeship at Newport workshops my final year was the Electrical Engineering Branch.*

5.8 Electrical Engineering Branch.

My time at the Electrical Engineering Branch was my final year, 1965. My pathway was along Batman Avenue to the central office that shared the building with the Overhead Depot and the Power Operations (PO) section. This was the control and monitoring centre for all the SEC 22,000-volt sub stations and 1500-volt suburban rail power distribution. Captured within an area that held the Electrical Running depot (drivers and guards) and maintenance fitters, it was a busy hub of rail working.

My introduction was basic and confirmation of what we do in this branch. Once more I arrived at a location better prepared for the trade and for change. The bonus, another year of electrical installations and equipment designated by the SEC as practical experience towards the 'A' grade licence. Within the hour I had met the leading hand, Barry Ely and issued with a leather linesmen's bag for my tools. Unlike the plant shop we carried our tools on our shoulder. He explained I would be working in the Flinders Street Station section and their priority the Princes Gate project. Its first phase completed and opened by Premier Bolt in June of 1964. We proceeded via the crew paths that led to the east end of the station and over the concourse to platform no1. This group of trade and apprentice's primary role were electrical installations, repair and replacement to all levels of the station, its platforms, the ERD and surrounds.

Billeted in a box.

To my surprise, the first image confronting me was my new amenities block, a large dated portable wooden building in the dimness of the Princes Bridge overhang. Measuring approximately 10 metres x 4 metres. Beyond the doorway was a meal table and lockers down each side for about 10 individuals, and yes it included a hand basin and running water. The standard pie warmer and urn shares the end shelf…this was home. The priority as previously mentioned was the provision of temporary lighting and power circuits for station working as the project progressed. My partner for the majority of the year was Bill Howard, an ex-Kiwi with previous experience in the commercial building industry. Bill who had in past years held a contractor's licence, sagely marked that the term 'wire jerker' was commonly used by the building industry for an electrician and the variety of work in this section would be less than at the Newport workshops. He was spot on.

Our work life could be hanging off ladders, steps or portable work platforms. The variety from office power points, ceiling fans to clogged pumps in the underground test pits. PVC cabling and plastic conduits now the norm replacing split and steel conduits in suitable locations.

What came over you?

I was in away paraded before the foreman on a misconduct charge. My story was simple. Over a period of some weeks our little amenities area tucked under the bridge overhang had become unacceptable from the point of cleanliness. I had previously advised that this was unhygienic and suggested that the MCC Health Department should be contacted. Granted one of the labourers cleaned once a day and emptied the bins but the presence of rats was visible. Unfortunately, a few local apprentices continued to throw food scraps about and when requested to clean up their mess responded poorly. 'Piss of Denman, you are only on loan'. Stepping away from my normal persona I suggested, 'If you wouldn't do it at home don't fucking do it here.' I ducked a swinging fist and might have run him into a locker with a head lock. On explanation my foreman was not happy and said he would consider my early return to my home branch. So be it. No winners, I waited out a week as my combatant was relocated to another section. There was no interaction, with or from the supervisor of apprentices, so the incident must have been locally labelled closed. The place was cleaner and the rats under control as we set up a 240-volt bare wire trap that fried them on contact overnight. The potential of a fire was never considered, with another version of the Pied Piper.

The year raced to a conclusion with endless 6 -day weeks with the occasional seven. Money was to be made and overtime plentiful. A working week might be replacing platform information board lamps to installations at the Drivers & Guards Depot and the continual temporary supply circuits for Princes Gate. I got to know every level of the Flinders Street Station building and all its many platforms from the St Kilda and Port Melbourne lines (light rail from 1987) to the milk dock at the western end of platform No 1. Hidden above the operations function of the station platforms was the home of the Victorian Railway Institute and many of its services. These included class rooms for station and guard safeworking briefs, the substantial lending and technical library, the gymnasium and the snooker/billiards tables. It was a hive of activity for members social and sporting activities. With branches at major country cities, it was a haven for many rail employees on relief duties or transfers. In the east the skyline was being interrupted as the two multi-story towers soared skyward, later to be known as the Gas & Fuel buildings. A year to celebrate, my 21st and the looming conclusion of my five -year apprenticeship. {Denman1965)

Next step, obviously a clerical error….in reach of my A grade licence the work type to achieve that was in the Plant Shop at Newport. It was shortly to become a war of words and correspondence to the CME on my transfer to the Train Lighting Depot.

CHAPTER 6

A College of Our Own

In 1922 the commissioners decided to establish their own technical school. The **Victorian Railway Technical College.** A temporary classroom was made available by partitioning a portion of the car painting shop. Staffed by a trade instructor on loan from the Education Department.

Old VR Technical school, near Newport station gates, circa 1960 (A Davis collection)

By March of 1923 the Victorian Railway Technical College had been built on a section of the workshops land near the Newport station. Reported in the *Public Records Victoria collection. February 1922* saw the first apprentices under the new scheme commence their training. They were interviewed by Mr. Nilsson, the Principal of the projected Victorian Railway Technical College. Classes commenced on February

27, 1922 in temporary accommodation at the paint shop, Newport Workshops until construction of the new technical college was completed. On March 11, 1923 the 160 students comprising the classes were transferred to the new college. The collage is then recorded as being closed due to the Great Depression to resume and open in April 1935 with fifty apprentices. Source: *Visions & Realisation, Volume 3, History of the Schools in the Port Philip Western Region.*

In 1927 at the annual conference of Technical Schools Association of Victoria Mr O. E. Nilsson, Principal of the Victorian Railway College presented a paper, titled the *Apprentice Training System of the Victorian Railways.* **Provided by Stuart Smithwick. edited extract**

In his introduction he writes. The question of the training of apprentices and the merits and demerits of the different schemes tried by various industry organisations in other parts of the world has occupied the attention of many people interested in the supply of our future skilled artisans. The aims of the system are:

1. to ensure an adequate supply of skilled artisans.
2. To encourage apprentices to take a thoughtful interest in their work, to develop initiative and pride of achievement and to become useful members of the community.
3. To enable a selection of apprentices of those suitable for the higher grades in the railway service.

Bonehead College. A term that seemed to be passed from year to year by a core of academic young men, but not by me. The college is controlled by the Council of the Victorian Railway Institute which reimburses the salaries of instructional staff on loan from the Education Department. The supervising body to the college is an advisory committee comprising members of the Education Department and officers selected by the rail commissioners. The members at October 1927 were:

S. H. Evans, Manager. Signal & Telegraph workshops – Chair. N. C Harris, Assistant Chief Mechanical Engineer. H. Forster, Engineer, Electrical Engineer's Branch, T.F. Brennan, acting Chairman Railways Staff Board, and E.P. Eltham, Senior Inspector, Technical schools.

Nilsson continued. Technical training of apprentices (1927 style) - When a lad has been selected by the Board of Selectors and has passed his medical and education examinations, he is started at one of the various workshops. He is enrolled as soon as possible at the school at Newport, or if he is employed at Ballarat or Bendigo at the School of Mines and Industries in that city. He is then required to attend classes as the commissioners may direct at such times hours of the day and night as he may require to be prescribed, during the complete course of training.

Grading of Apprentices – all apprentices are graded in to classes according to their educational qualifications and school examination results and general progress, Grading – **Senior**: Intermediate certificate or university leaving certificate or equivalent qualifications. **Intermediate**: junior technical certificate or university intermediate or equivalent. **Junior**: attendance at technical or high school but have not gained certificates and those who attended Elementary schools.

1st grade – common syllabus for first year course, metal trades, including car & wagon builders, moulders. Subjects -elementary science, mechanic, hydrostatics, electricity and magnetism and chemistry (2 hours) mathematics, algebra, arithmetic and mensuration. (2 hours) geometrical drawing (practical, plane & solid geometry & development. (2 hours)

2nd grade - common syllabus for 2nd year course, metal trades, including car & wagon builders, moulders. Subjects – mechanics, hydrostatics, and heat, electricity and magnetism (3 hours) solid geometry, mechanical drawing, dimensional sketching. (3 hours) mathematics, (algebra & trigonometry) (2 hours)

3rd grade – fitter & turner. Applied mechanics, heat engines, engineering drawing, applied mathematics and graphics.

3rd grade – boilermaker. Applied mechanics, heat engines, Iron steel and engineering alloys, engineering drawing & geometrical drawing and mathematics.

4th grade - fitter & turner. Applied mechanics, heat engines, engineering drawing and design. Iron steel and engineering alloys, applied mathematics.

Attendance at classes during working hours. Technical training is timetabled in ordinary working hours. Class times are held from 0800 – 1200 and from 1245 – 1645.

1st grade – 6 hours per week for all trades,
2nd grade – 8 hours per week for all but special trades,
3rd grade – 8 hours per week for main engineering trades plus 4 hours per week for all others.
4th grade – 8 hours per week (special course for advanced apprentices)

Attendance at evening technical school for the theory and practice of trade, 2-3 evening per week (grade1 only at present)

Syllabus. O.E. Nilsson, edited extract. The syllabus for the various trades is as far as possible the same as the Education Department. In addition to examinations set by the railway department, apprentices are encouraged to enter for the Education Departments examinations. As previously mentioned, the standard of the work reached at the end of the three year's course depends on the calibre of the students. Any work not completed in a year is carried on to the next.

Mathematics – the principles are taught with the application to problems likely to be met in the workshops. Algebra is treated as generalised arithmetic. Trigonometry is introduced in the second grade dealing with its application especially in machine shop practice and linked to the work in physics and mechanics.

Drawing – Geometrical and mechanical drawing – the apprentice is introduced to geometrical drawing development to determine points, lines and surfaces on the various views of a drawing. Application of drawings in plan, front and side elevations including sections and three dimensional. The apprentice is provided with simple workshop examples to sketch and then reproduce in suitable labelled and actioned drawings.

Elementary Science and Applied Mechanics – involve the apprentices in the theory and experimental work including, elementary science including mechanics, hydrostatics, heat, electricity and magnetism additional the use of vernier callipers and various forms of screw micrometres. Simple machines including their application in levers, pulleys, screw jacks and lifting gears to different uses in the workshop. The operation of pumps hydraulic jacks and accumulators and the effect of heat on various substances and materials and their application to railway working.

Heat Engines – the principles underlying the working of locomotives, steam turbines and internal combustion engines. The subject includes the study of various types of locomotive boilers, boiler mountings with their operation and construction of valves, value gears and valve settings. Locomotive superheaters and their management, and lubrication and usages.

1927 Victorian Railway apprentice syllabus for selected entry points.

Junior course. Lads entering with the following qualifications merit certificate and attendees at junior technical or high schools without obtaining certificates.

First year – elementary science taken to Junior Technical Certificate (JTC) standard in mechanics and hydrostatics and as far as possible in the time available JTC standard in electricity, magnetism and chemistry.

Mathematics – algebra, arithmetic and measurement.

Geometrical drawing, including practical plane and solid geometry and geometrical development.

2nd year - Mechanics, hydrostatics, heat. (The technical schools intermediate physics 'A' in Mechanics, hydrostatics and heat. Electricity and magnetism (Intermediate Certificate standard)

Mathematics – (preliminary mathematics, algebra and trigonometry special practical course).

Solid geometry, dimensional sketching and engineering drawing to grade 1. Solid geometry is continued from year1 to understand mechanical drawing.

3rd year – Applied mathematics the rest of physics 'a' course not included in 2nd year, and applied mechanics (special course)

Heat engines, grade 1, Engineering drawing, grade 11, Applied mathematics, (algebra and trigonometry, applied to engineering problems), Graphics (Education Department's syllabus).

Intermediate course. Lads entering with junior technical certificate, University intermediate certificate or equivalent.

First year – Mechanics, hydrostatics and heat. (Intermediate course treated as part of physics A syllabus). Electricity, magnetism to Intermediate standard.

Solid geometry, Dimensional sketching, engineering drawing to grade 1

Mathematics (preliminary mathematics, algebra, and trigonometry special practical Course)

2nd year – Applied Mechanics, (The rest of physics A course not included in Year 1, technical schools intermediate physics 'A' applied Mechanics 11

Mathematics – algebra and trigonometry to grade 1 standard.

Heat engines, grade 1   engineering drawing, grade 11, graphics.

3rd year – Applied mechanics, grade 11, applied mechanics 111

Heat engines, grade 11

Iron, steel and engineering alloys

Applied mathematics, (algebra and trigonometry, applied to engineering problems)

Graphics (Education Department's syllabus).

Senior course. Lads entering with junior technical certificate, Intermediate certificate or University leaving certificate or equivalent.

First year - physics A mechanics and Heat. Engineering drawing to grade 1

Mathematics, algebra, grade 1 and special practical course or grade 1

2nd year – Applied Mechanics, grade 11

Applied Mathematics – algebra and trigonometry to engineering problems.

Heat engines, grade 1 engineering drawing, grade 11, graphics.

3rd year – Applied mechanics, grade 111, applied mechanics 111

Heat engines, grade 11, engineering drawing and design, grade 111

Iron, steel and engineering alloys

Applied mathematics, (algebra and trigonometry, and elementary calculus applied to engineering problems)

Scholarships and prizes – every incentive is given to industrious lads to qualify for the higher positions in the service and the following scholarships and prizes are awarded annually.

Scholarships – those apprentices to the higher trades during the 3rd and 4th grade work who satisfactorily complete their technical course within the first three years of their apprenticeship, together with apprentices of lesser service who by reason of their educational attainments and proficiency are deemed worthy of being considered, are eligible to sit for scholarship examination. On the result of this exam a number, not more than three are awarded by the commissioners. Scholarship winners are nominated in either electrical or mechanical engineering. Successful diploma graduates are appointed as an engineering assistant. During the course of three years the collage fees are paid by the department. The apprentice graduate is required to enter into an agreement to remain in the service for a period of three years on completion of his award.

University free place - Apprentices of the higher trades with the necessary entrance qualifications are eligible for nomination by the commissioners for a free place at Melbourne University for either a degree or bachelor of electrical or mechanical engineering.

Apprentice Course recommendations

Course 'A' Fitters & Turners and Patternmakers

1st grade: 1. elementary science, mechanics, hydrostatics. Electricity & magnetism and chemistry. (2 hours) 2. geometrical drawings 9practical, plane and solid geometry and development (2 hours) 3. Mathematics, algebra, arithmetic and mensuration (2 hours)

2nd grade: mechanics, hydrostatics and heat. Electricity & magnetism (3 hours) solid geometry, mechanical drawing, dimensional sketching (3 hours) mathematics (Alg. & trig.) (2 hours)

3rd grade: heat engines (1 hour) engineering drawing (3 hours) applied mechanics (2 hours). applied mathematics (1 hour) graphics (1 hour)

4th grade: applied mechanics (1 hour) engineering drawing and design (3 hours). iron, steel & engineering alloys (1 hour) applied mechanics (2 hours) applied mathematics (1 hour)

Course 'B' Electrical Fitters

1st grade: same as course 'A' (common to fitters & Turners and Patternmakers)

2nd grade: same as course 'A' 2nd grade

3rd grade: electrical technology (1 hour) engineering drawing (3 hours) applied mechanics (2 hours) engineering drawing (3 hours). applied mathematics (1 hour) graphics (1 hour)

4th grade: electrical technology (1 hour) engineering drawing and design (3 hours). iron, steel & engineering alloys (1 hour) applied mechanics (2 hours) applied mathematics (1 hour)

Course 'C' Boilermakers

1st grade: same as course 'A' (common to Fitters & Turners and Patternmakers)

2nd grade: same as course 'A' 2nd grade

3rd grade: engineering plus geometrical drawing (3 hours). mathematics (1 hour) iron, steel & engineering alloys (1 hour) heat engines (1 hour) applied mechanics (2 hours)

Course 'D' Coppersmiths

1st grade: same as course 'A' (common to Fitters & Turners and Patternmakers)

2nd grade: same as course 'A' 2nd grade

3rd grade: engineering plus geometrical drawing (2 hours). Mathematics (1 hour) iron, steel &engineering alloys (1 hour)

Course 'E' Blacksmiths

1st grade: same as course 'A' (common to Fitters & Turners and Patternmakers)

2nd grade: same as course 'A' 2nd grade

3rd grade: engineering drawing (3 hours). Mathematics (1 hour)

Course 'F' Moulders

1st grade: same as course 'A' (common to Fitters & Turners and Patternmakers)

2nd grade: same as course 'A' 2nd grade

3rd grade: engineering drawing (3 hours). Mathematics (1 hour)

Course 'G' Car & Wagon builders

1st grade: same as course 'A' (common to Fitters & Turners and Patternmakers)

2nd grade: same as course 'A' 2nd grade

3rd grade: Solid Geometry, Building construction, (3 hours) Mathematics, Quantities, etc. (1 hour)

Course 'H' Painters 1927 proposal

1st grade: same as course 'A' (common to Fitters & Turners and Patternmakers)

2nd grade: special training at workshops or technical schools

3rd grade: special training at workshops or technical schools.

The VR painter. The railway painter is not only a good craftsman, but versatile and resourceful…painting anything from the Flinders Street station clock tower to bridges and gold lettering. They deftly apply their brushes to water tanks, bridges, signal gantries, station and departmental residences, name boards on sheds, flag boxes…an endless list, including repolishing furniture, paper hanging and kalsomining walls and ceilings. His apprenticeship lays the foundation of his trade and includes schooling and trade tests at Newport college or the Caulfield Technical school. *Edited, extract the Victorian Railway Newsletter, May 1951.*

Course 'I' Upholsterers

1st grade: same as course 'A' (common to Fitters & Turners and Patternmakers)

2nd grade: special training, theory & practice provided at the workshops.

3rd grade: special training, theory & practice provided at the workshops.

Course 'J' Plumbers

1st grade: same as course 'A' (common to Fitters & Turners and Patternmakers)

2nd grade: special training, theory & practice to be provided at technical schools.

3rd grade: special training, theory & practice to be provided at technical schools.

Course 'K' Lamp makers

1st grade: same as course 'A' (1st grade)

2nd grade: special instruction theory & practice at workshops or technical schools

3rd grade: special training theory & practice at workshops or technical schools.

Course 'L' Gas Fitters, Sheetmetal workers, Oxy welders

1st grade: same as course 'A' (common to Fitters & Turners and Patternmakers)

2nd grade: special training, theory & practice to be provided at technical schools.

3rd grade: special training, theory & practice to be provided at technical schools

Course 'M' Wood machinist

1st grade: same as course 'A' (common to Fitters & Turners and Patternmakers)

2nd grade: special training, theory & practice provided at the workshops.

3rd grade: special training, theory & practice provided at the workshops.

The following extracts *from O.E. Nilsson's Annual conference paper of the Technical School's Association (1927)* imply a combination of general education as well as core components of the various trades. *Extract pg. 137.*

All class work has a railway emphasis and is designed to help the student in his general work whether it is car & wagon building, boiler making, electrical fitting or general shop activities. Instruction is chiefly made up of tutorial lectures in conjunction with printed notes, film screenings and practical laboratory work. This phase of college activities is conducted by the principal and five full time instructors from the education department. Apprentices that wish to follow up a particular phase of their trade have a technical library at their disposal. An instructor in English is made available from the Footscray Technical College for eight hours each week for apprentices seeking to improve their vocabulary and written capabilities.

The trades were there from the earliest steam powered locomotives to the motive power of diesel and diesel electric engines. From open goods wagons to modern grain wagons to custom designed container units, as well as an endless succession of passenger carriages and trains. Over these years some trades were lost as improved technology or systems were introduced that required endless engineering and technical innovation. Name an industry trade and you could be involved in any of the engineering and work necessary in the workshops or in construction and servicing or for the thousands of kilometres of track, signalling systems and ancillary services that rail operation required.

Early examples of the commitment to apprentice training can be found from the *Victoria University archives. The Education Department's Inspectors report from December 1930,* providing commentary after their visit.

To the Railway Apprentice Technical school, Newport. (Principal Mr Grace) from the Education Department's Inspector: December 1930

Premises and equipment. the buildings and class rooms are well looked after.

Advisory committee. The committee appointed to control the school maintains close contact with the principal and its expert advice is at all times available.

A total number of apprentices is 51, a decrease of 25 on last year. No new apprentices have been taken on. The apprentices are divided into grades for courses. Intermediate B1, Senior B2, Intermediate C, Junior, and welders.

B1 – modified for apprentice boilermakers who have completed boiler making theory and drawing.

B2 – apprentice electrical fitters and fitter & turners' normal course.

Intermediate C – apprentice electrical fitters and fitter & turners' normal course.

Junior – blacksmithing and fitter & turner apprentices of insufficient ability to carry on higher classes.

Welders – attend this school, plus one-half day at the Working Men's College for oxyacetylene welding

Another earlier example details an extract from the Education Department's Inspectors report on October 7 & 8, 1924, detailing.

Grading of pupils as far as possible is based on their general progress and exam results. Apprentices would have been part of a day release program to attend the school at Newport while others attended colleges, like Ballarat School of Mines or local technical colleges.

Course of work.

1st Grade. - undertake the following subjects

Arithmetic and measurement, Algebra, Projection and development, Elementary science
1 hour every week, plus 2 hours alternative weeks

2nd Grade

Algebra	2 hours every week
Applied mechanics	3 "
Engineering drawing	3 "

3rd Grade

Algebra	1 hour every week
Applied mechanics	2 "
Applied electricity	2 "
Engineering drawing	2 "
Solid geometry	1 "

A good year – 1937 the Education Department's report

> To: Principal Victorian Railway College.
>
> From: A.W. Woodhouse, Secretary Education Department.
>
> Dear Sir, attached is the inspectors report on the 27th September 1937.
>
> A total of 177 apprentices under the direction of the principal. 149 in Melbourne, 14 each in Ballarat and Bendigo. Senior and intermediate attend classes for two half days each week. Junior apprentices attend for one half day each week and one additional half day each alternative week.
>
> Subjects- mathematics, Science, applied science and engineering drawing. Source: *Victoria University archives, November, 2024.*
>
> To: Principal Victorian Railway College.
>
> From: A.W. Woodhouse, Secretary Education Department.
>
> Dear Sir, attached is the inspectors report on the 17th august 1959.
>
> A local road construction will necessitate the demolition of the present building and plans for a new building within the railway workshops area are complete. The building will include classrooms for subject theory and a practical laboratory for metallurgy, applied mechanics and physics and electrical technology. Trades for accommodation include, boiler makers, car & wagon builders, electric fitters, interlocking fitters, locksmiths and weighbridge fitters. Subjects- mathematics, science, applied science and engineering drawing. Source: *Victoria University archives, November, 2024.*

Railway College for Railway Craftsmen, reads the heading from *Behind the Railway Scene, a Victorian Railway publication. (Date not shown)*

'You can see, therefore that angle B is equal to 40 degrees, says the instructor, pointing to the blackboard and a maze of symbols which might have been copied from an Egyptian sarcophagus. He pauses while the information sinks in. 'any questions?' then how many degrees are there in angle C?' Suddenly they have it. A dozen hands shoot up and the instructor nods approval. He takes the answer and the mathematics lesson goes on. Outside the classroom comes the clatter as a pilot engine drops a rake of trucks into a siding. In the adjoining class-rooms other instructors are teaching subjects to equally keen young men. All class work has a railway outlook designed to help the apprentice in general work of subjects as car and wagon building, boiler making, electrical fitting, heat engines and applied mechanics. This is the Victorian Railway College at Newport for railway apprentices.

Other comments were supportive.

The *Melbourne Sun* under the heading; Made at Newport…reports there is another workshop at Newport that has never built a loco, or welded a rail…but its products are, perhaps, something more valuable. It is the 'railways' own free technical school where hundreds of young apprentices are 'in class's' each year, learning to be tradesmen in the Newport tradition. *The Sun, September 13, 1954.*

They were there; A.J. CLARKE…*Bonehead College! Part of my training included one day a week in half day stints for three years at the Railway Technical College, known to railwaymen and apprentices alike as 'Bonehead' College. It was south-west of Newport station behind the signal box. This edifice was built in the 1920's and in 1959 had just received a second story and was just being used when it was decided by the 'powers that be' to build an overpass through the college site to replace the gates, so by 1960 it was demolished. School was at Flinders Street station while a new college was built west of the boiler Shop. The curriculum seemed quite adequate. The first year was in effect selected subjects as taught at intermediate level in the Victorian State junior technical schools. We studied, English, trade theory, trade science, geometry and trigonometry, algebra and trade drawing. Five subjects – trade theory 11, trade drawing, trade science, trade metallurgy and rail mechanics – comprised year 2.*

I wondered about the relevance of rail mechanics which mainly focused on the workings of the steam locomotives particularly as in 1959, the Victorian Railways had officially announced complete dieselisation by 1970. The third year's subjects narrowed down to trade theory 111, trade metallurgy and rail mechanics 11, which featured diesel locomotives.

TONY DAVIS was another at the original technical school and recalls…*at this time the VR had its own apprentice school near Newport station gates. We were the first apprentices to go in and it only lasted for 2 years when it was knocked down to make way for the overpass. We then attended classes at the VRI rooms at Flinders Street station.* **Temptation was at hand***. We were told on many occasions not to go to the pubs for lunch especially Young & Jacksons. Yet a number of us wanted to see Chloe.*

Chloe is the famous nude portrait and a Melbourne icon who hangs in the Chloe bar. Tony's on -job training was to cycle from various shops and reap a rich reward of wide work experiences. He had commenced at the Brake Shop, and spent time at the Railmotor Shop, the Roller Bearing Shop, the Erecting Shop, the Machine Shop, the Tool Room and the Drawing Office – all part of his apprenticeship journey.

Victorian Railway Technical College. - 1960

The opening of the **new** Victorian Railway Technical College in 1960 was to bring about another phase of change. A time line of approaching 40 years for thousands of apprentices of railway tradesmen and engineers was to find a new home.

Building for the Future was the lead in the *Victorian Railways Newsletter in September 1960*. The opening of the new V.R. technical College on July 4, marked a further development in the departments excellent system of apprentice training. Apprentices were first admitted to railway workshops at Williamstown in 1860. By 1905 the Victorian Railways were pioneering a system of apprentice instruction that sought to bring back all that was best in the 'guild" methods, modifying them to suit the conditions of the day.

The new college situated adjacent to the North Williamstown station was located on land within the rail premises along Champion Road. The buildings design encompasses 8,650 sq, feet in the main building and 6000 sq. feet in the practical trades section. The buildings layout includes various classrooms, a library and offices for the principal, administration and the supervisor of apprentices. More importantly an area set aside for exuberant young men to let of steam – a basketball court. The baton has changed with Mr J.A. Douglas as the new collage's first principal.

Newport Victorian Railway Technical College, circa 1961 (A Davis collection)

ROBIN STEWART, *trained as an apprentice electrical fitter and briefly recalls attending the college in 1967, but more about the recreations than the study. 'We played one rule, the ball had to go over the top of the ring. Basketball at lunch time. Great fun.'*

Additional benefits are the proximity of the new college to several manual training centres for practical training. The fitting and turning, welding and boiler making training centres are located adjacent and to the rear of the college. The electrical manual training centre is located in a shared part of the workshops West block.

Supervisor of Apprentices. There was also a new home in the collage for the Supervisor of Apprentices. Long before the national & state system established Apprentice Support Officers in the wider world of todays (2025) apprenticeships & traineeships the VR had our 'Super'. Roy Curtis, became a fixture in apprentice support and welfare for a period beyond 30 years. As befits the time period of paternalism and discipline the position of Supervisor of Apprentices was included as a feature of early VR advertisements. *'During the training period they will be in the care of the supervisor of apprentices who will over-see their progress and assist in any welfare issues.'* Roy Curtis is recorded on his retirement as commencing as an apprentice fitter & turner (1926) before a break in service to work for the Department of Labour at Geelong. (*August 1974 Rail News*) He returned to be offered the newly established position of Supervisor of Apprentices. He described the role as the liaison between the apprentice and management and a representative of parents. The next 'Super' was Robert Baillie before his later appointment to the Carriage Superintendent position at Newport Workshops. Bob brought new eyes to the 'welfare' of apprentice and modernised the position. Years later and Neville Morison won the position in1980 to around privatisation and relocated to Transport House. A notation in the Workshops Board Meeting, 8/11/1990, Personnel Report indicates N. Morison assisting the Newport Workshops to reach Quality Assurance compliance is to assist at Electrical Testing before proceeding to Northcote Bus and Preston Workshops. Implying a major change to the in-house apprentice support system. Both Bob Baillie (Car & Wagon builder) and Neville Morison (Fitter & Turner) had been part of the earlier Victorian Railway apprenticeship system.

RAY CRAMPTON had resigned in 1978 to start a career in the field of industrial relations. Much of his role as an apprentice officer is reflective of the 21st century in the support activities including wages and entitlements, schooling issues, financial issues and tackling bullying/discrimination and harassment in the workplace. Ray writes that; *I became an organiser with the ETU before stints for the National Tertiary Education Union, Federation Miscellaneous Union and Fire Fighters' Union before returning to the ETU.* Another success story of greener pastures. It is fitting that an ex Victorian Railway apprentice became an apprentice officer and training and development officer for the Electrical Trade Union.

To: Principal Victorian Railway College, c/o Station Master North Williamstown

From: A.W. Woodhouse, Secretary Education Department.

Dear Sir, attached is the inspectors report on the 6th October 1960

Premises and equipment. The occupancy of the recently completed school building which provides five spacious and attractive classrooms, a testing room, staff rooms and offices. The Principal and Apprentice supervisor has greatly improved the condition under which the school operates plus the sports area. Additional equipment includes 2 furnaces and quenching tanks, Vickers & Brinell hardness testing machines and a projector and drafting m/c, new switch and distribution boards and improved facilities for electrical testing.

A total of 356 of all grade apprentices attend both Newport and other colleges. 294 attend other schools, 119 at RMIT, 12 the Printing and graphics school, 19 the painting school, 4 at Collingwood Tech, 8 at Prahran Tech, 33 at Footscray, 52 at Bendigo and 47 at the Ballarat School of Mines.

Subjects- English & library, fitting & turning theory, mathematics & science, engineering subjects, applied mathematics and lab works and engineering drawing. Source: *Victoria University Archives, November, 2024*

Education Department, Treasury Place Melbourne G2, 18,19 August 1964

To: Principal Victorian Railway College, c/o station Master North Williamstown

Dear Sir, I forward for insertion in the school report book the inspectors report of the VRTC

Yours faithfully, W.A. Crellin, Secretary Education Department.

Premises and equipment. Buildings and surrounds, well, cleaned and maintained.

Enrolment: two hundred apprentices will be joining the service in 1965. It seems likely that the manual training of first year boiler makers will relocate from Footscray to here with an intake of 50 lads.

Examinations – 298 apprentices attended in 1963, approximately 30% gained credit passes and 45% gained the ordinary pass.

Subjects- English & library, fitting & turning theory, mathematics & science, engineering subjects, applied mathematics and lab works and engineering drawing. Source: *Victoria University Archives, November, 2024*.

A COLLEGE OF OUR OWN

HALF YEARLY FINAL REPORT — Dec./1963 N.T.C. 2

Apprentice: Owen Stanley WALDIE Class B.7.

To Parent or Guardian.
Dear Sir or Madam,
This report has been prepared on the progress made by your boy up to the last examinations. Would you please acknowledge the report by detaching the lower portion of this card, making any comment you wish, and return it to me at the College.
Yours faithfully,
J. A. Douglas, Principal.

KEY TO LETTERS USED: A Excellent; B Very Good; C Good—Satisfactory; D Fair—Can be improved; E Unsatisfactory

EXAMINATION RESULTS

Subject	Grade	Marks	Class Av.
Elec Fitting Theory	IV	47	
Elec Technology	II	76	
Railway Electronics		39	
Railways Elec prac.		Pass	

Average 54% | Pos'n in Class 13 in 15 | Rating C+

COLLEGE REPORT

Progress C | Behaviour A | Diligence C+
Times Late 0 | Half Days Absent 0 | Timekeeping Rating

Remarks: Satisfactory, but could have worked a little harder.

Principal

WORKSHOPS REPORT

Progress B | Conduct A | Aptitude B | Times Late — | Absences: Days 4 Part Days 6 | Timekeeping Rating C

Remarks: Progressing. Has ability but interest in his work wanes at times. Could apply himself more.

Manager

HALF YEARLY REPORT — JULY 1963 N.T.C. 2

Apprentice: Owen Stanley WALDIE Class B.7.

To Parent or Guardian.
Dear Sir or Madam,
This report has been prepared on the progress made by your boy up to the last examinations. Would you please acknowledge the report by detaching the lower portion of this card, making any comment you wish, and return it to me at the College.
Yours faithfully,
J. A. Douglas, Principal.

KEY TO LETTERS USED: A Excellent; B Very Good; C Good—Satisfactory; D Fair—Can be improved; E Unsatisfactory

EXAMINATION RESULTS

Subject	Grade	Marks	Class Av.
Elec. Fitting	IV	51	74
Elec. Technology	II	63	62
Rly Electronics		64	74

Average 60% | Pos'n in Class 13 in 17 | Rating B

COLLEGE REPORT

Progress C | Behaviour A | Diligence B+
Times Late — | Half Days Absent 2 | Timekeeping Rating A

Remarks: Making satisfactory progress.

Principal

WORKSHOPS REPORT

Progress C+ | Conduct B+ | Aptitude C+ | Times Late — | Absences: Days 1 Part Days 6 | Timekeeping Rating C

Remarks: Average, tries & shows some interest.

Manager

Half Yearly VR College Report, (O.Waldie collection) 1963

The Victorian Railways Technical College, Education Department of Victoria Technical schools;

Among the apprentice records of the *Victoria University Archives* employed by the State Transport Authority, 60 Market Street Melbourne.
Robert Stevenson – electrical mechanic, employer, State Transport Authority.
John Weir – electrical fitter, employer, State Transport Authority

Note: Since opening some 5000 apprentices have attended the VR Technical College to 1970 with the enrolment this year (1970), numbered four hundred.

Syllabus & Exam examples.

Electrical Wiring, Grade 2 Theory 1971- Extract *Victoria University archives*. (33 x 3-hour sessions)

Term 1. Introduction to electrical safety. DC applications. Generation of EMF. DC generators. Field connections. DC motors. Meters and instruments. Testing 7 revision.

Term 2. Meters & instruments. Earthing systems. Distribution systems. Lighting. Tariffs. Switch boards. Installation. Wiring practice. Cables and wiring. Heating. Testing & revision.

Term 3. Wiring regulations, review grade 1 topics. Revision grade 2 topics. Study of past SEC examination papers.

Technical schools - annual examination

Electrical Wiring Grade 2 Theory. Examples.

    Q1. A 5 H.P 240-volt dc motor takes 20 amperes when operated fully.

        (a) What is the efficiency of the motor?
        (b) What would be the cost of operation at full load if it ran for 8 hours/day for 20 days @ 5 cents/kilowatt hour. (14 marks)

    Q2. What is meant by the following terms?
        (a) accessory, (b) appliance, (c) service fuse, (d) sub-mains, (e) final sub -circuit.
        Draw a sketch of an installation showing the location of each item relative to each other.

Electrical Wiring Grade 2 Theory.

Extract, Q1. What is laid down with respect to –

    (a) The minimum size of a main earthing conductor?
    (b) List the devices required on a main switch board.
    (c) Cord line switches
    (d) Ceiling roses
    (e) Head lamps for boiler and similar enclosed spaces
    (f) Use of a lamp holder adaptor
    (g) The rating of a plug socket installed in a domestic premises.   (14 marks)

    Q2. What would you do if your mate was rendered unconscious due to an electric shock while holding an electric drill?

    Q3 What is meant by the characteristics curve of a DC generator?

    Q4 name 3 types of dc generators and what causes the pressure of a shunt wound generator running at constant speed to drop as the load increases.

Forget these bloody electrical fitters and such, if you were involved in another trade. The following examples are for a **turner & fitter or boilermaker & fabricator** and a different pathway.

Turner & Fitter, Syllabus 1964 - Extract - *Swinburne Technical College course notes.*

Metals used in trades: Metals and metallurgy would form a major component of your syllabus and divided in ferrous and non-ferrous.

Cast iron. steel, copper, brass, bronze, aluminium and bearing alloys. Cast iron is basically the properties of iron and carbon. (Fe about 97% and carbon about 3%) There are two principal types of cast iron – grey cast iron & white cast iron. Grey cast iron is low in tensile strength, but has a high compressive strength value making it suitable for machine bases, specifically lathe and other machine beds and car engines. White cast iron is formed when the carbon is chemically combined with the iron and forms a very hard constituent called cementite (iron carbon).it is extremely resistant to abrasion, and suitable for application as stone crusher jaws and rollers for steel rolling mills.

Steel. Can be classified into plain carbon steels and alloy steels.

Plain steels can be sub-divided into, (a) low carbo steel – carbon at 0.25% (b) medium carbon steel – carbon up to 0.5% and (c) high carbon steel up to 1.5%

Screw threads. – Classification of screw threads.

(a) **Power transmission.**
(b) **Screwed fastenings.**

'V' threads. Unsuitable for power transmission as the load component normal to the flank of the trad tends to burst the nut. 'V' threads are twice as strong in shear as square or acme due to the larger area at the root of the thread.

Whitworth threads – the British standard and the adopted standard of the Standards Association of Australia.

British Standard Whitworth (B.S.W.) bolt and screw standard thread for ¼ "diameter and over.

British Standard fine. (B.S.F) a finer pitch with applications for added strength and where vibration may occur.

British Standard Pipe. (B.S.P) the universal format for iron and steel pipes for water, gas and steam pipes and tubes.

American national threads. The American standard used in the USA.

(a) American national course – application for general engineering work
(b) American national fine – application in the automobile and aircraft industry
(c) SAE, extra fine – application in small appliance and fastening equipment.

Lathe operation – centre lathes accessory equipment, relating to chucks, face plates and steady rests.

(a) Setting up work in a chuck, jaws in the normal position, jaws reversed and jaws gripping inside.

The jaws of a centre lathe in their normal position are the set -up for common machining operations – outside diameter machined, facing, centre drilling, drilling, boring, reaming and tapping. Safety – projection of the material from the chuck jaws should be kept at a minimum.

Boring, usually when a hole is drilled with a common double fluted drill it lacks accuracy of size, roundness, parallelism and a good surface finish. Accurate specifications can be achieved by followed up operations with the use of multi fluted drills, D bits, and single and double ended boring tools.

(b) Use of collets.

In quantity production work, such as the production of bolts being machined from bar stock in a capstan or automatic lathe, this work is held in a specialist chuck called a collet. The common types of collet chucks are, push out and draw in collets suitable for holding round, square and hexagon section material.

(c) screw cutting.

Calculations for change gears when screw cutting. As the cutting tool always travels the distance of the lead for each revolution of the work, whether a single or multiple thread this term must be understood. The lead = $\frac{1}{T.P.I.}$ or T.P.I. = $\frac{1}{lead}$. Simple gearing: To obtain the required difference in speed between the lead screw and the main spindle to cut a given lead, the ratio between the teeth of the driving gear and the teeth of the driven gear must be the same ratio between the lead of the work to be cut and the lead of the lathe.

The formula to obtain change gears – $\frac{lead\ of\ work}{lead\ of\ machine}$ = ratio of $\frac{driver\ gear}{driven\ gear}$.

Calculate change gears to cut a 10 T.P.I. – lead screw of ¼ lead. Lead of work = 1/T.P.I. = 1/10. E.g. – $\frac{lead\ of\ work}{lead\ of\ machine} = \frac{driver\ gear}{driven\ gear}$. 4/10 = 2/5 x 10/10 = 20/50.

(d) Cutting a Vee thread. Pre checks of the following – 1. Check the lathe slides for undue tightness or slackness. 2. Check lathe spindle speed. 3. Check tumbler gear position to suit hand or thread size to be cut. 4. Check gears and or gear box lever position. 5. If the work is between centres, check that the drive carriage is tightly fastened to the work. 6. Check tool angles. Note: the cutting tool must have sharp cutting angles. 7. Check saddle movement by hand. 8. Check diameter of work.

Cutting the thread, - start lathe, engage clasp nuts and take a light cut. Back the tool off the work using the cross-slide screw, disengage the clasp nuts and return the saddle to the start point. Check the pitch with a screw pitch gauge. Continue until the graduated collar indicates the full screw depth. Finish cuts should be .001 deep. And a final pitch check or to mating part if available.

Steel fabricator/boiler maker. Syllabus 1964. Oxy- Welding Department Methods of welding. Extract - *Swinburne Technical College course notes.*

Introduction - Welding can be described as (1) the uniting or joining of two or more pieces of metal – heated to a high temperature level that they become plastic – by means of blows of a hammer or pressure. (11) joining metals by fusing or reducing them to a molten condition at the right junction that enables on solidification of the metal to form a sound joint. The former (1) termed plastic welds refers to forge welds and electric resistance welding such as butt, seam, spot etc while the later (!!) fusion welds apply to gas welding processes, electric arc welding and thermit welding.

Butt welding – the method consists of joining pieces end to end and securing complete fusion of the entire cross section of the pieces. The line of weld being transverse to the length of the pieces. Applied to wires, rods, bars, plates, tubes or pieces of similar shape.

Seam welding or line welding – the welding of longitudinal seams in sheet metal, by either abutting or overlapping. Its general application is the making of tubes, containers, such as milk cans etc.

Spot welding – consists of welding sheets, strips by spots when bringing together and heating small sections of the sheets between copper or other suitable electrodes points under pressure. Application for sheet metal containers, stove parts, lamp shades, frames.

Electro- percussive - is a process of electronically welding separate metal parts by drawing an arc between the parts to be welded, thus heating them to the required temperature when they are brought together with percussive force. It is applicable to automobile parts, cutting tools and hardware.

Electric Welding Theory Exam Grade 11 extract STC.1967

All questions to be answered   time allowed: 2 hours

1. (a) outline briefly preparation procedure which a welder operator should observe with regards to equipment, material, weld rod selection prior to actually welding
   (b) What effect does excess amperage have on a fillet weld?
   (h) State the amperage range for 6-gauge conventual electrodes.

2. (a) Name three metals which are readily welded using the electric arc process
   (b) Name two internal defects which occur in weld metal
   (c) Sketch and label an ideal fillet weld showing the following leg length, toe, face and throat depth.

3. As a welder operator you are required to hand weld 200 feet of butt welding on ½ inch thick material. Explain what procedures you would adopt to weld this job using the trade names of the electrodes used.

4. Explain the main functions of the electrode coating

5. Explain the different welding characteristics of the following electrode types (a) cellulose type (b) low hydrogen, (c) rutile (type3)

6. What personal equipment should a welding operator have when welding, using 8 # iron powder electrodes.

7. Name 5 safety precautions a welder should adopt to prevent risks of electric shock.

8. Give details of 2 areas which you consider as hazardous locations when using either oxy-acetylene or electric arc equipment.

9. What are welding codes? Explain how they assist the welding industry.

A new age had entered the system, among them;

Craig Stevens – boilermaker, employer, **State Transport Authority.**
Boilermaker & structural steel fabrication   subjects – electrical arc welding grade1, theory & practice. electrical arc welding grade11, theory & practice. electrical arc welding grade111, theory & practice, work-study 1, (methods study) work-study 11, (implementation) - pass.

Graham Woods – boilermaker, employer, **State Transport Authority**
Boiler making & structural steel fabrication - pass

Apprentice Education - Newport Technical College

The Newport Technical College was built on a section of the railway workshops land, west of Shea Street and reputedly leased on a 99-year lease. *The Victoria University archive* summary states that the Newport Technical College was established as a division of the Footscray Institute of Technology in March of 1979. The Newport College of TAFE was formally established in November 1982 when the Newport Technical College separated from the Footscray Institute of Technology. It also incorporated the Victorian Railway Technical Collage which had provided dedicated training for Victorian Railway apprentices. Its primary purpose was to cater for a wider demographic with courses expanded to include pre-and post-apprenticeship, technicians' certificates and community based short courses. The new college will cater for about 1000 students. Among them 340 metal and welding and machine tool trade apprentices. The Newport College of TAFE formally ceased in May 1991, when it merged with Footscray College of TAFE to form Gellibrand College of TAFE. The site in Champion Road is now vacant.

Twenty years later the apprentice fitter & turner is still at the wheel, with changes and technologies to his trade syllabus. 1984. (assume T = technical)

An extract of subjects included from the Newport Technical College (TAFE) records included. Subjects – mathematics 1 T, science 1 T. English 1 T, drafting 1 T, – mathematics 2 T, science 2 T. English 2 T, drafting 2 T, metallurgy 1T, applied heat 1 T, mechanics 1 T, mechanics 2 T, drafting 1 M, drafting 2 M, engineering practices M.

Others in the grade of blacksmithing in year 3 of their apprenticeship's are completing trade theory 3, trade practice 3 and trade science 3. (*Newport Tech. (TAFE) Collage. Annual school report for year ending 1987*)

Brett Symons - Electrical fitter, employer, **Public Transport Corporation**, V/line Newport Workshops, Champion Road, Newport.
Certificate in Engineering – modules: Occupational health & safety, computing in engineering, turning 1, Machining, Milling, Hand & power tools, drawing interpretation, Drilling & drills, Tool sharpening off hand tools.

Apprentice Carpentry – unit examples: Newport TAFE 1990

Site setting out – domestic, site setting out – industrial. Leveling instruments, strip footings, pad footings.

Scaffolding regulations, scaffolding frames, scaffolding tubes.

Framing – timber framing manual, framing ceilings – domestic, framing deep joints.

Gable roofs, simple hip roofs, flat roofs, suspended ceilings, window frames, floor sheets, wall cladding & cupboard installations.

V/Line apprentices continued different programs – trade: Certificate in Engineering, Mechanical, Fabricating & Electrical/Electronics

Sample ITC – Annual Report, 8 -May - 1992

Subject – module -unit	Code	results
Occupational Health & Safety	NBB02	*** P
Machining	NBB06	*** P
Welding & Thermal Cutting	NBB09	*** P

Changes continued as the Education Department rationalised the identity of Newport TAFE to a wider western suburb's community to be renamed the **Western Metropolitan College of TAFE (Newport campus).**

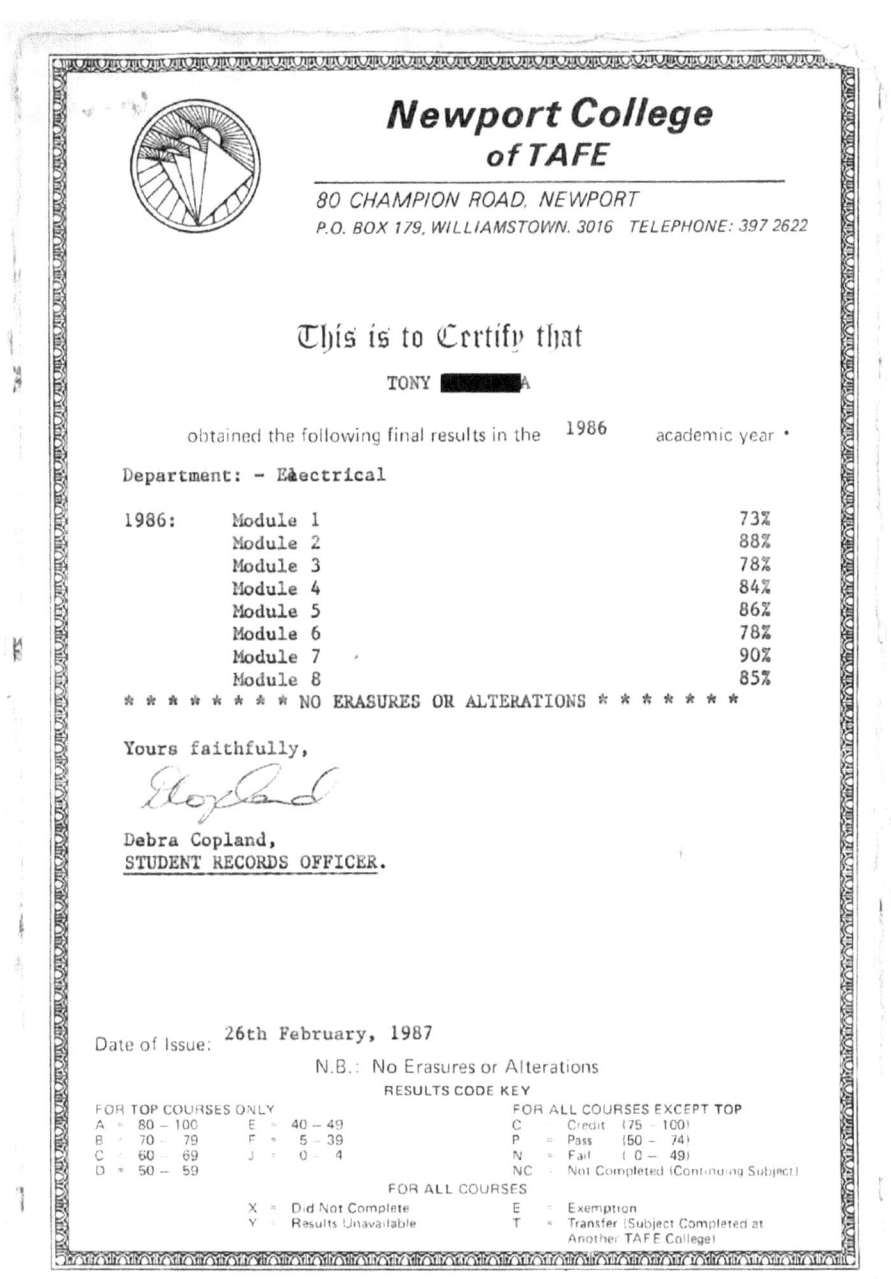

Newport College of TAFE, apprentice results

Newport College of TAFE formally ceased to exist in May of 1991 when it merged with Footscray college of TAFE to form Gellibrand College of TAFE. In August 1991 it was renamed Western Metropolitan College of TAFE

CHAPTER 7

A World of Change, and Change again

In the Report of Victorian Railways Board, (1979) the following branch structure exists: the Chief Traffic Manager – **Chief Civil Engineer, Chief Mechanical Engineer, Chief Electrical Engineer**, Chief Freight Manager, Comptroller of Accounts, Comptroller of Stores, Chief Marketing Manager, Director of Planning, Director Management Controls, **Manager of Personnel**, Secretary of Railways, Manager Trading & Catering Services.

From November 1979 the **Electrical Engineering** assumed responsibility of the Way & Works Signals Division in recognition of the increase sophistication of electrical and electronic signalling. It maintained responsible for linesmen and electrical mechanics in suburban station electrical maintenance and installation and electrical fitters in signalling. The signals division continued its program of level crossing protection. The Caulfield Signal School was soon to relocated to an area of the Newport workshops.

The **Way & Works** apprentice on-job training remained unchanged – apprentice fitter and turners and electrical fitters in signals & telegraph and metro & country and permanent way materials depots. Note the Spencer Street Workshops and Spotswood Workshops were now transferred to the Workshops Branch.

These structural changes set in place by the Victorian Railway Board continued their response to impact the commercial and economic pressure on the business. These changes set in place the business model that was to be the fore-runner of a core business approach and further introduce technology in stream lining operations

The Workshops Branch was formed mid-June 1979 with the responsibility of all workshops which had previously been under Branch control. Its mandate consolidated the rebuilding and manufacturing activities as distinct from field maintenance which remained under the control of the operating branches. With the government confirming service delivery plans the construction and building of 36 modern air-conditioned carriages for the Geelong and Ballarat lines commenced. This contract as well as the manufacture of an additional stainless steel suburban trains consolidated the role of the workshops. Additional work included the refurbished and inclusion of air-conditioning for country sets by obsolete Harris cars (asbestos removed) for country units.

The report of the *Victorian Railways Board for the year ending 30th June,1981* indicated further refinement to the business structure with inclusion of the **Chief Workshops Manager** responsible for all workshops activities. The summary of its first full year of operations since its establishment 1980/1981, indicated many improvements in productivity were achieved… these decisions would also impact the skill base required by the business and their relevant trades. This responsibility would include apprentice training and the manual training centres at Newport. (Authors thoughts)

The apprentice manual training centres at Newport and workshop on-job locations had a NEW BOSS; the Chief Workshops Manager.

What did it mean to the apprentice – a new employer name on their payslip and initially some minor impact as the work continued for the train fleet and infrastructure equipment service and maintenance. Yet change was occurring in the wider world at every level of the organisation. The VicRail apprentice now attended the wider education colleges with the closure of the VR Technical college. Like the disappearance of the coal heaps and steam generated locomotives from earlier generations the business was rapidly adopting newer technology and structural reform. Implementing aspects of the earlier Lonie Report the new *1983 Transport Act* initiated major reforms to the transport portfolio. It abolished long term transport agencies including the Victorian Railways, (VicRail) the Melbourne and Metropolitan Tramways Board and the Country Roads Board. For the rail industry, the Act established **the State Transport Authority** and the **Metropolitan Transit Authority** and a new direction in modernisation and structural reform.

Still on song. 'It is the firm intension of the State Transport Authority to continue to recruit, train and employ sufficient apprentices to meet our needs so that we can provide a safe and efficient transport system in this State". This was the message of STA chairman, Mr Keith Fitzmaurice when he addressed a gathering of management, apprentices and parents at the 1983 apprentice prize presentation at Newport Collage. Both he and the Chairman of the Apprentice Advisory Committee, Bill Wilkins stressed that the successful completion of an apprenticeship is 'just one step along the path" and noted that there is room in the new organisation for young men of talent…'

In 1983, Chief General Manager, Workshops, Dick Terrell said as a new comer to the V/Line organisation he had met tradesmen in the railways whom he believed were second to none. For those young people thinking in terms of their future he pointed out that tomorrow belongs to those prepared to gain technological qualifications.

Apprentices continued to be employed as the industry dynamics continued to change.

Needs Analysis – Manpower & Training Appraisal.

Workshops Board Meeting No.24. extract. **Personnel Report;**
Workshops Division – Apprentice Training Centres Improvement Programme. Newport Workshops. Preliminary appraisal. – January 1986

The training of apprentices has been an established practice in V/line throughout the whole of its existence. Traditional apprenticeships consist of 4 years of on-the-job with the apprentice working alongside an experienced tradesman for the entire period of his apprenticeship.

In recent years the method changed with the first year off-the-job which takes place in a formal practical classes and technical training at a training centre at Newport workshops. The scheme is administered by the Department of Employment and Industrial Affairs who set the standard for the equipment and facilities. Off-the-job attracts a government subsidy of approximately $250,000 per annum.

Alternatives (1) continue the present scheme – off-the-job for first year V/Line apprentices and on-the-job for the remaining three years. (this will involve some capital expenditure)

> (2) change to four years on-the job-training. (No capital expenditure, the loss of government subsidy) considered inferior to alternative (1)

> (3) give up apprentice training completely. (No capital expenditure, serious loss of trade skills and possible union disruption.)

> (4) continue present system but transfer the apprentice to an outside organisation for the off-the-job training.

> (5) Continue the present system and host outside apprentices in their first year (off-the-job) program.

Update: Apprentice Training Centres Improvement program: the Boiler Shop canteen location is suitable for refurbishing for the relocation of the Electrical Training Centre. After a detailed appraisal a target date of June 1987 is achievable after the opening of the new employee canteen. Extract. Manager Personnel.

Workshops Personnel Group Report – January 1987, extract in part.

A total of 122 apprentices have been recruited by the Authority in 1987. 102 actually indentured and 90 will spend their first year at Newport. The State Additional Apprenticeship Scheme (SAAS) has been finalised enabling 42 additional apprentices to commence on Wednesday, 28 January.

Private Industry: the Authority has accepted four private indentured apprentices to be trained in the Newport training centres bringing $20,000 in revenue. A further 5 apprentices from the Group Apprentice scheme (GAS) have been accepted to be trained at the Boiler Makers Training Centre. This revenue stream will finance the Boiler Makers T/C for the year.

The following examples are of the key selection panels involved in the selection and interview process. Disclaimer – Owen Waldie commenced as an electrical fitter apprentice in 1961. His apprenticeship journey is included but his involvement with apprentice selection was to occur many years into his career.

OWEN had followed his career path through the trade and supervisory grades. While working at the Electrical workshops he was invited to be part of the selection panel for electrical apprentices. He commenced this role in 1980 and continued to 1994.

His records show the business of apprentice selection was a primary activity, year on year. The selected panels for V/line were assembled for locations at Ballarat and Bendigo but mainly Melbourne centric. E.g.; interview will be conducted on the 14th Floor, Transport House, 589 Collins Street. commencing at 0830 – 15.30 at ½ hour intervals.

Panel members were representatives of specific trades and specialists in the current roles of the industry.

Panel 1 - Linesmen. J. Tawton, N. Kritikos. 30/9 – 3/10/1985

Panel 2 - Elect. Fitters. (W/S) O Waldie, L Pumphrey. 30/9 – 15/10/1985

Panel 3 – Fitters & Turners (W/S & Plant) A. Rodda, N. Morison. 30/9 – 15/10/1985

Panel 4 – Carpenters & Joiners (Carriage) R. Baillie, W. Warren. 4/10 & 7/10 incl.1985

Panel 5 – B/Makers. & S.S. Fab. N. O'Neill, A. Sowter, 8/10 & 9/10/1985

Panel 6 – Elect. Fitters (Sigs) L. Hill, R. Gallagher. 16/10 – 21/10/1985

Panel 7 – Electrical Mechanics. R. Hanan, P. Wiseman. 17/10 & 18/10/1985

Panel 8 – Coppersmiths, Moulders, Painters, Upholsters. N. Morison, W. Warren, 17/10 – 21/10/1985

Panel 9 – Refrigeration Mechanic. R. Hanan, R. Martin. 21/10/1985

OWEN *related that the selection process was always an experience with the panel asking a series of questions that included details of the job against the preparation of individual applicants. Some may have followed these themes…Q. have you undertaken any work experience and if so what type and duration. Q you have selected an electrical fitter as your first preference, what do you know about the work? Q. Can you explain the main reasons why you applied for an apprenticeship at the Victorian Railways/V/Line.*

Each youth brought with them their application for apprenticeship that formed part of the inter-play between the parties. Additionally, the panel would confirm the work role and current apprentice rate of pay.

Year 1 – junior $195.95, adult $348.60, year 2 – junior $256.40 (1993)
Living away from home allowance year 1 – $68.85 per week, year 2 plus $9.40 per week. This application provides a record of their education level/results and any work experience. Importantly their reason for seeking the apprenticeship.

Selected extracts from completed apprentice interview records reads in part;

Applicant A – forgot to bring reports, unsure of himself and did not read the electrical fitting section, forgot what he had applied for, subject results indicate he needs to keep going at school, prompted to ask questions. Estimate of effectiveness understanding of trade. Weak. (options strong – average – weak -wrong choice) rating 3 of 10

Applicant B – satisfactory school report in trade subjects, school reports read 'spasmodic' performance, understood the work of electrical fitter, good reference from part time work, confident with average presentation. Understanding of trade good, rating 5 of 10.

Applicant C – school results below average, substandard for maths and English. Forgot to bring a personal reference. Part time work as an apprentice gardener. 1st preference is as a carpenter and joiner. Neatly dressed but lacked confidence in the work role in the industry. Rating 4 of 10

Applicant D – Wangaratta lad with above average school results, credit result in maths and electric circuitry. Trade knowledge high and work experience in the metal industry. Would come to Melbourne if selected. Rating 6 of 10

OWEN continued...*'our task was to basically weed out the ill prepared and rate the talent in descending order. Those who combined some knowledge of the trade (first preference) and interviewed well would clearly be in the top percentile. Others judged as not suitably would be advised in the coming weeks. Occasionally a youth would be offered an allied trade other than his/her first preference. Each panel at days end would review their assessments and rate the applicants on a suitability scale and that became the criteria for a future job offer. On the conclusion of all interviews the recommendations of the panel would be forwarded to the Personnel Branch or employment department of the day. Owen remembers the first female apprentices from their interviews, among them Owena Shewring as a fitter & turner (Newport Wheel Shop) and Sue Devonport (electrical fitter) for signal's maintenance (Way & Works).*

Yearly the pre – advertising apprentice campaign would involve the manpower needs of the industry. Example in part. Public Transport Corporation

Memo from; General Manager Workshops Division (V/Line) (the Met)
Subject: Apprentice intake.
To ensure that deadlines are met, please advise your apprentice intake requirements, both trade and numbers by June I, 1990. Any proposed changes in structures or work practices due to structural, or change programmes. The Impact of technological changes which may affect work force numbers. Polices relating to sub-contracting, which may impact workloads. Retirement of trades person. Anticipated tradespersons turnover and any environmental factors that may be expected to impact the availability of trades staff. Anticipated workload for 1990-2
J Barry, GM Workshops

Outside the fence – the 1973 Training/Technical Education Revolution.

Inspired by the Kangan report recommendations that defined the importance of the training system and their funding. Australia's training system became known nationally as 'Technical and Further Education' (TAFE). The period from 1973 covers some of the most significant changes in Australia's apprentice systems.

The 1980's began a period of major national economic and educational reforms. These reforms were initiated and perused by consecutive federal governments. In Victoria the junior technical schools that had existed from 1912 cease as separate educational institutions. The students of junior technical schools were absorbed into the high school system. With some degree of rationalisation, the facilities and infrastructure of the junior technical schools were taken over by the technical & further education colleges to provide vocational and post- secondary education. The initiatives initially advanced by the Kangan report saw the rapid development of apprentice training and the development of traineeships. This period also saw further changes to the VET sector and the development of national VET curricula. The priorities of the then Fraser government for TAFE was to improve the quantity and quality of training for tradespeople and expanded TAFE role in programs for youth.

End of an Era. The year 1979 saw railway apprentices (core trades) join mainline education under the wider technical college system, not entirely new as many before had attended a range of technical colleges for specialised skills training. The entry of non-government providers into the training market, providing an alternative to apprentices and employees. It was during this period that all curriculum development had to provide, and training adhere to clearly stated competencies for students. Formal adoption of competency-based training and assessment, was to become a produce of all apprenticeship trade training. What is a competency- the consistent application of knowledge and skills to the standard of performance required in the workplace.

In 1981, apprenticeship information pamphlets were printed by the **Industrial Training Commission** on behalf of the **Metal Trade Industry**.
General – trade schooling, trade teaching at a technical school is compulsory for all apprentices and for most trades this extends over three years of the **full four – year apprenticeship.** There are two forms of schooling, day release and block release.

Work examples for Boiler Maker and/or Structural Steel fabrication apprentice – steel construction is a branch of engineering which involves, the making of boilers, cutting, forming and connecting of standard rolled steel sections, and a variety of finished products.

Work examples of fitter and turner or machinist – cuts and shapes metal to a required design and exact size then fits all those parts together. A variety of machines include lathes, millers, shapers, borers and planers plus hand and power operated tools.

The **Electrical Industry** trades also provided advice for apprentices with their information pamphlet.

Work examples for electrical fitting and/or armature winding – the electrical fitter may work in workshops, power stations and laboratories where with the aid of machine and hand tools they are engaged in the manufacture, assembly and or overhaul of electrical equipment including generators, motors and switchboards. This may also include the erection and maintenance of electrical equipment on site.

Armature winder specialising in the test, repair and rewinds of generators, electrical motors, magnetos and associated equipment. An Electrical mechanic generally specialises in the installation of electrical wiring for lighting, heating and power systems for houses, factories and commercial buildings. A Linesman generally involved in the erection, fixing and maintenance and repair of over/head power lines, sub stations and public lighting

CHAPTER 8

The Manual Training Centres

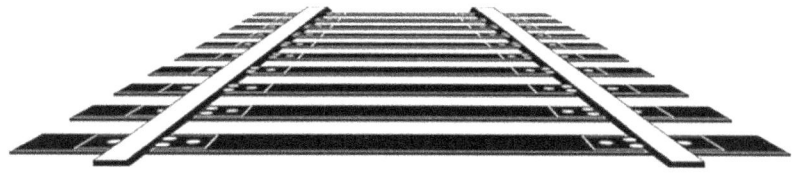

The training centres had now become the entry point for all apprentices in the core trades from 1961.

Edited version VR to V/Line, pg.50

The manual training centres for metal trade apprentices in the first year had been set up at Newport near the technical college. It was progressively extended until all apprentices in all trades were receiving skills training in their first year and continued on a selected day release in their two subsequent years.

Every apprentice attended the education departments school term framework on a day release program. 2nd and 3rd year apprentices attended the training centres on either a ½ or full day per fortnight against their program. All first-year apprentices in there on job training worked the same hours as the workshops or depot

Yet before the establishment of the skill centres metal trade apprentices were provided with hand skills in the form of the chipping block. **Tony Davis (1957)** recalls, *'during our first year we had this fitting exercise one afternoon, one day a week. It involved a grey cast iron bock 5"x5"x5" inch(125mm). Using a hammer and cold chisel, I, (We) had to remove a ½" of cast from 5 sides before filing and scraping it flat and level. On one surface we had to mark out using marking blue and a surface gauge a centre 1/1/2" wide and then chisel and file to a depth of ½ ". This was completed to a template gauge. The final task was to drill and tap four studs in the centre of the quadrants before sign off by the instructor'. 'We were on a placement cycle over the first four years and told that in our 5th year we could choose were we wanted to work if there was a vacancy.'*

OWEN WALDIE related a similar experience as a '61 electrical fitter apprentice. The 'block' chipping exercise was done on a half day morning release in a section of the fitting shop at Newport. Based at Jolimont, Owen would catch the 'shops' train to join his peers under Jock's tutelage. Each block was hand chipped in a mini wire enclosure with safety screens on three sides. The end result was exacting and demanding to fit the template gauge before drilling, tapping and fitting the studs.

At the time of writing, it has been difficult to establish the formal rationale that introduced skill centres within the Victorian Railways. The first consideration is the Advisory Council on Technical Education or the various Trade Committees providing the criteria. Unquestionably it was driven by some external body as similar skill centres paralleled the VR within other State government departments and instrumentalities. The *VR Newsletter of October 1964* records the following...

The School Council maintains a liberal and progressive interest on the needs of the apprentices and an active interest in the college. Some significant advances are being made...The report on Manual Training within the Victorian Railways, irrespective of its adoption or otherwise is further evidence of the earnestness with which problems are being considered.

Although the VR held some degree of autonomy other utilities were also highly engaged in skill centres for apprentice training, the State Electrical Commission, the Gas & Fuel Department, the Melbourne Metropolitan Tramway Board and the Williamstown Navel Dockyards. The Royal Australian Navy advertised their apprentice training section at the Williamstown dockyards as follows; the school is equipped with modern tools, machinery and equipment in which metal fabrication and steel construction, sheet metal work with electrical mechanics, plumbers, and fitter & turners and coppersmiths are trained for the first 12 months. For the remaining 3 years the apprentice is rotated in various workshops applicable to their trades. Formal technical trade education occurs either I day a week or one week's block release depending on the trade. *Navy News pamphlet 1986* The author in his role as the senior instructor (ETC) in the period of the late 1970's visited the SEC and the Army Training School for Apprentices at Balcombe. Note: An item in Training advisors report for the Industrial Training Commission of Victoria, (1979) provided the following; The current awareness by industry for the need of well-co-ordinated training programs is apparent as group cooperative training schemes are increasing including off the job programs. General Motors Holden was additionally building their skills training centre complete with machine tools and equipment. It was reported for completion in 1980 with an intake of eighty apprentices.

Post '61 - The training centres.

NORM SWANWICK'S reminiscences remain a vivid picture in his mind regarding the layout of the electrical training centre. *The ETC was located over near the Geelong line and was half a workshop but I can't recall the other half (Fitting Shop). During the first twelve months, we undertook routine bench work, and machine work learning to operate, lathes, drills, grinders etc. On another day we would be trained on practical work involving electric wiring. As far as tools go, it was pretty basic. There would have been about a dozen benches with two of us per bench where we mainly filed away at various bits of metal. I don't remember all the projects we worked on but the square, plumb bob and g clamp comes to mind. One big project we did towards the end of the year was optional and was a car battery charger. Each bench had a tool locker with hand files, marking out tools, a square, and safety spectacles. There was*

Award night medallion, N. Swanwick

a main tool store where other special tools were kept (master surface plates) and one of us would be rostered into the store daily. Along one side there were several screened off boards where we would undertake various wiring assignments. About a third of the centre contained several lathes, drills, grinders etc; then of course was the dreaded chipping area where we did the block. I remember our group had chipping on Fridays. Once a week we would undertake chipping which involved chiselling and filing away on a great block of cast iron. The electrical fitters' group which was the bulk of the apprentices mixed with half a dozen electrical mechanics and a couple of train lighting technicians who eventually had their apprentices reclassified to electrical fitters. We had a large recreation area and there was a couple of handball courts we could spend our lunchtimes playing. There was enough area to kick as football or soccer ball and play soccer. Sever times a week we would head across to the VR tech college for our theory training. We were divided into three groups depending on our secondary school results and year.

The top group had the opportunity to be awarded an engineering scholarship based on outstanding results. I was at the training centre during my first year and returned for a day once a fortnight during our 2nd and 3rd years. It was mainly to continue our training on the application of the lathes. In our third year we undertook an external exam at the training centre overseen by an external examiner. This exam involved a lot of turning work and some minor bench work. We had three hours to complete the exam and it was a sort of solenoid. Not many completed the task but nobody to my memory failed.

A listing of instructor's names is recorded in multiple issues. Under the heading of *Future VR Craftsmen, VR Newsletter March 1961.*

A series of photographs depict apprentices undertaking various hand skills under the watchful eyes of instructors J. Mitchell and N.J. Emmett with senior instructor S. E. Curwood in the metal trades training centre. Instructor A. J. McGilton shares a marking out problem with apprentice J Anderson in the Car & Wagon builders/Carpenters training centre.

How did they put up with us.

The roll call of apprentice instructors is sadly incomplete but a few can be recalled and include, Cliff Simonds, Car & Wagon, Ken Gennifer, senior instructor ETC, instructors, Alf Robinson, Alan Daws, Ron Little, Kevin McPoyle, Dennis Denman, Graham Button, Merv Carson, Lindsay Hatley, George Saliba, Graeme Copeland. Arthur Pregar, Jim Poulton, Neil Brinsmead, Jack Connelly MTC and Les Hill, David Frost, Wayne Collins, John Tawton, Noel Arnott at the Caulfield/Newport Signals School. Linesmen instructors, Ted Summers, Don Brown and Ron Page.

Training centre generic layout

The initial locations of the manual training centres were adjacent to the 'new' technical college purpose built and opened in 1960. The centres were trade designated as the boiler maker/ structural welding apprentice training centre, and the turner & fitters apprentice training centre. The other two core trades, the electrical apprentice training centre was initially located in the West Block in a section of the fitting shop and the car & wagon builders in the East Block car shop. Early in the 1970's the ETC was relocated to the East Block utilising an area of the Carriage Shop. In the early 1980's the ETC was moved adjacent to the MTC and BM/MF centres after the closure of the Victorian Railway Technical College.

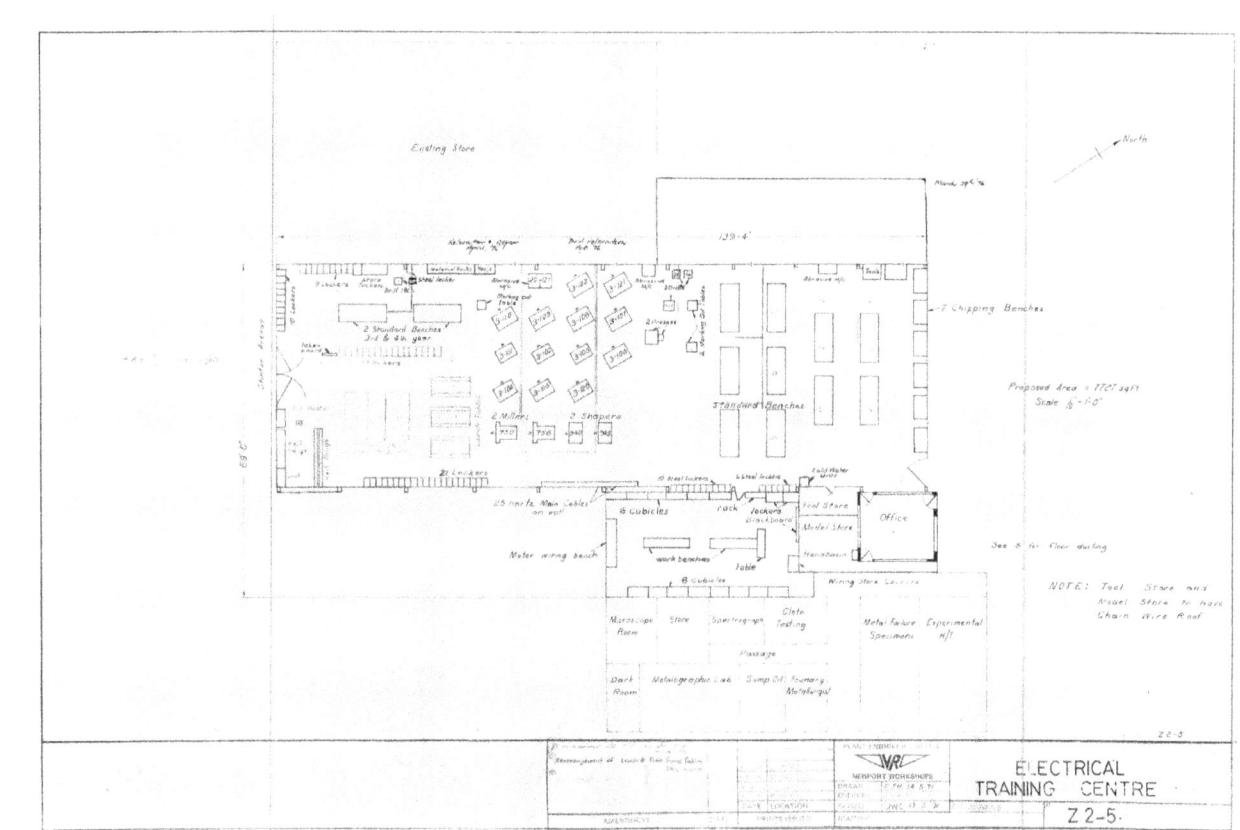

Electrical Training Centre layout drawing, circa 1977 (D.Denman collection)

Each centre was set up in a box or rectangular area appropriate for the trade The initial two centres were green field set ups. Similar in layout within an open plan, including the instructor's office/administration and tool/material store and designated separate work areas. Examples of the MTC and ETC included a separate area for chipping benches, a separate area for machine/lathe/shaping and drilling and a central bench area to accommodate hand skills.

Each bench occupying 6 apprentices, 3 on each side with a separate tool locker and a 4-inch (100 mm) open jaw vice. The tool locker inventory for the metal trades held the following, a set of 10-inch (250mm) files, flat, half round and round. A metal scribe, a square, dividers, a 6 "rule, 16-ounce ball peen hammer, hacksaw and safety googles and spectacles. An area for clothes lockers and amenities was isolated from the working space.

In 1968 the Fitters & Turners' training centre's machine and equipment inventory is listed as; 10 – chipping blocks benches, 8 – 6-inch centre lathes, 8 – 41/2-inch centre lathes, 2 – millers, 2 – shapers, 2 – marking off tables, 1 – cylindrical grinder, 1 – power hacksaw, 3 pedestal drills, 1 – press, 1 – slotter.

The skills program: in today's language the skills program was designed to provide the introduction of skill sets, both hand and machine skills that included the making of selected models or tools. Skills training was the key and a program to accelerate skills promulgated for the majority of intakes who had applied from technical schools. An element of self-paced skill achievement was in the selection of tools and equipment made in the apprentice program.

Models varied to suit trade skills but the mechanical/electrical apprentices list includes, a square, drill gauges, wheel pullers, plum bob. set of 'G' clamps, small surface plate, a 4" wheel and axle rail set, depth gauge, metal tap/reamer tool holder and tow bar ball. The electrical apprentices additionally completed an electrical soldering iron and copper/pvc head mallet.

Activities examples included making a square to accurately measure a 90-degree angle. Component parts two. A section of mild steel approximately ½ inch by 6 inches and a blade of approximately 1/8 inch by 8 inches.

How to: Provided with a blueprint and metal sections the skill set is to file flat and square surfaces and to fit the blade at right angles. Activity 1 – file and scrapping, then check against a flat surface of a master plate. This is done by rubbing each component part over a surface plate and referencing the high points of marking blue and continuing this progress until approved. Activity 2 - the end section now requires a machine process that requires a milling cut to enable the two pieces of metal to be joined to form the square. Activity 3 – is fitting the blade by drilling holes to enable rivets to bind the two sections. Activity 4 – is surface cleaning and a final check against a master square. Sign off by an instructor. (interaction and progress checks would be a continuous process)

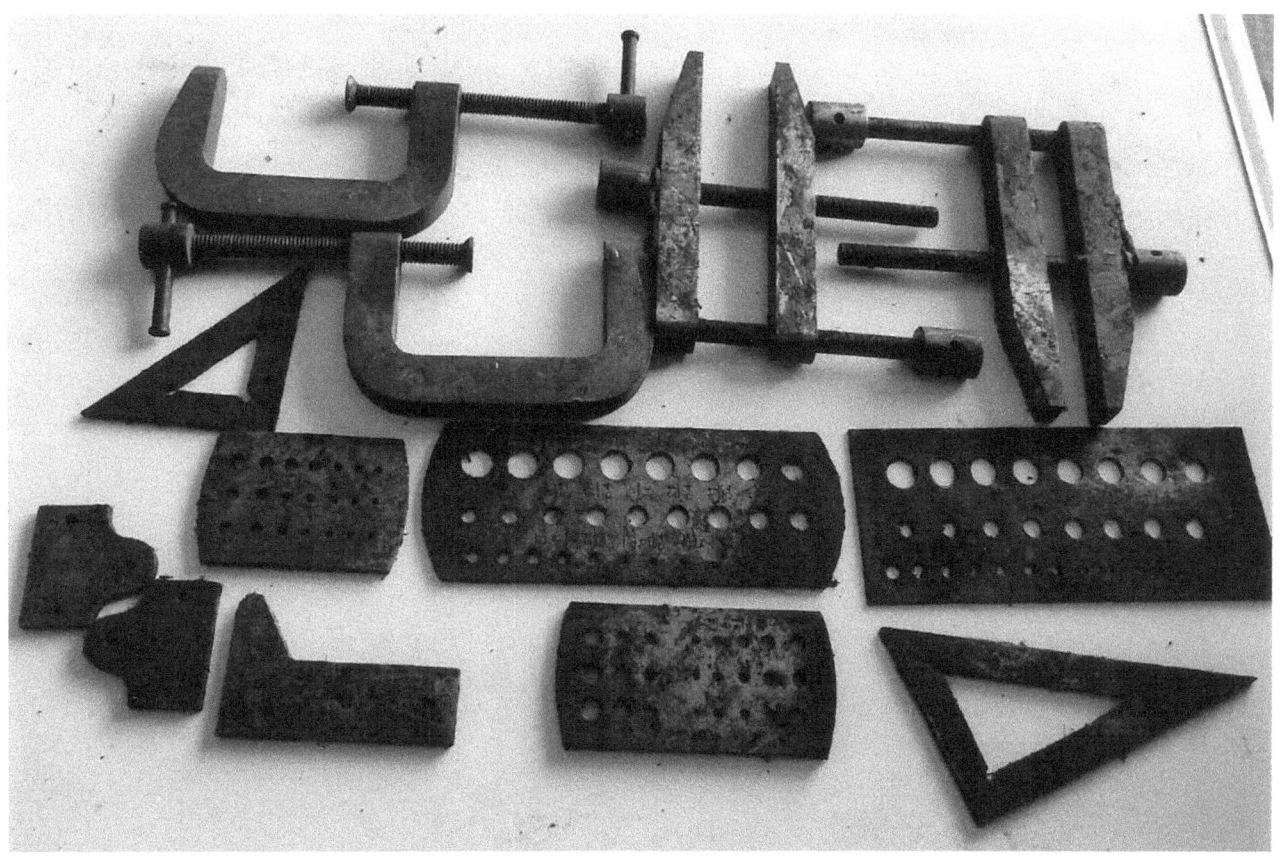

Apprentice models & tools examples, (Bruce Nevandt collection)

STUART SMITHWICK commenced his apprenticeship in 1985 (4 years) at the Fitting & Machining training centre. He writes, *my rail journey started on the 22nd of January 1985. A pimply faced, just sixteen-year-old walked through the gates of the Newport railway workshops. Following the other young blokes that got off the train at North Willy (North Williamstown) to find our way to the Fitting and Machining training centre that would be the workplace for the next twelve months. There was a mix of city and country guys from across the state. There were thirty-two fitting and turning apprentices that year and about 140 odd across the various trades. One fella only lasted a couple of days and got homesick. They must have had someone who had just missed the cut as he arrived the following week. Some of the nick names I recall were Magoo, Tiny, Doc, Benny, Blinky, If, Rambo, Junior, Poots and Meat. The instructors were Alan Daws, Jim Poulton, Neil Brinsmead and Merv Carson. They must have had thick skin to put up with our crap day in day out. I'm not sure if all the apprentices felt like me but it was monotonous. Filing and scraping day in, day out wore you out both physically and mentally. Occasional turns on the machines made for a change.*

One highlight *was going to the engine build shop (8 road) to sort nuts and bolts for a few hours each week. I'm sure the training centre instructors had secret meetings to set a path for each lad. Possibly the move to each shop was the test to see what skills were best suited for the department. During this period there was a day a week at Newport TAFE which continued to our third year.*

My second year was out in the big world of the shops. My first stint was in the Roller Bearing shop…hot and greasy is how I remember it. After three months, off to another location. The paper war dictated our movement and a memo would arrive for the next assignment. Report to the Foreman Turnery at 7.24 am sharp on Monday morning. I went through most of the shops at Newport with two stints at Jolimont Workshops. I probably enjoyed the locomotive (Erecting shop) the most. A second period in the turnery in my third year was the final move staying there for the bulk of my time at Newport. I remained in the turnery for the next thirty years, although that involved periods in the wheel and Loco shops. I took voluntary redundancy in 2018. Looking back, I still use the skills I learnt in the training centre with the best being patience.

Apprentice models & tools examples, (Bruce Nevandt collection)

Disclaimer D. DENMAN attended his apprentice training period at RMIT and on-job at the workshops. From early 1970 he first acted as a relief trade instructor at the Electrical Training Centre West Block site. From 1974 – July 1979 as the senior instructor at the ETC's carriage shop location.

Reflections. *My first period was at the West Block for short periods involved in the hand skills program. Instructing and supporting, occasionally demonstrating filing and scraping techniques. Reviewing the component parts of the file from the safety edge to the cutting surfaces or belly or face of the file. In truth I was out of my depth as my skill set was in electrical installations and equipment maintenance. The constant in the daily tool or model was the work bench. On most days this was the work point where the grunt and bite of hand files and patient surface scraping was your lot. One model was a small surface plate that had to be filed and scrapped to the master plate finish. This final finish was the result of repeated scrapping of high spots indicted by marking blue from the master plate. How I appreciated the RMIT program all those years early.*

First impressions. *I arrived to the team of Ken Gennifer Senior Instructor, Ron (Doc.) Little, hand skills, Alan Daws, machine skills, Alf Robinson electrical skills and my lot as a swing man. The ETC set up was an office and tool room with an open plan area divided into three distinct independent work areas. The machine section included the lathes, pedestal drills, shapers and a few milling machines and a large powered steel cutting saw. This area was a go/ no go location with safety googles/spectacles, hair nets if required and no loose clothing a mandatory condition. The main section was the multiple bench workstations set up for hand tool operation. Each bench combined individual tool lockers and 4" engineers vice.*

Author, ETC instruction, circa 1978

6 apprentices to a bench – 3 on each side. Arranged within this area were engineering stands positioned to enable marking out and precision tool use. A separate area with wire enclosed booths was used for the block chipping. Ron Little had journeyed from that 1937 apprentice turner & fitter apprentice to skills instructor. Ron (Doc.) Little was the driving force behind the hand skills program and to which I was to become initially 2nd banana. Doc was old school and if the outcome was to be flat and square it was non-negotiable. The section designated for electrical board work was separate with multiple metal booth frames. Here Alf Robinson was able to provide electrical circuitry design and application utilising both conduit and TPS cables and different switching arrangements. A series of benches with 240-volt supply enabled single phase motor working and associated control equipment. Additional variety was the construction and wiring of an electric soldering iron.

In some ways the ETC, real or imagined operated independently from the wider world. There had been no formal change over in my role as senior instructor outside this is the program. No documents were on hand to formalise the program other than the requirement of a half yearly report of individual apprentice's progress. The program was repeatable from one year to another. Sort of set in stone or appropriately set in mild steel or cast iron with little input from the industry on any changed needs. During my entire time as senior instructor at the ETC, the

Apprentice Advisory Committee provided no advice or contact on training input or progress. (authors recollection). The first-year apprentice was captured to hand and machine skills developed across the range of models that made up the activities for the year. 2nd and 3rd year apprentices followed a half day block release period mainly in machine operation skills.

A year of hand & machine skills (B. Nevandt collection)

Each complementary to the theory content and experiments designated by the education department and apprenticeship guidelines. Independent to a fault and curious, I arranged to visit various metropolitan locations to seek input from electrical supervisors on their skill needs. Their feedback enabled some direction in a wider variety to consider non-ferrous working and electrical equipment and products. Notwithstanding the primary purpose of the ETC in skills training the wider world of electrical technology was being introduced daily. After an informal chat with Jim Kain, the Principal of the VR College about looking outward he arranged a contact at RMIT. Added to this approach I had arranged to visit other organisations involved in apprentice skill training. The Army apprentice school at Balcombe and the State Electricity Commission apprentice centre to observe their programs. The exchange of programs and some model drawings enabled the introduction of minor changes enabling nonferrous working and other materials including plastics.

The benefits would include different skill sets in tool and drill sharpening and machine cutting speeds. All was achieved by making a small soft head mallet using 2-inch (50mm) aluminium bar cut to 3 inches (75mm) long. Drilled and tapped to enable end caps, one of brass one of hard plastic. With the head pre drilled the cane handle was fitted by the car builder apprentices. One small model/tool had opened the door to a learning experience and co-operation between trade centres. The assistance of Cliff Clarke (car builder instructor) was invaluable. We also sort outside work that might provide some change and variety. As my previous position was within the plant shop, I was aware of work that could be undertaken under supervision with benefits to the plant shop with stores inventory. They presently made consumables like welding cables with fittings and extension leads with protective lamps. Our offer to produce these items on their behalf was accepted. My thanks to the electrical foreman John Richards. They supplied the cables and fitting and the training centre the labour. A win, win result for both parties.

Metrification. Our next step was to review our metrification program to our lathes in machine/turning work. We had initially fitted conversion adaptors on the lathes which was adequate for our needs, notwithstanding that training lathe operatives was not our primary objectives, the machining of tool and model sections required exacting tolerances. One option was to replace old with new and a 'needs' case was written up and forwarded to the Apprentice Advisory Committee via the CME's office (Les Rolls acting CME). Someone in high office supported the submission and at days end approval was granted for replacement Hercus lathes.

The bloody block. Another task to which every generation of Victorian Railway apprentices to the metal trades would have in common was the infernal chipping block. Every comment would undoubtably revolve around hand abrasions and visits to the shops nurse. Previously overlooked as skill errors or collateral damage my view was different. A skill, (in my view) that should have been relegated with steam was still on the books. In the ETC the task involved chipping about a ½ inch off the face of a 5x5x5 inch (125mm) cast iron block. My concerns included, the personal injury suffered and injury statistic but equally important time efficiency. The compromise was to use the shaper machine to minimise the block surface to 50 % with the remainder to be hand chipped. The surface then filed and scraped to flat and level to a surface plate standard. The chipping skill maintained the instances of hand abrasions declined and the nurse complimentary on reduced visits.

The Bloody block. Where else but the Victorian Railways.

Band-Aids to First-Aid certificates. *One thing followed another and the chief ambulance officer was only a phone call away. The rail industry had a long history of first aid practitioners and competitions. Theses competitions were a Calander event held at Mt Evelyn where teams competed for individual and team honours. The winners eligible to represent the Victorian Railways in the interstate rail comps. My thought process was to provide first aid training to all the electrical apprentices before they commenced at their work location. approval was sought and confirmed from the Apprentice Advisory Committee, most possibly the CME as it was his turf. The affirmative response set in motion first aid training, examination and certification. Training by memory occurred in the old canteen location including all instructors for a couple hours over 10 weeks. The first aid program utilised emergency response to accidents and incidents, including patient and responder care, electrical shock conditions, shock and bleeding control. Adult and child recusation procedures and CPR using model manikins. Bandaging and sling usage and practical application. A small success but others were to follow.*

Drown or smother. *Another highlight is in need of recording. The induction of each apprentice with a session of fire risk, fire application and suppression. This operation was managed and conducted by the local in-house firemen* *with a talk and demonstration of hoses and extinguishers. In groups of 12 to 15, apprentices were taken from our compound to the oval. Central to the shops it was a large area of open space maintained and mowed for meal break recreation. Regardless of how they left they always returned resembling drowned rats. The exercise included fire suppression of both material (wood scraps) and oil fires in a half 44-gallon drum. The finale was having two or three apprentices rolling out a 3" ((75mm) hose. Hit the tap and watch as they attempt to hold and direct a high-pressure hose. The results spectacular and the firemen appreciative of their work. Though wet, no apprentice was ever lost.*

Don't tell – Just do. *Fifteen years after the introduction of the training centres it might well have been questioned if the apprentice program was purpose fit to suit the changes impacting the rail industry. Yet, there is no evidence or recollections of questions being asked and the quality of skilled apprentices continued. Efficiencies and cost reduction had become the driver of service delivery and the industry's work roles. These changes abundantly visible in the latest technology and products utilised by the core trades in rolling stock and infrastructure. Plastics and fibre glass replacing many timber fittings in car fitting. Rubber insulted cabling replaced with PVC and TPS. In fabrication, thermal and wire feed welding normal and turnery work modernised with CNC (computer numerical control) programmed lathes. Fire proof and waterproof environments introducing MI mineral insulated cable – or pyro cable. Solid – state electronics introduced for motor control. Somewhat out of sight of management both myself and Kevin McPoyle after negotiating an extension of space from the Carriage Superintendent, Les Mills (a chunk of the car shop storage area) decided to interpret skills as reflecting the needs of today's (1977) electrical industry and technology We decided to relocate the booths for electrical board work and build half a house.*

Half a house. *A little initiative, materials and labour and we were away. The timber was requisitioned against our cost centres and the car builder apprentices had the opportunity greater than their models. Under supervision we built half of a house frame, two parallel walls and an end wall to industry standards at about 4 metres with a window and door opening. A portion of each frame was covered with chip board and the majority wall surface left open. All battened down and secured, it grew in the space of a week and was years ahead of this application of the trade. This vehicle complimented the apprentices board work in simple circuits with the building frame enabling the experience from point of entry (fuse board) to different circuit environments. In some ways we were interpreting the changes in the industry and applying these to skills appropriate to apprentice training. A new degree of variety had been introduced without any loss to the program. The cadre of high achievers were rewarded with early release to their workplaces and the recognition of accelerated skills would become the norm. Who knows if we enhanced the progress of that period of apprentice. I like to think for the majority…yes*

I took up a position in the Corporate Training area in mid-June 1979 leaving my association with Newport Workshops and apprentice training. The years following saw both Graham Button and Graeme Copeland at the helm. The pathway from the Plant shop and holder of an 'A; grade certificate confirmed for the senior instructor and far from my eyeline. Changes continued with the closure of the VR Technical College and in the following years as the ETC was relocated.

In 1987 the Electrical Training Centre was relocated to the former refurbished Boiler Shop canteen location consolidating the location of the core skill training centres. The manual training centres final days are unclear but surely linked to a period prior to the privatisation of the workshops.

CHAPTER 9

STA - Scholarships and Awards

Technical College Prizes – Subject to good conduct, tuition, regular attendance, zeal and industry in the service of the State Transport Authority, those apprentices who each year of the period of tuition, are adjudged first, second and third highest in order of merit among all apprentices in their trade are awarded monetary prizes providing they obtain not less than 75% of the possible marks in their final term examinations.

Apprenticeship awards, VRI ballroom 1976, Deputy General Manager, Mr McCallum told apprentices that they had the opportunity in the railways to go as far as possible. There are opportunities for scholarships; if you try hard enough, they are there for you. (*VR Newsletter 1976, extract*)

Scholarships – apprentices who, because of their scholastic attainment are permitted to undertake a special technical course, and who satisfactorily fulfil the requirements of that course, will be eligible for such numbers of scholarships, under certain circumstances as the State Transport Authority may determine and such scholarship winners will be nominated as students in electrical, mechanical or civil engineering.

Congratulations to all prize winners who realised the top college scholastic results within the Victorian Railways, V/line or State apprenticeships awards. The following contributors were recognised as the outstanding apprentice of their year. Tony Davis, (Fitter & Turner, Victorian Railways)1960. Norm Swanwick, (Electrical Fitting, V.R. Technical College) 1969. Both were winners of the apprentice awards (Bronze medallion) as the best of the apprentices of all trades for which training is provided, of the

Apprentice Commission of Victoria. Scott Gould – 1st & 3rd apprentice of the year medallions for signal maintenance. The medallions for Victorian Railway awards were commissioned and introduced in 1980 and designed by sculptor, Michael Meszaros. The bronze medallion design features a hand holding a file and a puzzle piece, featuring a track section depicting a rail line.

Michael Meszaros, OAM, contributed his recollections from 1980. The brief was to express something important, relevant and central about apprentices, the railways and the importance of the apprenticeship course within the railway system. At the time, there was by memory, 23 apprenticeship courses within the railways comprising most trades needed for the successful functioning of the railways. These ranged from fitting and turning to clockmaking and much in between. These factors lay beneath my thinking in arriving at the design. I always try to avoid what I call the 'shopping list approach', by which I mean using a lot of little illustrations of the elements which make up a subject. I rather try to find some underlying principle which ties all those details together. In any case, I came to the conclusion that since all the apprentice courses were essential to the proper running of the railways, they created, in a sense a complete picture of the railways. Combined each apprenticeship skill worked together to make the railway runs successfully. My solution was a jigsaw puzzle where the image on the puzzle was a railway track laid on ballast. The idea of many pieces linked together to make a complete picture seemed an appropriate symbol of this linkage and the importance of each piece.

Victorian Railways Apprentice Award medallion, M. Meszaros OAM design

The second element of in my thinking was to express the refined skills needed for each trade and the element of the skill being carried out by a person who put them into action. To express this, I two hands carefully filing the last piece of the jigsaw piece, to make it fit perfectly into position. The medal was first made in the size of the apprentice of the Year Award.in 7.5 inches diameter, and this was cast in bronze with a separate cast bronze inscription plate, which was I also designed and made in the same style and material as the medal. This was presented mounted on a timber panel, in a lined timber case, made by.my cabinet maker, Sophus Bruhn. The bronze casting was made by the foundry of C.F. Burnell. The small medals, 2.5 inches diameter were struck by the royal Australian mint in Canberra and presented in three versions – **gold** plated for the best in each trade, silver plated for second and bronze for the third.

The silver and bronze medals were finished with a dark petunia, which displayed the modelling to advantage. Gold cannot be patinated, and I always thought it was the least satisfying from an artistic point of view. The original was made by modelling it in plasticine. A plaster mould was the cast from this and the texture of the ballast added at this point, plus some work on refining the modelling. A plaster cast was made from the mould into which I engraved the lines defining the jigsaw pieces, this was the pattern for the bronze casting and also for the mint to do the reduction and striking. I was invited to the first presentation, and was informed that I would be needed to speak in two minutes. I had forgotten that I had been asked some months before, and so I was unprepared. In those two minutes, I had the thought that I had been trained academically as an architect as well as being trained as an informal apprentice with my sculptor father. It was the apprenticeship training with which I was making my living…this was well received.

The New Breed. Personnel Group report for the Workshops Board, No.72 in August 1991 noted the Apprentice awards were presented at the Newport TAFE. Forty-two apprentices were presented with prizes. The winner of the V/Line apprentice of the year and Roy Curtis Memorial Award was Ms Michelle Hines, (Sheetmetal Worker 1st class) Ballarat Workshops with special awards to Ms Christina Pearce, (Painter & Decorator) Ballarat Workshops and Slade Davis, (Fitter & Turner) Freight Division.

9.1   Railways of Australia Competitions.

Beyond the walls of individual rail systems were annual competitions conducted for nominated apprentices (1st in State competition) representing each rail States. Annually a different state hosted the competition for the core apprenticeships. NSW rail, QLD rail, SA/National rail, WA and the V/Line (Victorian Railways).

OWEN WALDIE continued his participation in other aspects of the rail apprentice; including employment selection interviews and as the V/Line representative judge in ROA competitions. His progression was from an adjudicating judge to head judge for the trade of electrical fitters for the State rail systems. V/line hosted the ROA competitions at the Newport TAFE in 1987, and then at NSW Rail Chullora facility/workshops in 1991. Trades represented in the ROA competitions included fitter and turners, bricklayers, carpenters and electrical fitters.

Rules as unforgiven as ever; i.e. electrical fitters' competitors will commence and finish their work as instructed by the judges. The familiarisation period is to be used to examine the project plan, equipment, and materials.

This competition has been designed to test your ability to apply your basic trade skills to complete a project over an 8-hour period. Among the instructions; the interpretation of circuit drawings and layout diagram, measure and set out the conductors and apparatus on the basis of circuit and layout diagrams, cutting and sawing conduits, cables and apparatus of plastic and metal (junction boxes, fuse boards, switch/dimmer, earth stakes and water pipe, the use of TPS cable and soldering connections.

Equipment; test equipment, electric hand tools, steps, draw in snake, bender, stock and die set. Safety equipment, foot and eye protection.

R.O.A. Work skill competition, Newport college of TAFE. 1987

V/Line electrical apprentices work skill competition.

CHAPTER 10

The passing of the Victorian Railways

The State-owned railways had operated since the mid-19th century after the failure of the privately operated company of Melbourne & Hobson Bay Rail Company. History records that the then State parliament enacted the *Victorian Railways Commissioners Act of 1883* to construct, maintain and manage the state's railways. The staff of the Department of Railways came under the authority of the Railway Commissioners. All through that period of initial explosive community growth the rail industry reached nearly every corner of the State to meet grain and wool export markets. Within the State's capital of Melbourne, the growth of community suburbs demanded rail links and faster and improved services. These primary roles were the visible face of the RAIL who additionally operated a laundry, a printing works, a refreshment service and workshop canteens, the list was endless. The Victorian Railways also ran the Victorian Government Tourist Bureau (1926 – 1959), the Mount Buffalo Chalet (1925- 1985), the State Coal mine at Wonthaggi, and the Newport Power stations A & B.

Events large and small altered the face of rail services that were once seen as essential to both the regional and urban communities. The drivers of change combined rail traffic rationalisation and burdening deficits. The Railways amendment Act 1972 passed the management from the Victorian Railway Commissioners to a Victorian Railway Board siting a modern structure to manage change. From 1974 the Victorian Railways traded as VicRail, before later successive governments responding to commercial and economic pressures introduced the State Transport Authority (STA) trading as V/Line and the Metropolitan Transit Authority (MTA), (1983) bringing to closure 100 years of the benevolent rail institution, the Victorian Railways. The MTA continued with this trading name until the Public Transport Authority (the Met) was formed some six years later in 1989. V/line Passenger was franchised to National Express, returning to government ownership as V/Line Passenger Corporation in 2003.

Privatisation of the rail industry was to follow as the Kennett Government tendered for service providers. In 1998 the suburban rail network was divided into integrated business units of the Public Transport corporation as Hillside Trains and Bayside Trains. Bayside was privatised in August 1999 as a subsidiary of National Express. Hillside Trains as a subsidiary of Connex. Today, (2025) the suburban rail system is consolidated under one provider, Metro, a wholly owned MTR corporation of John Holland Group and UGL Rail, a division of United Group Limited.

These drums of change finalised the role of service delivery from the State to Service providers under term delivery contracts for rail, tram and bus transport. An extract from the *Memorandum of understanding between the Government of Victoria and the rail unions (specified) 1993*.

Infrastructure services core services will remain in house.
These core services are: signalling and communication, track and civil, tram infrastructure and rail electrical (heavy rail and light rail). **Workshops savings** – the unions agree to implement the proposed changes as recommended by INDEC, subject to consultation. Training of PTC staff in all aspects of safeworking will be retained in-house. **All other training could be contracted out.**

Apprentice Training. The inevitable march of time, economics and technology. The Training for apprentices in the Victorian Railways has undertaken many changes and parallels the technological changes of the rail transport industry over a hundred years. It also mirrors the social and political times of the period which saw changes to the Victorian Railways structure from a government bureaucracy to a commercial entity. Change and innovation in the late 20th century became the catch phrase of governments worldwide leading in part to the 'System to a Service' policy of the 1993 Kennett, Victorian State Government that commenced the transition to private service providers.

The history of the Victorian Railways is of a diverse spread of activities in the provision of public rail services and much more, including its construction, maintenance and servicing. It also includes a commitment to their employee's wellbeing in training and education opportunities. The trades and technical training were historically the domains of the Way & Works, Electrical and Rolling Stock Branches prior to Workshops Division of the State Transport Authority and their workplace locations. Prior to the apprentice undertaking his first year in a skills program at the Newport Training Centres, the individual tradesman was the apprentice's prime instructor. In reality it never changed as the remaining years of an apprenticeship was on-the-job. The variation over the years relevant to the rail business activities. The wheels of progress had continued to turn as the impact of major drivers with terms of competitiveness and core business had led to major government reports and recommendations. *In truth the wheels of major elements of apprentice training for the Victorian Railways were past*. Unprecedented national economics and educational reforms were enacted. The railway apprentice was swept along with these changes as his work place and work type changed. It was the world of the rail industry before the formalisation of learning by a combination of Government reforms, Industry Committees, Training Commissions, the National Public Transport Training Board, and TAFE to enable Australian wide trade and transport transferrable qualifications.

The stories shared here might be a starting point rather than an end. They lived the Victorian Railway's apprenticeship system that successfully trained thousands of young men and later some young women. Each a personal story in an industry of changing technology that defined their apprenticeship years.

Today, an apprenticeship is complete when the require competencies, delivered and assessed by the RTO (Recognised Training Organisation) and confirmed in the workplace. The RTO must confirm workplace competencies with the employer. *(Victoria State Government information.2025).*

What's on your apprentice papers?

On my records (**Denman,1965**) of apprenticeship there is no reference to the Apprentice Commission of Victoria even though they were the presiding authority. Clearly issued on the completion of my apprenticeship certificate is the employer - the Victorian Railways. Probably the norm of those years with apprentices employed by the other major government departments the same or similar on their completion. Simply explained as the organisation you were indentured to became the training provider within the guidelines of the Apprentice Commission. As in the case of government instrumentalities i.e., the Gas & Fuel Corporation, the State Electricity Commission, The Melbourne Metropolitan Tram Board, and the Williamstown dockyard. <u>Depending on the 'times' rail apprentices</u> from the nineteen eighties received their trade completion of apprenticeship notification from the Apprentice Commission or the Industrial Training Commission of Victoria. This was issued on completion of studies from the relevant TAFE organisation and confirmation of workplace on-job work by the employer (V/line or the Met)

Apprentice Completion Certificate.

```
G. 242                    VICTORIAN RAILWAYS.              No. 1948
                                                    Rolling Stock Branch
                                                    Melbourne 20/ 1 /19 66.

        Certificate of Completion of Apprenticeship

    This is to Certify that  Owen Stanley WALDIE
    whose signature appears in the margin, satisfactorily
    completed his Course of Training as an Apprentice
    Electrical Fitter,            on the Fifteenth      day
    of   January,      19 66.

                                          .......................................
    138—46                                      Head of Branch.
```

Signature of Holder O S Waldie

Victorian Railways, Certificate of Completion of Apprenticeship

Sources. The stories are recollections of the listed contributors. Primary and secondary sources were provided by articles within the magazines and publications of the Victorian Railway's magazine, *Rail Ways, V/Line News, STA and other publications, including the Newport Journal* and internet sources of *State Government Acts*.

Contributors CV's

Norm Swanwick – V.R. – Electronic Engineering, Department of Defence
Owen Waldie – V.R./V/Line – Train Lighting Depot Inspector/Quality Assurance
Anthony Davis – V.R. - Education Department, technical trade teacher.
Dennis Denman – V.R./PTC - apprentice training/MET training manager.
Stuart Smithwick – V/Line/Clyde Downer group.
Scott Gould – State Transport Authority - Signal Maintenance Manager, Metro.
Ray Crampton – V.R. – ETU, Fire fighters Union, ETU Apprentice Officer, Training and Development Officer
Owen Murray – V.R. – Way & Works, Eastern Region district fitter.
Terry Riley – V.R. – turner & fitter
Bruce Nevandt – V.R – Diesel maintainer, Geelong/South Dynon
Harry Stevens – VR. - V/line – Diesel maintainer - South Dynon
Andy Barros – VR -V/Line – Electrical fitter – JWS/Epping Depot

YOUR STORY

Name   Apprenticeship...........................

Year commenced..................   Year completed...........................

Departmental number, optional...

Organisational name, Victorian Railways, State Transport Authority, (V/line) the Met, Public Transport Corporation.

<u>Year 1</u>   workplace, work type

<u>Year 2</u>   workplace, work type

<u>Year 3</u>   workplace, work type

College attended...............................
<u>Year 4</u>   workplace, work type

<u>Year 5</u>   workplace, work type

Other roles.. if resigned......................................

Apprentice Honour Roll:

Some among the many. The list is not inclusive, but a sample of names, the year of their birthdates and <u>starting work classification</u>. The names have been taken from a personnel search of V/line's data base September 1988 – series 41, held at the Victorian Public Records Office and other research sources. The many others from later periods and those that moved into private enterprise and commercial life after concluding their apprenticeship are sadly not included.

Name	date of birth	commencement classification
Abbott, John Alfred	30/12/1882	App. Fitter & Turner
Ablett, Barry Winston.	25/2/1945	App. Blacksmith
Ahlstrom, Brian	14/31944	App. Boilermaker
Ainsworth, Joseph.	15/2/1922	App. Fitter & Turner
Aingimea, Paul	15/8/1949	App. Fitter & Turner
Allen, David.	8/8/1925	App. Boilermaker
Allibon, William.	19/8/1927	App. Fitter & Turner.
Arnold, Leonard	29/8/1950	App. Fitter & Turner.
Ardizzon, Enzo	19/11/1943	App. Electrical Mechanic
Augustine, Desmond	28/5/1922	App. Boilermaker
Austin, Malcolm	19/11/1943	App. Electrical Fitter.
Bachitow, Victor	21/5/1940	App. Fitter & Turner
Baillie, Robert John	1/1/1934	App. Car & Wagon builder (SofA)
Baker, Kevin.	16/11/1932	App. Printer
Baker, Raymond	n/a	App. Upholsterer
Baldwin, Ivan	n/a	App. Welder
Ball, George	2/11/1940	App. Painter
Barby, Ronald	1910	App. C &W Bldr.
Barclay, Eric	1938	App. Fitter & Turner
Barker, James	11/11/1922	App. Painter
Barker, Ronald.	1942	App. Boilermaker.
Calverley, John	29/12/1941	App. Car & Wag. Bldr.

Name	Date	Role
Calvert, David*	11/11/1901	App. Iron machinist
Cameron, Alexander	23/3/1904	App. Blacksmith
Cameron, Donald	15/6/1922	App. Boilermaker.
Cameron, Ronald	1/8/1944	App. Fitter & Turner
Cameron, William	29/11/1941	App. Car & Wagon Bldr.
Camp, Terence	2/6/1946	App. Boilermaker
Campbell, Peter	22/6/1941	App. Car & Wagon bldr.
Chapman, William	11/2/1917	App Fitter & Turner. (Workshop M'ger.)
Christesen, Aubrey	**15/10/1898**	**App. Boilermaker *appointed 17/11/1915**
Curtis, George	**11/2/1888**	**App. Fitter & Turner (appointed, 7/2/1905)**
Curtis, Roy	**n/a**	**Fitter & Turner (SofA)**
Davey, John	21/9/1938	App. Boilermaker
David, Clifford*	**12/10/1899**	**App. Boilermaker (appointed 10/11/1915)**
Davis Geoffrey	6/7/1928	App. Carpenter
Daws, Alan.	30/8/1933	App. Turner & Fitter (trade instructor)
Day, Norman	14/8/1944	App. Car & Wagon Bldr.
Denis, John	27/8/1933	App. Elec. Fitter
Denman, Dennis	4/9/1944	App. Electrical Mechanic (1961)
Deluca, Domen	14/6/1944	App. Fitter & Turner
Doran, John	30/12/1923	App. Blacksmith
Dorgan, Fredrick	14/7/1901	App. Moulder
Duncan, Maxwell	19/5/1945	App. Boilermaker
Duggan, Basil	4/9/1938	App. Car & Wagon Bldr.
Duggan, Kevin	31/8/1940	App. Car painter
Eaton, Arthur	3/11/1923	App. Fitter & Turner
Eaton, Robert	29/11/1936	App. Elec. Mechanic.
Eaton, Ronald	30/5/1925	App. Coppersmith
Eddy, Robert	29/11/1909	App. Carpenter
Edney, George	23/5/1923	App. Fitter & Turner

Edwards, Brian	8/10/1937	App. Interlock Fitter
Edwards, Kenneth	5/4/1944	App. Elec. Fitter
Edwards, Stuart	2/8/1951	App. Fitter & Turner
Elker, Raymond	6/8/1925	App. Fitter & Turner
Elliot, William	**18/6/1898**	**App. Patternmaker**
Fell, Alan	19/1/1937	App. Coppersmith
Finlayson, John	4/8/1904	App. Wood machinist
Fiolet, Hendrick	9/5/1943	App. Elec. Fitter
Firth, Allan	9/5/1921	App. Elec. Fitter. (Chief EE)
Forty, Cecil	**10/2/1899**	**App. Car & Wagon Bldr.**
Forster, Godfrey	**6/4/1899**	**App. Fitter & Turner**
Foster, Stephen	30/3/1945	App. Car & Wagon Bldr.
Fowler, James	**22/9/1886**	**App. Fitter & Turner**
Gallacher, Robert	6/12/1929	App. " "
Galletley, Graeme	14/4/1940	App. Car & Wagon bldr.
Galletly, W.O	n/a	App. Fitter & Turner (CME)
Gamble, Donald	15/2/1937	App. Elec. Mechanic
Gardiner, Ralph	25/5/1932	App. Elec. Fitter.
Gasperino, Laurance	**17/12/1897**	**App. Boilermaker**
Gatehouse, Athol	14/4/1904	App. Iron machinist.
Gates, Robert	17/5/1910	App. Fitter & Turner
Gauld, graham	15/5/1943	App. Elec. Fitter
Gaven, Peter	27/12/1934	App. " '
Giblett, Kenneth		22/4/1941 App. " "
Haberman, Gordon	11/8/1930	app. Car painter
Hall, Keith	12/11/1943	App. Carpenter
Hanan, Richard	15/8/1930	App. Elec. Mechanic
Handcock, john	13/6/1933	App. Coppersmith
Hanson, Terrence	28/4/1940	App. Letterpress Machinist.

Hansford, Charles	20/1/1908	App. Elec. Fitter* JWS M'ger.
Hardeman, Raymond	2/1/1906	App Car & Wag bldr
Hayes, Vaughan,	29/4/1926	App. Elec. Fitter
Hennessy, Michael	**21/6/1860**	**App. Fitter (Hobson Bay rail)**
Hughes, Maxwell	7/8/1928	App. interlock Fitter.
Hodges, Ian	n/a	App. Elect. Fitter.(Commissioner)
Ivers, Frederick	14/111951	App. Fitter & Turner
Irving. Alan	28/3/1928	App. Elect. Fitter.
Irving, Leslie	19/4/1939	App. Fitter & Turner
Irving, Bruce	n/a	App. Unknown ** source N. Harris
Jack, Albert	8/3/1928	App. Fitter & Turner
Jack, Franklin	9/2/1932	App. Fitter & Turner
Jack, Robert	13/5/1923	App. Fitter & Turner
Jack, roger	4/12/1938	App. Boilermaker
Jack, Russell	13/1/1935	App. Boilermaker
Jackson, Alan	25/5/1950	App. Fitter & Turner
Jaensch, Jack	25/9/1912	App. Painter
Jakymezuk, Steven	9/11/1941	App. Elect. Fitter.
James, Murray	18/1/1943	App. Elec. Mechanic
Kauffman, Conrad	19/9/1910	App. Fitter & Turner
Kayrooz, Anthony	20/1/1942	App. Elec. Mechanic
Keane, Stanley Francis	29/9/1918	App. Fitter & Turner -CME.
Kelly, Bernard	13/10/1936	App. Electrical Fitter.
Kelly, George	7/6/1907	App. Fitter & Turner
Kelly, john	6/4/1905	App. Fitter & Turner
Kelly, Neil	11/12/1941	App. Carpenter
Keener, Robert	7/10/1950	App. Fitter & Turner
Kift, John Berriman.	28/12/1933	App. Electrical Fitter.
Keng, Michael	n/a	App. Electrical Fitter.

Lack, John	n/a	App. Mech. Fitter.
La Fontaine	25/11/1935	App. Boilermaker
Lacy, Michael	21/10/1932	App. Electrical Fitter.
Laird, john	14/11/1937	App. Plumber
Lane, Thomas	1/2/1938	App. Boilermaker
Lane, William	1/5/1939	App. Boilermaker
Langcake, Thomas	1/10/1940	App Car & Wagon Bldr.
Langdon, James	29/10/1943	App. Fitter & Turner
Little, Ronald	30/1/1922	App. Turner & Fitter (trade instructor ETC)
Lythgo, Robert	n/a	App. Car & Wagon Bldr.
Mace, Pierce	28/11/1937	App. Spring maker
MacGibbon, Trevor	23/3/1944	App. Plumber
McInnes, Alan	29/9/1950	App. Fitter & Turner
Madex, Robert	30/11/1943	App. Painter.
Maguire, William.	15/12/1941	App. Elect. Fitter
Malvista, Heinz	16/6/1944	App. Elect. Fitter.
Manfield, Henley	24/10/1908	App. Carpenter
Milne, Ronald	21/11/1924	App. Elec. Fitter
Mahoney, Hugh	3/2/1935	App Car & Wagon Bldr.
Morison, Neville	n/a	App. Fitter & Turner (SofA)
McCall, John	19/2/1950	App. Fitter & Turner
McSparron, Robert	17/6/1950	App. Fitter & Turner
Murray Owen	n/a	App Fitter & Turner
Nanscowen, Peter	4/2/1947	App. Elec. Fitter
Nash, William	14/2/1940	App. Elec. Fitter
Naugle, Leo	13/9/1904	App. Fitter & Turner
Nelson, Ernest	14/3/1924	App. Fitter & Turner
Newell, George	21/7/1926	App. Tinsmith
Nicholls, Harold	5/9/1940	App. Sailmaker

Nicholson, Alfred	26/1/1919	App. Fitter & Turner GM
Nicholson, James	11/9/1941	App. Boilermaker
Odgers, Geoffrey	6/4/1950	App. Fitter & Turner
O'Loughlin, William	10/4/1935	App. Fitter & Turner
Oliver, Geoffrey	13/5/1949	App. Fitter & Turner
O'Neil, Noel	8/10/1938	App. Boilermaker
O'Riordan, Terrance	4/3/1921	App. Upholsterer
O'Shea, Michael	20/1/1950	App. Fitter & Turner
Parsons Christopher	14/11/1937	App. Engine Blacksmith
Patterson, William	16/1/1922	App. Coppersmith
Paton, Kevin	29/8/1938	App. Sailmaker
Payne, Edwin	31/3/1925	App. Interlock Fitter
Perrin, Anthony	21/7/1950	App. Fitter & Turner
Pinkerton, Kenneth	19/6/1950	App. Fitter & Turner - TBC
Quirk, Ian	2/12/1941	App. Fitter & Turner
Rae, Stewart	19/5/1933	App. Tinsmith
Rankin, Charles	**11/7/1894**	**App. Fitter & Turner**
Rankine, William	**11/8/1942**	App. Fitter & Turner
Rayner, Alwyn	18/5/1942	App. Moulder
Riley, James.	8/11/1926	App. Electrical Fitter. (1942)
Roach, R	n/a	App. Fitter & Turner
Rolls Leslie.	8/10/1923	App. Electrical Fitter. * CME
Rodda, Albert William	n/a	App. Fitter & Turner
Rudolph. Ernie	n/a	App. Elec. Fitter (1937)
Roseburgh, Thomas	18/12/1949	App. Fitter & Turner - TBC
Sanders, Roy	29/12/1927	App. Weighbridge Fitter
Sawyer, George	10/10/1932	App. Elec. Fitter
Scheurer, Norman	22/3/1923	App. Boilermaker
Stevens, Craig	20/11/1963	App. Boilermaker & fabricator.

Scott, David	6/8/1933	App. Tinsmith
Stevenson, Robert Scott	30/1/1969	App. Elect Mech.
Smithwick, Stuart	n/a	App. Elec Fitter (1985)
Swanwick, Norman	n/a	App Electrical Fitter (1966)
Swift, Graeme.	29/8/1931	App. Fitter & Turner* TBC
Tancredi, Michael	9/11/1937	App. Boilermaker
Taylor, Geoffrey	27/5/1924	App. Boilermaker
Taylor, John	10/5/1941	App. Engine Boilermaker
Thompson, Kenneth	5/10/1950	App. Fitter & Turner
Turk, Maurice	n/a	App. Patternmaker – TBC
Uhe, F.H	1/7/1936	App. Elec. Fitter
Van Berkel, Graeme	5/4/1939	App. Fitter & Turner
Vasily, Mili	10/10/1939	App. Elec. Fitter
Vassallo, Carmel	26/4/1944	App. Fitter & Turner
Vincent, Arthur	27/3/1902	App. Fitter & Turner
Virgona, Antonia	23/1/1945	App. Elect Mech.- TBC
Wakefield, graham	11/1/1942	App. Elec. Fitter
Walker, Ian	21/4/1938	App. Fitter & Turner
Wallace, William	9/10/1926	App. Elec. Fitter
Waters, Derrick	22/4/1946	App. Carpenter
Watson, Arthur	8/1/1937	App. Patternmaker
Waldie, Owen	4/2/1945	App. Elec Fitter
Wheatland, Andrew.	n/a	App. Electrical Fitter
Willmot, Peter	25/7/1950	App. Fitter & Turner
Wilkins, William	2/5/1931	App. Electrical Fitter, CEE
Yarwood, Douglas	16/2/1937	App. Boilermaker
Yean, Desmond	13/10/1938	App. Fitter & Turner
Youens, Jack	11/4/1921	App. Boilermaker
Young, Keith	7/3/1923	App. Fitter & Turner

Young, Robert	29/11/1903	App. Wood machinist
Youren, Richard	27/12/1946	App. Boilermaker -
Zala, Jeffery	24/9/1950	App. Fitter & Turner
Zerbst, Raymond	30/4/1951	App. Fitter & Turner
Zdybel, Stanislaw	18/1/1951	App. Fitter & Turner -

A Scrapbook History of Apprenticeship Training in the Victorian Railways

1960 - 1984

Compiled by Norm Swanwick
Apprentice Electrical Fitter 1966 - 1971

December 2024

INTRODUCTION:

While reading a May 2024 edition of Rail Digest magazine I came across an article about an open day and the closure of the Newport Railways workshop back in the late 1980's. I had undertaken part of my apprenticeship training back in the 1960's at Newport which included attending the Victorian Railways Technical College located within the workshop's precinct. Nostalgia overtook me and I decided to investigate what had happened to the College only to discover that it had seen its last classes in 1980 and was eventually demolished. Railway apprenticeship training had been transferred to the recently built Newport College of TAFE which itself was eventually closed and demolished. Part of the Workshops has been leased to private industry which now took over the role of maintaining railways (now V/Line) rolling stock. The original historic part of the workshops is leased by Steamrail Victoria to house and maintain a variety of heritage steam, diesel and electric rolling stock. My research took me up to 1984 and I was unable to obtain any further information after that date although apprentices were still being trained. I suspect that eventually with the workshops being closed and the maintenance of rolling stock being now undertaken by private industry, apprenticeship training by V/Line had ceased or at least had been reduced considerably.

SOURCES:

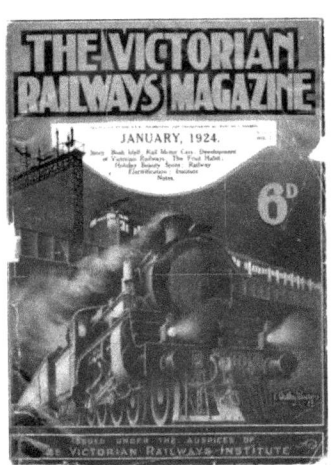

Most of the information contained in this document has been extracted from the monthly staff magazines published by the Victorian Railways. The first edition appeared in 1924 and was known as the "Victorian Railways Magazine" and had a cover price of 6d and was issued under the auspices of the Victorian Railways Institute. In 1931 it was known as the "Victorian Railways Newsletter" which it continued to be called up to June 1973 when it again changed its title to "Victorian Rail Ways" and continued to be published under this title until around 1983 when it became known as "V/Line News". For a brief period in 1983, it was published under the title STA News (State Transport Authority). Most copies of the magazine from 1924 to 1979 are available online. March 1981 to June 1983 Railways Magazines are available at the National Library in Canberra and the V/Line December 1983 to March 1991 are also available at the National Library. Various issues of the magazines are available for sale on eBay and I was fortunate to be able to obtain a number of the 1980 editions of the Railways magazine which appear to be unavailable elsewhere.

Unfortunately, the quality of most of the pictures appearing in this report is not the greatest as most were taken from online scanned images.

BRIEF HISTORY OF THE VICTORIAN RAILWAYS

1856   Victorian Railways Department established by the Government.
1874   Victorian Railways became VicRail as a trading name. 1976 New VicRail logo introduced.
1983   30 June VicRail ceases to exist.
        1 July State Transport Authority (STA) & Metropolitan Transit Authority come into being. STA announces its new livery & logo V/Line.
1997   V/Line split into V/Line Passenger and V/Line Freight.
1999   V/Line Freight sold to Rail America and known as Freight Victoria.
2000   Freight Victoria changes its name to Freight Australia.
2004   Pacific National assumes control of Freight Australia.

BRIEF HISTORY OF NEWPORT RAILWAY WORKSHOPS

The Newport Railway Workshops were the main railway workshops for the Victorian Railways for 100 years (1889 – 1980s), employing up to 5000 people at its peak. The workshops built and maintained locomotives and rolling stock, as well as manufacturing much of its own machinery, tools, many railway items and tarpaulins.

Brief History of Newport Railway Workshops

1854   Australia's first railway opens between Melbourne and Port Melbourne.
1857   First Railway Workshops were built at Port Gellibrand, Williamstown.
1882   A railway carriage workshop was built in Melbourne Road, Newport.
1884   Williamstown Workshops soon outgrew its limited site. A new workshop site was chosen in Champion Road Newport to replace the small Williamstown Workshop.
1886-88   The Newport Workshops were based on the British Railway Workshop designs, practices and principles. These buildings are now considered to be one of the finest surviving examples of late Victorian Railway Workshop Architecture in the world.
1887-90-1910   Tarpaulin shed was constructed in the Northern section of the site to produce tarps for perishable goods in open wagons. In just four years in 1890, it was doubled in size. Twenty years later in 1910, it was doubled in size again.
1893   Manufacture of locomotives commenced at Newport Workshops greatly expanding the operations of the workshops.
1895   Carriage workshops transferred to Newport Workshops.
1902-15   this period saw a major expansion of the workshops, as the Victorian Railways modernised its operations. Both East and West Block were extended to double the size of the workshop area.
1937   The Spirit of Progress was constructed at Newport Workshops. This was Australia's first fully air-conditioned all steel passenger train.

1939-45 Newport Workshops were used to construct military equipment during WW2 – including Bren Gun Carriers, aircraft fuselages, ship hulls and 3' 6" gauge railway equipment used throughout Australia during the war. The workshops worked around the clock, day and night shifts, and employed a staff of 5000, of which 35% were women.

1950s End of manufacture of locomotives at Newport Workshops. Its role reverted back to the maintenance of locomotives, rolling stock, and railway equipment.

1980s The older parts of Newport Workshops had reached the end of its usefulness. There was limited potential to turn a 19th Century workshop into a modern facility. By the end of the 1980s, large areas of Newport were no longer in use.

1993 Steamrail, 707 Operations, and DERMPAV moved their operations into West Block at Newport Workshops.

The Heritage significance and importance of the Newport Railway Workshops

1988 V/Line commissioned C & M J Doring Pty Ltd, consulting engineers, to undertake a Heritage study of Newport Workshops from 1888 to 1988. This report found: *"There can be no doubt that Newport is one of the best surviving 19th-century railway workshops in the world and one of the country's most outstanding items of Industrial heritage."*

1992 Joan Kirner, Australia's first female State Premier and former State Member for Williamstown and her state Labour government, recognised the importance and Heritage significance of the Newport Workshops.

A working party, established by the Kirner Government, recommended that the Newport Workshops be made a Heritage Rail Precinct called "Railworks", where operating heritage railway operators and a railway museum could be established.

1993 Railworks was established and the Public Transport Commission of Victoria granted tenure to Steamrail, 707 Operations and DERMPAV in West Block at Newport Workshops.

1994 Heritage Victoria added the Newport Railway Workshops to the Victorian Heritage Register (H1000). A citation from the heritage listing states that: *"The workshops are one of the best surviving 19th-century railway workshops in the world."*

1997 The National Trust of Victoria classified the Newport Railway Workshops B4019, stating that:*"The magnitude and variety of buildings, industrial processes, and trade skills practiced at this site and the extensive collection of working machinery, qualifies the workshops to be of prime national importance."* The Hobson Bay City Council has also listed Newport Workshops as heritage buildings (H065) under their planning scheme.

2000 Heritage Victoria, VicTrack, and the Department of Infrastructure on behalf of the Minister for Transport, commissioned Helen Lardner Conservation and Design to undertake a Conservation Management Plan for the Newport Workshops. The report concluded that: –*"The Newport Workshops are of high Local, State and National Heritage Significance."*

2018 VicTrack advised Steamrail and all other not-for-profit organisations at the Newport Workshops that their current leases would not be renewed when they finished in April 2020.

2019 Following Steamrail's representation to VicTrack, a new lease is currently being negotiated. For how long, and what conditions would apply is unknown, so Steamrail and the Newport Workshop's future is uncertain.

The future of Newport Railway Workshops

The Newport Railway Workshops has the potential to become one of Victoria and Australia's most significant tourist attractions, generating jobs, investment and growth locally, in the State, and throughout Australia.

With such a strong link to Victoria and Australia's heritage, Newport Workshops should be designated as Victoria's Rail Heritage Precinct and used only for heritage rail activities. This would give Steamrail long-term tenure to enable it to remain viable and continue to undertake heavy steam maintenance for all heritage railways in Victoria.

Newport Railway Workshops Central Block & Clock Tower/Admin Offices

Aerial Views of the Newport Workshops

HISTORY OF VICTORIAN RAILWAYS TECHNICAL COLLEGE

Apprentices were first admitted to the railway workshops at Williamstown in 1860. For the first 25 years of the railway's existence, the number of apprentices taken on was very small. From 1905 until 1922, a special course for railway apprentices was conducted at the Working Men's College now the Royal Melbourne Institute of Technology.

1905 railway apprentices were the first to attend the old Workingman's College (now the RMIT)

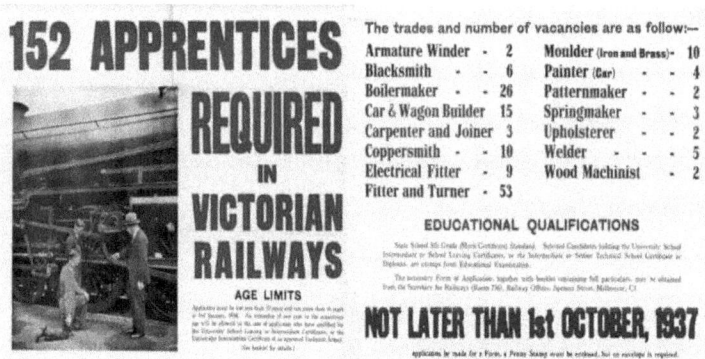

1937 newspaper advertisements for Railway apprentices

February 1922 saw the first apprentices under the new scheme commence their training. They were interviewed by Mr. Nilsson, the Principal of the projected Victorian Railways Technical College. Classes commenced on February 27, 1922, in temporary accommodation at the paint shop, Newport Workshops, until construction of the new Technical College was completed. On 11 March 1923, the 160 students comprising the classes were transferred from the Workshops to the Technical College that was officially opened by Mr. Commissioner Shannon.

Newport VR Technical College 1922

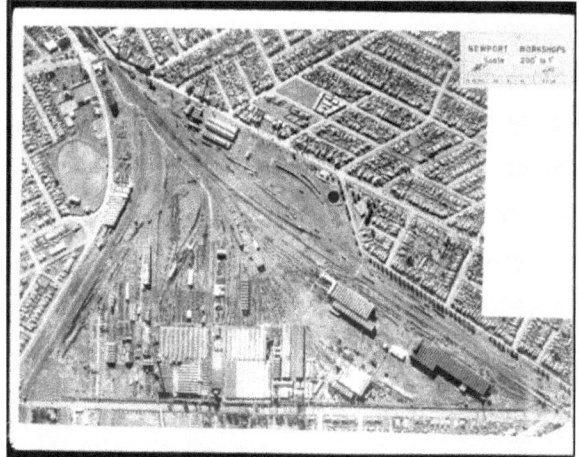

Newport Railway Workshops 1950 showing the location of the college.

Apprentices at Newport Technical College **Apprentices Training at Newport Workshop**

Public Records Office Victoria Collection

1925

The Victorian Railways Magazine, October, 1925. 557

Sound Technical Training for Apprentices

Some of the boys at the Railways Technical College, Newport. Instructors Messrs. A. R. Lukeis, O. Nillson, and W. Grace in white in front.

Scientific training is the basis of a skilled trade or a profession. The Victorian Railways Commissioners realised this when they established the Victorian Railways Technical College at Newport. Mr. O. Nillson, the head instructor, here reviews the work of the College.

THE Railways Commissioners have always insisted on apprentices at the Newport Railway Workshops receiving a sound technical training.

There are dozens of officers now in high positions in the service who received their early training as apprentices in the Department. The following may be mentioned:—Mr. Commissioner Shannon, Mr. A. E. Smith, Chief Mechanical Engineer; Mr. H. P. Colwell, Chief Electrical Engineer; Mr. Shea, Chief Mechanical Engineer of South Australian Railways; Mr. P. Leslie, Workshops Manager, Way and Works Branch; Mr. G. Curtis, of the Betterment Board; to mention but a few.

Before 1922 all railway apprentices in the metropolitan districts attended the Workingmen's College, but to save loss of time incurred in travelling, the Commissioners established a school at the Newport Workshops.

In 1923, Mr. Commissioner Shannon opened the new college, situated near the Newport station, and at the present time 272 apprentices are enrolled.

Since the school was opened, 445 apprentices have been registered.

In the first year at the College, all apprentices do the same course, which includes algebra, arithmetic, mensuration, elementary science, solid geometry and geometrical development. In the second year the syllabus for the iron trades is mathematics, applied mechanics and engineering drawing, while apprentices such as painters, upholsterers, and wood machinists do a modified course more suitable to their particular trade. In the third year, the main course is mathematics, electricity, mechanics and steam, solid geometry, graphics and engineering drawing, while the apprentices doing the modified courses attend the Workingmen's College.

Although a definite amount of work is thus laid down to be completed for each year, we often find it possible to *(Continued on page 602)*

There may be a future Chief Mechanical Engineer among these lads—Apprentices at the Newport Railway Workshops and Students of the Victorian Railways Technical College.

A SCRAPBOOK HISTORY OF APPRENTICESHIP TRAINING IN THE VICTORIAN RAILWAYS

1957

Railway apprentices at the V. R. Technical College, Newport, after the annual presentation of awards. In the centre are Messrs. H. Tran, Principal of the College, P. Farnan, then Chairman of the Staff Board, and R. Curtis, Supervisor of Apprentices.

V.R. APPRENTICES FILL TOP POSTS

THROUGHOUT the whole of industry, the V.R. trained apprentice has a first-rate reputation. That reputation has been built up by sound training. In 1905, the Department was pioneering a system of apprentice instruction which sought to bring back all that was best in the old trade guild methods, modifying them to suit modern conditions.

UNDER the V.R. training scheme, emphasis is laid not only on making a lad an efficient employee, but also in ensuring that he becomes a skilled tradesman, taking a personal pride in his work.

The thoroughness of this training in the Department's metropolitan and country workshops is proved by the number of former apprentices who have risen to the highest positions in various branches of the service. The present Chief Mechanical Engineer, Mr. G. F. Brown, and the Assistant C.M.E., Mr. W. O. Galletly, began their railway careers as apprentices, as did many other senior officers in the Rolling Stock Branch. Indeed, all around the system can be found successful apprentices who have climbed high in the service.

Among the apprentices of the pioneer 1905 school were such men as Mr. H. P. Colwell, former Chief Electrical Engineer, and Mr. J. Fowler, former Member of the Staff Board. The 1908 group included Mr. A. C. Ahlston, former Chief Mechanical Engineer.

Most successful apprentice in recent years is Assistant Engineer William Wilkins, who joined the railways as a lad labourer in the Electrical Engineering Branch and, later, was accepted as an apprentice. He did so well at the Newport Technical College that he won a Commissioners' scholarship entitling him to undertake a diploma course in electrical engineering at the Royal Melbourne Technical College.

In his fourth year, he won the prize awarded to the best electrical engineering student, and subsequently brought further honours to himself and the Department by obtaining his fellowship diploma in electrical engineering, and winning the two coveted awards of the year—the Professor Kernot medal and the Hans Ernst prize.

Latest apprentices to draw attention to the high standard of the Department's apprentice training system are Donald Cracknell and George Chamings, who were selected by the Apprenticeship Commission of Victoria as the outstanding apprentices in their respective trades. (see page 13.)

Spectacular advancement to high positions in private industry by former Victorian Railways apprentices also lends support to the claim that the Department's training system is second to none, and is recognized as such by industry generally.

Prominent industrialist and business leader, Sir Fred Thorpe, was a Victorian Railways apprentice fitter and turner. In the last war he was Director of Machine Tools and Gauges, and was also on the Advisory Committee to the Minister of Defence Production.

Mr. Charles M. Cock, who became Chief Electrical Engineer of the Southern Railway Company, England, in pre-nationalization days, and then Chief Electrical Engineer of British Railways, is now General Manager of Traction for English Electric Co. Ltd. He was a V.R. apprentice fitter and turner.

Mr. Fred Shea, one-time Chief Mechanical Engineer of South Australian Government Railways, and now Director of Engineering of Clyde Industries Ltd., is another former V.R. apprentice who rose to a high position in private industry.

These quoted cases go to prove that, in a land of opportunity, the Railways continue to lead their apprentices along the pathway to success.

July 1957

A SCRAPBOOK HISTORY OF APPRENTICESHIP TRAINING IN THE VICTORIAN RAILWAYS

OPENING OF THE NEW COLLEGE JULY 1960

New Victorian Railways Technical College Opens at Newport:

The opening of the new VR Technical College at Newport took place on 4 July 1960. The College was opened by Sir Arthur Warner, Minister of Transport. Sixty of the original VR Technical College's first batch of students were special guests at the College opening ceremony.

The New College:

(Above) New building for Newport Technical College nears completion on its site at Newport Workshops.

The construction, in 1960, of an overpass to enable road traffic to operate with greater freedom over the busy Melbourne Road crossing at Newport necessitated the removal of the Technical College, that had been the training centre for thousands of Railway tradesmen.

The new College was sited close to the actual workshop activities. Practical training was undertaken in several manual training centres. The fitting and turning, welding and boiler making training centres were located in two new buildings at a short distance at the rear of the college. The electrical manual training centre was located in an older shared workshop building on the far side of the Newport workshops near the Melbourne – Geelong railway line.

The first Principal of the new college was Mr. J. A. Douglas. The college also contained an office for a Supervisor of Apprentices, an experienced railway officer who was once an apprentice himself. His duties were to look after the welfare of apprentices, help them in their work, assist in solving their personal problems and exercise general supervision over their training. The first Supervisor of Apprentices to be located in the new College was Mr. R Curtis.

Trade classes were conducted at selected Technical Colleges where instructions could not be given at the VR Technical College Facility. Some of these included Bricklaying at Collingwood Technical College, Upholsterers at Prahran Technical College and sheet metal, Painter and Carpenter at Footscray Technical College.

After nearly 60 years of training apprentices, the Victorian Railways Technical College closed it's doors in late 1980. Apprentice training was transferred to the new Newport Technical College of TAFE located on leased railway land in Champion Rd in North Williamstown.

It should be noted that apprenticeship training also took place in a number of other Railway Workshops, especially Bendigo & Ballarat. After completing the first year of manual training, apprentices were then transferred to various workshops to undertake on-the-job training.

College Principals & Supervisors of Apprentices:

Principals		**Apprentice Supervisor**	
1961-63	J.A. Douglas	1960-74	R W Curtis (retired February 1974)
1964-65	H. Slinger	1974-79	Bob Bailey
1966-75	J. Kain (retired Sept 75)	1979-83	N A Morrison
1976-80	Ken Hall		

A SCRAPBOOK HISTORY OF APPRENTICESHIP TRAINING IN THE VICTORIAN RAILWAYS

Mr. Nilsson (centre) greets some of the men who were amongst the first apprentices at the original Technical College. (From left). Messrs. J. Burke, C. Burke, J. Crawford and G. Coulthard.

NEW V.R. TECHNICAL COLLEGE OPENED

"IF you have served your time in the Victorian Railways as an apprentice, nobody queries your training. It is the hall mark of a craftsman's excellence". That high tribute to the railway apprenticeship system was paid by Mr. O. E. Nilsson (Chief Inspector of Technical Schools and President of the Apprenticeship Commission) at the opening of the Victorian Railways modern Technical College at Newport on July 4. A Railway Technical College had been functioning continuously since 1922, and Mr. Nilsson was the first Principal.

APPLAUSE greeted the announcement by Mr. L. G. David (Chairman of the Staff Board and Chairman of the Apprentice Advisory Committee) that 60 of the original V.R. Technical College's first batch of students were special guests at the College opening ceremony.

Mr. E. H. Brownbill (Chairman of Commissioners) said it was appropriate that the new Technical College came into being 100 years after apprentices first began training at the old railway workshops at Williamstown.

"We take pride", he said, "in the fact that our apprenticeship training can compare with the best in Australia.

"Since its inception the College has taught many apprentices who had risen to responsible V.R. administrative positions. One was Mr. Commissioner G. F. Brown, who provided definite evidence that the basic training received at the College amounted to something."

Other apprentices from the Rolling Stock Branch who had done well were Mr. S. F. Keane (Superintendent of Locomotive Maintenance), Mr. P. J. Dance (Investigating Engineer), Mr. C. Hansford (Assistant Workshops Manager, Jolimont), Mr. A Stronell (Rolling Stock Engineer) and Mr. J. Smyth (District Rolling Stock Superintendent, Bendigo).

In the Electrical Engineering Branch, successful former apprentices were Mr. I. G. Hodges (Engineer of Electrical Tests) and Mr. L. Flower (Lighting and Power Superintendent).

Apprentices who have climbed high in the Way and Works Branch were Mr. G. F. Woolley (one of the first students, and now Signal and Telegraph Engineer), Mr. A. A. Phair (Machinery and Water Supply Engineer), Mr. E. J. Gooding (Metropolitan District Engineer), Mr. L. McCallum (Acting Engineer of Special Works), Mr. K. C. Cousin (another of the original apprentices, and now Acting Asistant Signal and Telegraph Engineer), Mr. R. J. Gallacher (Acting Engineer-in-Charge, North-east Standardization), Mr. J. Brodie (District Engineer, Geelong), Mr. J. Emmins (Acting Engineer of Structural Design), Mr. K. Smith (Engineer, Class 1), Mr. C. Clayton (Construction Engineer, Signal and Telegraph Division and another of Mr. Nilsson's first boys), Mr. W. Stokes (Workshops Manager, Spotswood) and Mr. P. Gibb (Assistant Workshops Manager, Spotswood).

Declaring the College officially opened, the Minister of Transport (Sir Arthur Warner) said he hoped the railways and the community generally would benefit from the improved standards of technical training embodied in the new Technical College.

As a memento of the historic occasion, Sir Arthur was presented with a set of book-ends carved to represent a Spanish galleon and Mr. Nilsson received a coffee table. Both presents were the work of railway apprentices.

(In next month's *News Letter* the history of the College will be traced.)

Sir Arthur Warner, Minister of Transport (left) receives a memento from Mr. J. A. Douglas, Principal of the College.

August 1960

A SCRAPBOOK HISTORY OF APPRENTICESHIP TRAINING IN THE VICTORIAN RAILWAYS

BUILDING FOR THE FUTURE

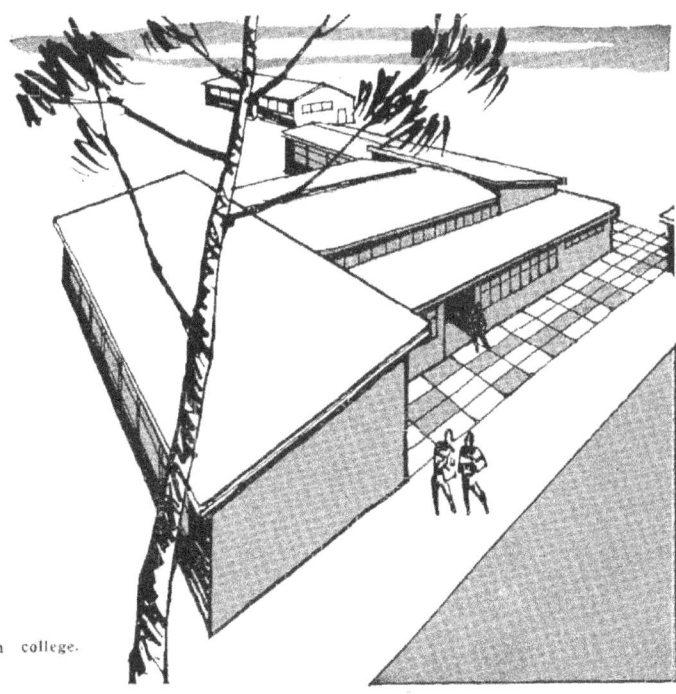

AN artist's impression of the new modern college.

OPENING of the new V.R. Technical College, on July 4, marked a further development in the Department's excellent system of apprentice training. Apprentices were first admitted to railway workshops at Williamstown in 1860. The pioneer in this grade was Thomas Hale Woodroffe, who subsequently became Chief Mechanical Engineer, and also acted as a Commissioner for a period.

AN apprentice was accepted on recommendation and selection as to suitability; training covered seven years, the first without pay. No form of indenture bond was executed, and, on completion of the term, the apprentice was raised to journeyman status and retained in the Department, if suitable.

For probably the first 25 years of the railways' existence, the number of apprentices taken on was very small. However, as the lines extended and workshop capacity increased, the intake of apprentices also increased.

By 1905 the Victorian Railways were pioneering a system of apprentice instruction that sought to bring back all that was best in the "guild" methods, modifying them to suit the conditions of the time.

The emphasis was laid on training lads not only to become efficient employees, but also to ensure that they became skilled tradesmen taking a personal pride in their work.

From that year until 1922, a special course for railway apprentices was conducted at the Working Men's College, now the Royal Melbourne Technical College.

February 1922 saw the first apprentices under the new scheme commence their training. They were interviewed by Mr. Nilsson, the Principal of the projected Victorian Railways Technical College and graded into five classes covering Arithmetic and Mensuration, Mathematics, Elementary Science, Projections and Geometrical Development.

Classes commenced on February 27, 1922, in temporary accommodation at the Paint Shop, Newport Workshops, until construction of the new Technical College was completed. On March 11, 1923, the 160 students comprising the classes were transferred from the Workshops to the Technical College that was officially opened by Mr. Commissioner Shannon.

The construction, in 1960, of an overpass to enable road traffic to operate with greater freedom over the busy Melbourne Road crossing at Newport necessitated the removal of the Technical College, that had been the training centre for thousands of railway tradesmen and engineers.

The new College is sited close to actual workshops activities. Practical trade instruction in turning and fitting, electrical fitting, and welding can now be given in a separate section of the college instead of being conducted in various sections of the Newport Workshops.

Provision has been made to accommodate the Supervisor of Apprentices and his staff in the new building, thus affording even closer collaboration than previously between the college staff and this officer.

Every effort has been made to provide ample provision for future requirements; the 8,650 sq. feet of floor space in the main college building and 6,000 sq. feet in the practical trades section compares more than favourably with the 7,200 sq. feet of the old building.

The Victorian Railways News Letter

A SCRAPBOOK HISTORY OF APPRENTICESHIP TRAINING IN THE VICTORIAN RAILWAYS

Adequate provision has been made for recreation.

During their first three years on the job, about 300 to 400 apprentices in the metropolitan area in the grades of Fitter and Turner, Electrical Fitter, Boilermaker, Car and Wagon Builder, or Sailmaker spend from eight to ten hours weekly at the College.

All class work has a railway emphasis and is designed to help the student in his general work whether it is car and wagon building, boilermaking, electrical fitting, or general machine shop activities.

When apprentices enrol, they are graded according to their educational qualifications and commence in a class at the appropriate level. Separate classes are provided for Car and Wagon Builders, Boilermakers, Turner and Fitters and Electrical Fitters. Each apprentice shares in the educational programme common to his group and, in addition, receives special training in his own chosen occupation.

At the present time, training is divided into technical courses for those capable of reaching professional status, and trade courses. A technical course covers three years of the Education Department's Certificate course and up to Diploma standard in certain subjects, while the trade course is similar to the Education Department's Apprenticeship Commission Trade Course.

A new course to be known as a Technician's Course for outstanding Trade Course students is being planned. This course will be similar to the Education Department's Technicians' Certificate Course.

Trade classes are conducted at selected Technical Colleges where instructions cannot be given with Departmental facilities. Students attending these centres are provided with free rail travel.

The centres at which students attend are:

School of Printing and Graphic Arts.
Printing.

Prahran Technical College.
Upholsterers, French Polisher.

Collingwood Technical College.
Bricklayer, Electroplater.

Footscray Technical College.
Boilermaker, Tinsmith and Sheetmetal Worker, Plumber, Gas Fitter, Moulder, Blacksmith, Car Painter and Painter, Carpenter and Joiner, Coppersmith, Electric Mechanic, Moulder, Patternmaker, Springmaker.

Every year scholarships are awarded to outstanding pupils at the V.R. Technical College for a degree course at the Melbourne University and full time diploma courses at any chosen Technical College.

During their studies the trainees are paid a salary, all tuition fees are met, and they retain full railway privileges such as pass concessions, sick leave payments, and so on.

On graduation they are appointed to the professional staff of the Department. Since the college was founded, 115 scholarships have been awarded.

Other awards are made for diligence, proficiency, regular attendance at school and workshop, and examination results above 60 per cent. For 1959 a total of £300 was awarded by the Commissioners in the form of trade proficiency awards to 54 apprentices.

Certificates are issued to apprentices on successful completion of their school course.

Instruction is chiefly made up of tutorial lectures in conjunction with printed notes, film screenings and practical laboratory work. This phase of college activities is conducted by the Principal and five full time instructors from the Education Department. Apprentices who wish to follow up a particular phase of their trade have a technical library at their disposal. For those who desire to extend their education there is an English library designed to improve their vocabulary and writing capabilities. An instructor in English is made available from the Footscray Technical College for eight hours each week to instruct first year students.

Throughout industry the railway-trained apprentices has a first-rate reputation. This has come from the recognition that an apprentice is an individual—not just a name. From the first day that he enters the Department he is watched by a Supervisor of Apprentices, an experienced railway officer who was once an apprentice himself. His duties are to look after the welfare of apprentices, help them in their work, assist in solving their personal problems and exercise a general supervision over their training.

It is this personal interest that has helped to maintain the high standard of students passing through the Victorian Railways Technical College, as it is felt that the future of the Department is to a great extent, in the hands of its apprentices.

High administrative positions in every technical branch of the railways are occupied by former railway apprentices while one of the present Commissioners, Mr. G. F. Brown, is also a product of the Victorian Railways Technical College.

The aim of the College can, perhaps, be best explained by giving a favourite quotation from its first principal's notebook:

" There is room at the top. Men who can fill responsible posts are wanted in the Railways Department. It is fear, doubt, pessimism, and lack of ambition that keeps men down.
" Nothing can stop the man from succeeding who has the will to succeed and the energy to work."

CLASS room tuition, combined with practical trade instruction, gives apprentices every chance to succeed to the highest posts in the V.R. service.

September 1960

Awards:

Every year, scholarships were awarded to outstanding pupils at the VR Technical College for a degree course at Melbourne University and full-time diploma courses at any chosen Technical College. Since the college was founded in 1922 and up to the opening of the new College, 115 scholarships have been awarded.

Each year a group of apprentices were awarded a cash prize for outstanding work during the year. These awards took into account an apprentice's diligence, proficiency, regular attendance at college and workshop and examination results above 60 per cent.

Each year during Apprenticeship Week, the Apprenticeship Commission of Victoria would award Bronze Medallions to the state's Outstanding Apprentices in each trade. A medallion was also awarded to the Outstanding Apprentice (all trades) employed in the Victorian Railways who undertook their training at the Victorian Railways Technical College. A number of railway apprentices have over the years won the state award for an outstanding apprentice in their trade. These awards were usually presented in May each year during Apprenticeship Week. The presentation ceremony was normally held in May in the Melbourne Town Hall and the medallions on most occasions were presented by the Governor of Victoria and in May 1968 by the Duke of Edinburgh.

The award for the Outstanding Apprentice of the Year attending the Victorian Railways Technical College appears to have come to an end in 1973. For the next few years, no individual top honour award was made. However, annual prize awards were still made to VR apprentices who achieved top marks in their various trades and now included apprentices from all the various workshops and technical colleges. The Apprentice of the Year was reinstated in 1977 and now all apprentices in the Victorian Railways were eligible to receive this award.

A full list of all known winners of the Victorian Railways Apprentice of the Year and State Apprentice of the Year can be found at the back of this document. A shield which contained the names of the various winners was located on the entry wall of the Newport Victorian Railways Technical College. What happened to the shield when the College closed I do not know. Most likely it was discarded or is gathering dust in a basement somewhere.

Apprenticeship Week Open Days:

The Newport college and its associated manual training centres would participate in Apprenticeship Week by holding an open day. All trades would participate in various exhibits and visitors could see apprentices at work on their normal trade training exercises. The open days were normally held over three days and would attract a large number of visitors including school students and various dignitaries.

It appears that these Apprenticeship Week open days at the Newport training facilities were no longer held after 1969. Although there is a record of a small display being held at the Melbourne Town Hall as part of Apprenticeship Week in 1974.

THE YEAR 1960

New Apprentices:

For the 1960 intake of apprentices, 776 applications were received. Of these 244 were accepted. Most will undertake their training in Melbourne but some will do their training at the Ballarat or Bendigo workshops.

Holiday Camp:

Two apprentices were selected to attend a holiday camp at Somers. The aim of the camp was to bring together apprentices from industries and schools to help them develop qualities of leadership. In later years these leadership camps were conducted by the Inter-Church Trade and Industry Mission and normally held at Hall in the Grampians. Commission In 1960 they were Maurice Turk apprentice patternmaker and John Lack an apprentice mechanical fitter.

Bronze Medallion Awarded:

Apprentice tinsmith and sheet metal worker, Colin Welsford, of Spotswood Workshops, won a bronze medallion for the best exhibit in the sheet metal trade held as part of an apprenticeship display in the National Museum.

Apprentice of the Year:

The apprentice of the year for 1959 (announced in 1960) was Neil Embling, a photo-engraver.

Scholarship Winners.

Six scholarships were awarded to apprentices considered capable of undertaking full-time study of professional courses in either civil, electrical or mechanical engineering.

Next Years Vacancies:

Vacancies for 272 railway apprentices were advertised Statewide in August. Applications closed on 31 October. A booklet was published dealing with apprenticeship opportunities with copies being available from most stations. Successful applicants from the country would receive a living away from home allowance to cover their board.

1960-2

MORE SCHOLARSHIPS FOR APPRENTICES

Mr. Turk

Apprentices' Awards

APPRENTICE Tinsmith and Sheet Metal Worker Colin Welsford, of Spotswood Workshops, won a bronze medallion for the best exhibit in the Sheet Metal trade for 1960, his entry being judged equal first with that of another apprentice. The entry, a brass hand signal lamp, was included in the apprenticeship display at the National Museum. Mr. Welsford has had brilliant results in his apprenticeship examinations—topping his class during the last three years with percentages of 95, 98 and 99, as well as securing a Commissioners' prize each year.

Incidentally, the "Apprentice of the Year"—Mr. Neil Embling, a photo-engraver—is the son of Mr. A. C. Embling, District Rolling Stock Superintendent at Ballarat.

SIX scholarships—the greatest number for some time—have been awarded this year to apprentices whose work during their period of training has shown they would be capable of undertaking a professional course. Five of the successful lads attended senior classes at the V.R. Technical College and one studied at the Ballarat School of Mines. All have now begun full time study in their courses of civil, electrical or mechanical engineering at their chosen colleges. On completion of these, they will be available for appointment to the professional staff of the Department.

From Italy, in 1951, came Michael Beatrice, who, after obtaining his Junior Technical Certificate joined the Railways as an apprentice electrical fitter. He is studying for his Electrical Engineering Diploma at Footscray Technical College.

Kenneth Powell began as an apprentice car and wagon builder. In his first year in the Trade Course at the V.R. College, he topped his class and was awarded a Commissioners' Prize. At Caulfield Technical College he is doing Civil Engineering.

Two other lads who will also be at Caulfield Technical College are Stephan Jakymczuk and Leonard Waters. Stephan began his education in Germany, completed it in Australia and started in the Department as an apprentice electrical fitter. In his first year he won a Commissioners' prize, and, last year, topped his class. Leonard obtained his Intermediate Technical Certificate at Wonthaggi Technical School and began as an apprentice electrical fitter in 1958.

A Ballarat lad, Paul Kennedy was dux of the Ballarat Workshops apprentices in his first year on car and wagon building, won a Commissioners' Prize and came first in his carpentry course at Ballarat School of Mines. Paul has now begun studying for his Civil Engineering Diploma at Royal Melbourne Technical College.

Educated at the Hamilton High School, John Arnott, an apprentice fitter and turner was another winner of a Commissioners' Prize in his first year. He is doing mechanical engineering at Swinburne Technical College.

Apprentices in Camp

"THE best holiday we have ever had" was the summing up of two 17-year-old railway apprentices who recently were selected to attend a holiday camp at Somers.

The lads, Maurice Turk, apprentice patternmaker of Newport, and John Lack, apprentice mechanical fitter of the Ironworks Division, represented the Department at the annual Lord Somers camp, that overlooks Western Port.

Maurice is keenly interested in cycling and swimming (holding the Royal Life Saving Bronze Medallion) and has been an active member of the Scout movement for nine years.

Since attending the camp, he has commenced playing basketball for Power House, the camp's Melbourne team name.

John, too, has taken up new sports—rugby and athletics—with Power House. He also swims and plays tennis, table tennis, and soccer.

Twenty-four railway lads have attended the camp since the scheme was introduced in 1949; two being selected to attend each year. The camp was founded in 1929 by Lord Somers, then Governor of Victoria.

Aim of the camp is to bring together 100 boys from industries and schools to help them develop qualities of leadership and respect for the other's viewpoint and their fellow men.

Mr. Welsford

Mr. Lack

April 1960

THE YEAR 1961

Record Intake of Apprentices:

Mr. R. Curtis (Supervisor of Apprentices) meets the lads for the first time.

FOR 219 lads, January 16, was a significant day in their lives; chosen from 579 applicants, they were apprentices beginning their V.R. careers. It was the record intake of apprentices in the Department's history. Warmly greeting the lads at the V.R.I., Melbourne, Mr. E. P. Rogan (Commissioner) congratulated them on choosing a tradesman's career because, with the present technological progress, their employment scope was greater than ever.

"Nowhere else in Australia" he said, "are the apprentice training facilities so comprehensive as in the Victorian Railways. We are the State's biggest single industrial undertaking and the Department is giving an indispensable service. The high quality of that service has been proved by the way we are handling the wheat harvest. We rose to the occasion, despite the critics, as we have always done. But we are not complacent, for what we do today we aim to do better tomorrow".

Mr. Rogan spoke of the new centre for apprenticeship training at Newport Workshops—the recently erected Technical College and the new training school that will cover both the thereotetical and practical sides for the first 12 months of the lads' apprenticeship. "Provision of these facilities", he stressed, "represents our forward thinking, and the Commissioners hope you will all dedicate yourselves to forward thinging".

Members of the Apprentices' Board of Selectors (Messrs. W. Walker, Member of the Staff Board—and Chairman of Selectors—K. A. Smith, Engineer, Way and Works Branch, and A. Chalmers, Rolling Stock Staff Section) addressed the lads. Mr. Walker emphasized the great personal satisfaction it would be to the selectors to discover, as time went by, that all the 219 lads had succeeded.

Messrs. R. Curtis (Supervisor of Apprentices) and W. E. Elliott (General Secretary, V.R.I.) also spoke.

Scholarship Winners.

Four scholarships were awarded to four apprentices to undertake four-year full-time Associate Diploma courses at various colleges.

From left: W.J. Maguire, K.G. Thompson & F.G. Buratta
(Apprentice Electrical fitters) & R.J. Fallon (Apprentice Boilermaker.
Centre: Mr. J.A. Douglas (Principal Newport Technical College)

Apprentice Prize Winners for 1960 (presented in 1961) & Increased Allowances

Prizewinning V.R. apprentices with Messrs. C. S. Morris (Chairman, Staff Board), J. A. Douglas (Principal, V.R. Technical College) and R Curtis (Supervisor of Apprentices). See story below.

1961 - 2

Increased Allowances for Apprentices

"The increased proficiency allowances recently approved for apprentices were highlighted by the Chairman of the Staff Board, Mr C. S. Morris at the recent presentation of 79 prizes awarded to railway apprentices by the Department.

The excellent training given in the railway workshops is reflected in their successful results. This year, in competition with other apprentices at technical colleges, VR lads gained 18 prizes and also four scholarships – the latter being awarded by the Commonwealth Bank for post-apprenticeship studies. Another two of the apprentices achieved the coveted distinction of Outstanding Apprentice for their trade. They were App. Moulder Lance Widders and App. Tinsmith and Sheet Metal Worker Colin Welsford.

Apprentices, whose scholastic results and conduct, etc. at college meet certain prescribed standards, will, under the new scheme, be paid allowances ranging up to 12/- a week. Previously, they were limited to a maximum of 3/- a week.

An interesting feature of the new system is that the awards will be paid in lump sums, twice yearly, instead of being included as at present, in the fortnightly wages. Payments will be made following each half-yearly review.

The first payment of the increased allowances will be made early in 1962 and will be based on the results of the latter half of 1961. The present allowances will continue to the end of this year" (extract from the August 61 Victorian Railways Newsletter)

Apprentices of the Year for 1960

From Left: Colin Welsford (Sheetmetal) and Lance Widers (Moulding) Outstanding apprentices in their trades in Victoria. Anthony Davis (Fitting & Turning) Apprentice of the Year (V.R. Technical College). Mr G.F. Brown Deputy Chairman of Commissioners.

1961 - 3

1961 Open Day (Held in April).

First to be held in the new Manual training centres and the VR Technical College.

For use in a passenger carriage, a partition is being moulded by Apprentice Car and Wagon Builder, I. Hazelgrove.

In their mid-day break, apprentices revel in a game of basket-ball at the Newport Technical College.

Apprentice Upholsterer G. Ragh is attaching webbing to a small seat frame prior to stringing.

Under the guidance of Instructor A. J. McGilton a problem is being worked out by Apprentice Car and Wagon Builder, J. Anderson.

Apprentice Vacancy Record

"Just over a thousand applications were received for the 203 railway apprentices required for 1962. This is the largest number of applicants in any year since the end of the war."

THE YEAR 1962

New Apprentices welcomed

Mr. Rogan with a group of the new apprentices

180 new apprentices were welcomed by Mr Commissioner Rogan at the VRI on January 22.

During the weeks before the closing date for applications, departmental staff visited 62 technical and 47 high schools throughout the state. Consequently. When applications closed, 1114 boys were in the running for the 1962 intake. To handle this response, eight selection centres were set up in main provincial towns in addition to the normal metropolitan centre.

Of the 180 chosen, 60 are country boys and 19 are new Australians who have been educated in Australian schools. There is also a proportion of railwaymen's sons. Twenty-five apprentices will be trained at Ballarat and Bendigo workshops.

All told there are 24 trades represented in this year's intake. Last year a special manual training centre was opened at Newport Workshops.

Outstanding Apprentice for 1961 (awarded in 1962)

Apprentice Fitter and Turner Allen G. Bourquin is congratulated by Mr. G. F. Brown (Deputy Chairman) on his selection as the outstanding railway apprentice attending the V.R. Technical College during 1961. The award was presented to Allen by the Governor, Sir Dallas Brooks, at the Melbourne Town Hall during the recent Apprenticeship Week. Allen comes from Anakie (about 12 miles from Lara) and began his apprenticeship in 1959 at Newport Workshops.

1962 - 2

1962 Apprentice Prize Winners for 1961

Group of prize-winning apprentices who were presented with $400 prize money for their work during 1961. In centre of second row are (from left) Mr. R. W. Curtis (Supervisor of Apprentices), Mr. C. S. Morris (Chairman of Staff Board) and Mr. J. A. Douglas (Principal, V.R. Technical College).

Apprentice fitter and Turner E. G. Wilson working on a model of S class steam locomotive restored by apprentices at Newport Workshops.

THE YEAR 1963 — NEW APPRENTICES WELCOMED

WELCOMED TO FAMILY

Staff Board Chairman Mr. C. S. Morris pointed out features of Flinders Street Station to this group of Mildura district apprentices.

(Below) Fifteen-year-old twins Ray and Ron Cooney, of Broadmeadows, who will both train as tinsmiths.

They came from near and far.....

ONE hundred and sixty lads started their Departmental careers recently and became members of a "family" of 1,000 railway apprentices.

The V.R.I. Ballroom, Melbourne, was the location for the annual intake of apprentices who will each complete five years training in one of 17 different trade courses.

The simple, yet impressive welcoming ceremony will undoubtedly remain long in the memory of the lads, especially as they were brought together in such a large group for probably the only time in their railway career.

Several Departmental officers warmly welcomed the lads into the railways, and the Commissioners were represented by Mr. C. S. Morris, Chairman of the Staff Board.

He told them "For most of you, today is your first job. We, who have been with the Department for many years, know that you will receive a most thorough training. On behalf of the Commissioners, I welcome and congratulate you, firstly for choosing a railway career, and secondly, for having been selected as railway apprentices".

Some applicants came from the most remote corners of the state, as well as from New South Wales. Of the 902 applications received, 562 came from the metropolitan areas and 340 from country districts. Twelve apprentices have started training at Bendigo, 14 at Ballarat and the remainder in Melbourne.

This year there was an increased number of apprentices who were not Australian born. Countries of birth included Germany, Egypt, Greece, England, Scotland and Italy.

Peter Dickie, Hamilton; Francis Lane, Wakool, N.S.W.; David Anderson, Mildura; Murray Bertram, Murrayville; David Klemtz, Paynesville; Eric Gunstone, North Altona; Fantino Camilleri, Glenroy.

The Victorian Railways News Letter

A SCRAPBOOK HISTORY OF APPRENTICESHIP TRAINING IN THE VICTORIAN RAILWAYS

1963 – 2

"Apprentice Lady"

WHEN this year's group of 160 apprentices was welcomed on the boys' first day in the railways, it was an all male audience at the V.R.I. hall, Melbourne, with one exception—Miss Marie Cahill.

Often referred to as "The apprentice lady", Miss Cahill (right) is a behind-the-scenes employee of the Apprenticeship Selection Committee and is responsible for handling the applications and processing all the paper work for each apprentice.

A Rolling Stock branch typiste, Miss Cahill has, for the past nine years, been on loan annually to the Secretary's branch for three months.

In addition to checking details shown on the application, Miss Cahill personally sees each apprentice at least three times, culminating in the big day when all lads are assembled at the V.R.I. hall on their first railway working day.

Parents often accompany country lads, and are quickly put at ease by Miss Cahill regarding accommodation and other personal items. She can also explain to parents where their son will train, as she has visited the V.R. college at Newport. She often meets apprentices who have completed their training and is always interested to learn of their progress.

A keen traveller, Miss Cahill has visited most Australian states, and her next trip will be to Central Australia. For relaxation, she plays tennis with a church group at Box Hill, of which she is secretary. She also plays squash and basketball.

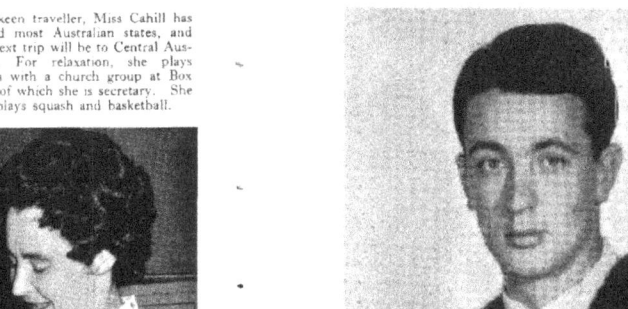

Robert John Stewart, who was adjudged best apprentice for 1962 at the V.R. Technical College, is in his fourth year as an apprentice electrical fitter, and, at present, works at the Signal and Telegraph Division, North Melbourne. The award is made by the Apprenticeship Commission of Victoria and is open only to youths attending the V.R. Technical College.

Apprentices

FOR the 175 railway apprenticeships to be filled this year, 901 applications were received. Of these, 339 were from the country and 562 from suburban areas. Those selected will begin their training on January 21.

Mr. R. Hunter, Senior Mathematics and Science Instructor at Newport Technical College, uses models to teach solid trigonometry to apprentices (from left) D. Ferguson, G. Dyioba, A. Hill and J. Emery. Models were made from welding rod at the Coppersmith Shop, Newport, by Apprentice N. Hunter. They have been cadmium plated to prevent corrosion and enable parts to be coloured.

MODEL FOR SHOW: At Newport Workshops, Apprentice Electrical Fitter Peter McGrath makes an adjustment to a 1/12th scale working model that will demonstrate how bogie exchange operates. The model, which was made by apprentices at Newport Workshops, will have its first public display at the Department's exhibit in the Royal Agricultural Show this month.

1963 – 3 OPEN DAY

TRADES BEHIND THE TRAIN

AS the Department's contribution to Apprenticeship Week, the V.R. Technical College and the apprentice manual training centres at Newport Workshops were open for public inspection last month.

General view of exhibits in the electrical display.

Graeme, an apprentice fitter and turner, demonstrates the use of a surface gauge to his parents Mr. and Mrs. D. Whitaker (left). At right is Mr. J. A. Douglas, College Principal.

At the college was a fascinating display that revealed something of the great variety of skills needed to operate a modern railway system. It was a cross section of the crafts behind the train. In the various rooms were exhibits of work from 25 grades of apprentices—a variety that few other industries in the State could equal. Also in the area was the Department's mobile display featuring its model railway and supplying general railway information.

Attracting much attention were the nine accurate 1/12th scale models of a diesel-electric locomotive, roomette, sitting carriage and various freight vehicles. Most were built by apprentices.

The display, as a whole, was educational on three levels:

- to apprentices who saw what youths in other trades were doing;

A SCRAPBOOK HISTORY OF APPRENTICESHIP TRAINING IN THE VICTORIAN RAILWAYS

1963-4

- to their parents (and also Departmental supervisors) who could see the sound training the lads were receiving;
- to members of the public who could realize the "brains behind the trains".

All of the youths' parents were invited, and—considering the display was held during the week—quite a large number accepted. Indeed, in one training centre where there are 48 lads, the parents of 45 of them came. Some arrived from as far as Wangaratta, and even from Murrayville, 356 miles away. While there, parents were able to meet their lads' supervisors and talk over any problems that the youths might have.

All the apprentices in the metropolitan area and groups from Bendigo North and Ballarat North Workshops were invited. The latter two groups comprised those who had not visited one of the previous displays.

At regular intervals, buses left the College to take visitors to the manual training centres where they saw apprentices engaged on their normal trade training projects.

Educational experts were considerably impressed by the display; and members of the public commented favourably on the way in which information was so readily supplied by the youths in charge of the various exhibits.

As well as the Newport exhibition, there was an eye-catching display—*Trades Behind Trains*—at the Victorian Government Tourist Bureau in Collins Street. It featured a 1/12th scale model diesel-electric locomotive made by V.R. apprentices, and modern railway equipment that the boys would eventually maintain as qualified tradesmen.

The 1/12th scale models on exhibition.

Instructor D. Martin shows a teaching aid to Mrs. N. Arkley. At right is her son Robert, an apprentice fitter and turner.

THE YEAR 1964

APPRENTICES WELCOMED

Apprentice Fitter and Turner Ronald Hope (6 ft. 8 in.) meets Apprentice Electrical Fitter Martin Vloedmans (4 ft. 2 in.). They were among the 208 new apprentices who were officially welcomed to the Department last month by the Chairman of the Staff Board, Mr. C. S. Morris.

Apprentice Electrical Fitter K. R. Pepperell operates a cathode-ray oscilloscope. He was selected as the outstanding Railway Apprentice attending the V.R. Technical College last year.

Apprentices wanted

THERE will be vacancies in the Department for 280 apprentices, including 15 for Bendigo and 17 for Ballarat, to start next year. The apprenticeships are in 22 trades, giving a wide choice to applicants.

The closing date for receipt of applications is October 19, this year.

Successful applicants will begin a five-year apprenticeship on January 18 next.

Prizes for Apprentices

V.R. apprentices with (centre, front row) Messrs. H. Slinger (College Principal), C. S. Morris (Chairman of Staff Board), and R. W. Curtis (Supervisor of Apprentices). The occasion was the presentation of prizes, last month, by Mr. Morris. Prizes to the value of £450 were won by 80 of the apprentices.

A SCRAPBOOK HISTORY OF APPRENTICESHIP TRAINING IN THE VICTORIAN RAILWAYS

1964 – 2 OPEN DAY

APPRENTICESHIP WEEK DEPARTMENTAL DISPLAYS

AS the employer of 1,000 apprentices, the Department made its annual contribution to Apprenticeship Week by holding displays at Newport, Ballarat and Bendigo Workshops, Geelong and Melbourne.

At Newport Workshops, for the first time, visitors had a choice of attending during either the day or evening. Day sessions were held on Tuesday and Wednesday, May 12 and 13, when the College and five manual training centres at the Workshops were open for inspection between 9 a.m. and 5 p.m. Evening sessions were held on the Monday and Tuesday, from 6.30 to 9 p.m., but only the College and the nearby Fitters and Turners Training Centre were then open for inspection.

Among main features of the display were the Department's large 1/12th scale models of locomotives and other rolling stock, its TT scale model railway, and the mobile exhibit where general information of railway interest was distributed. Buses, at regular intervals, took visitors on tours of the five manual training centres.

Twenty-five trades were involved in the display. Although this was the first time that an evening inspection was possible, nearly 350 visitors attended during the evening sessions. Altogether, 900 adults and 600 school pupils visited the display. Included among them were representatives of leading industrial concerns and public utilities, as well as parents of the apprentices. Some of the parents showed their keen interest by coming long distances to attend the display.

Groups from schools and colleges were among the visitors. Third-year Apprentice Fitter and Turner L. De Luca gives a demonstration of engineering drawing to a group from Sunshine North Technical School.

Apprentice Electrical Fitter K. R. Pepperell operates a cathode-ray oscilloscope. He was selected as the outstanding Railway Apprentice attending the V.R. Technical College last year.

WHO IS HE?

The Victorian Railways Returned Servicemen's Section is looking for a man.

HE is the last remaining member of the V.R. staff who enlisted for service in the armed forces (land, sea or air) during the 1914–18 war.

The ranks of these men are thinning rapidly. Obviously, there cannot be many left in the Department. The retirement of the last of them will mark the end of an era.

So, the V.R. Returned Servicemen's Section is very interested to get in touch with the remaining members of the staff who enlisted for that war.

The Secretary, Mr. R. E. Erwin, will be glad to hear from them. He is in the Eastern District Engineer's office, Room 12, Flinders Street (auto. 2468).

June 1964

A SCRAPBOOK HISTORY OF APPRENTICESHIP TRAINING IN THE VICTORIAN RAILWAYS

HOW GOOD IS V.R. TECHNICAL COLLEGE?

RECENTLY the Education Department's Board of Inspection made a report on the Victorian Railways Technical College. Extracts from the report are published below.

BUILDINGS AND GROUNDS

The buildings are well cleaned and well maintained, both within and without, it being a real pleasure to find apprentices actively co-operating in the care of furniture and equipment and in proper disposal of litter.

The building of a new bookstall will enable the provision of more storage room for various types of equipment and cleaning material, while the approved extensions will make necessary provision for a new classroom, larger staff-room and Apprentice Supervisor room, as well as for a more fitting office for the Principal.

The Railway authorities are to be congratulated on their forward policies in the matter of accommodation and general developments.

EXAMINATIONS

It is interesting to observe that of the 298 apprentices attending the College in 1963, approximately 30% gained Credit Pass and 45% gained Ordinary Pass.

These results are most encouraging.

ORGANIZATION AND SUPERVISION

The school gives the impression of being efficiently organized and very well supervised.

The Principal's excellent report shows evidence of careful thinking and analysis, a clear perception of the needs of the institution, and a readiness to act on initiative where the need for progress or reform becomes apparent.

Courses have quickly been re-aligned to meet new diploma pre-requisites, while approved practical work is being recommended for certain trades.

The decision to insist on apprentices passing all subjects before becoming eligible for a College Certificate should certainly raise the status of that award.

Teachers were well prepared to go before their classes, there was a pleasing relationship between instructors and apprentices, and the lads evinced a very good attitude towards their studies. Books and equipment were being sensibly used, cyclostyled material being relevant and effective. Due use is being made of visual education methods.

The present steps being taken to establish a library are applauded; ultimately instructors in all subjects should give consideration to the incorporation of library research in their teaching programmes.

Leaving Technical Certificate classes were being well taught and responding suitably to the challenge of the work. As more science equipment becomes available the course in Leaving Physics will gain in value and effectiveness.

GENERAL

The tone of the school is wholesome and the spirit healthy. Generally there is an air of progress and purpose, a reflection of good staff co-operation and unity of aim.

The School Council maintains a liberal and progressive outlook on the needs of the apprentices and an active interest in the development of the College. Some significant advances are being made and it would appear that sincere thought is given to the provision of every possible opportunity to interested boys. The report on "Manual Training within the Victorian Railways", irrespective of its adoption or otherwise, is further evidence of the earnestness with which problems are being considered. It will be interesting, indeed, to watch developments.

PRINCIPAL'S OPINION

MR. H. SLINGER, Principal of the V.R. Technical College has had 28 years of experience in apprenticeship training during which he has had close contacts with all Victorian industrial organizations that provide apprentice training. He is also conversant with such schemes in other States, in England, and several other overseas countries. Asked for his opinion of V.R. apprentice training, Mr. Slinger contributed the following article.

In my experience I have not found better opportunities offered to trade apprentices than those which exist in the Victorian Railways Department. Here are some of the advantages our apprentices have:

COLLEGE FACILITIES

Apprentices in trades where large numbers are concerned receive all their training at our own College and Manual Training Centres situated in the Newport Workshops area. The College is modern, well-equipped, and staffed by fully qualified teachers from the Education Department.

The great advantages of this set-up are that teachers have a means of obtaining very close supervision of apprentices, that time is not lost travelling to outside schools, that a better relationship between teacher and student can be obtained, and that a greater opportunity exists to foster the team spirit which is so important in an organization such as ours. The proximity of the College to most workshop areas makes it possible to arrange timetables that are not so exhausting as those which have to be used in outside schools.

This type of College is, to my knowledge, the only one of its kind in Victoria, and one of the few in the world.

(Victorian Railways apprentices who are situated in the country workshops, and metropolitan apprentices in trades where small groups are concerned, attend outside schools and colleges).

SCHOOLING OPPORTUNITIES

Apprentices are carefully graded on intake and given courses which suit their abilities. By this means it is possible for the apprentice to

156   *The Victorian Railways News Letter*

A SCRAPBOOK HISTORY OF APPRENTICESHIP TRAINING IN THE VICTORIAN RAILWAYS

qualify for a Diploma or Certificate through scholarships which are awarded each year. Those who may not be successful in gaining a scholarship will at least be trained to the standard of Leaving Technical Certificate in addition to their normal qualifications. This applies equally well to apprentices at Ballarat North and Bendigo North.

An important point to note is that apprentices who left day school before gaining an Intermediate or higher certificate are not excluded from this course provided they show aptitude in their course at the V.R.T.C.

Apprentices in trades which normally do not lead to Diplomas and who attend outside schools may study Technician courses as applied to their chosen trade.

The trade and special courses are designed to be completed in three years as compared with four years for apprentices in other organizations. This gives our apprentice the advantage that in his fourth and fifth years he has time available to improve his qualifications if so desired. In certain cases tuition fees are paid by this Department.

A comparison of schooling and specialized manual training hours for Victorian Railway apprentices and apprentices in most outside firms shows the following:

	Victorian Railways	Most Outside Firms
1st yr.—	up to 40 hrs. weekly	8 hrs. weekly
2nd yr.—	up to 19 hrs. ,,	8 ,, ,, ,,
3rd yr.—	up to 15 hrs. ,,	4 ,, ,, ,,
4th yr.—		4 ,, ,, ,,
Total	74	24

This arrangement of schooling compares very favourably with the Royal Aircraft Establishment at Farnborough, England, where their intake for 1962-63 was 15 for diploma and degree training, 23 for advanced trade training and 83 for ordinary trade.

The Victorian Railway intake for 1964 was 13 for diploma training 19 for advanced trade training and 173 for ordinary trade.

The Victorian Railways and R.A.E. are the only two organizations, to my knowledge, which conduct training for apprentices along these lines.

MANUAL TRAINING

Several manual training centres have been set up at Newport, where most apprentices are taught the rudiments of their trade. The apprentice spends the whole of his first year between the training centre and the College while the three trades with most apprentices are to be given manual training also in their second and third years. These centres also help to develop a good team spirit and a correct attitude towards other people.

INCENTIVES FOR AN APPRENTICE

- The opportunity to obtain the best qualifications according to his ability.
- Proficiency Allowances which are up to 2·4 times higher than the Apprenticeship Commission Allowance.
- Commissioners' prizes to the value of about £500 per year.
- Concession fares and passes.

Since my appointment to the position of Principal, I have been more and more impressed with the training our apprentices receive, and also with the progressive attitude of our Commissioners, Staff Board, and Advisory Committee, which has made Victorian Railways trained tradesmen held in such high regard throughout Australia.

£7¼ MILLION FOR WORKS

THE Department has been allocated £7¼ million for the current works programme. This will provide for further improvements to suburban lines, more *Harris Trains*, diesel locomotives and rolling stock, installation of more boom barriers and flashing lights, and the replacement of certain level crossings by grade separation.

Money for advance planning for the proposed city underground railway will again be increased by £5,000 to £35,000, while another £10,000 will be available for preliminary rail works to provide connexions to the underground railway.

Money will also be available to finish new railway stations at Gowrie and Epping, and for improved lighting in country carriages and heating rail motors.

Principal features of the programme are:—

- £490,000 for major improvement works on the Burnley group of lines. This will allow completion of the third track, signalled for two-way running, between Hawthorn and East Camberwell; completion of the final section of duplication between Syndal and Glen Waverley, and further progress on the building of two additional tracks between Richmond and Burnley.
- £260,000 to start the first stage of re-constructing the Melbourne freight and passenger yard.
- £140,000 for work on the new Spencer Street station, to complete the public car park, southern passenger entrance ramp, and the greater part of the passenger and parcels subway systems.
- £130,000 for duplication work on the Geelong line—completing the section between Rock Loop and Laverton and starting preliminary work between Newport South Junction and Rock Loop.
- £120,000 to improve terminal facilities in the Dynon area to cope with the continued growth of freight traffic resulting from the Melbourne–Albury–Sydney standard gauge line.
- £18,000 to start preliminary work for automatic signalling between Essendon and Broadmeadows.
- £225,000 as this Department's share of the cost of grade separation work at level crossings.

For track relaying and renewing points and crossings, £1,620,000 will be available. One hundred and thirty-five miles of country lines and 5 miles of suburban lines will be relaid, and 55 miles of country lines reconditioned.

Main expenditure on rolling stock will be:

- £1,180,000 towards the second order of 30 modern *Harris Trains*.
- £1,015,000 to buy diesel locomotives already ordered. During the year it is planned to place in service the final 11 of 20 T class 900 h.p. locomotives and the first 17 of 25 Y class 650 h.p units.
- £795,000 for building, in Demental workshops, rolling stock of various types for both broad and standard gauge traffic.

October 1964

A SCRAPBOOK HISTORY OF APPRENTICESHIP TRAINING IN THE VICTORIAN RAILWAYS

THE YEAR 1965

APPRENTICES: Among the 230 railway apprentices who were welcomed to the Department last month by the Secretary for Railways, Mr. W. Walker (left) were 15½-year-old twins Peter and John Gibb (right). The twins, who come from Box Hill, are apprentice boilermakers.

Apprentice success

LAST month, Apprentice Bricklayer Robert Bennett was presented with first prize for apprentice bricklayers attending Collingwood Technical School. He is the first apprentice in his trade, while in the employ of the Department, to achieve such a distinction.

Mr. Bennett

Prize winning, however, is nothing new for Robert. In 1961, when he began his apprenticeship, he was awarded a Commissioners' prize for obtaining top results among apprentices, of any year, in his trade. He was also awarded the Beazley prize for top results among first-year apprentices attending Collingwood Technical School. In 1962 and 1963, he also gained Commissioners' prizes and, last year, shared one—an equal first—and was also the year's outstanding apprentice in his trade. Robert is in the Special Works division of the Way and Works Branch. which he worked during the latter part of his career included the design of S.O.P. carriages, steel buffet cars and No. 5 State Car. Mr. Malthouse retired last month.

Duke's award

APPRENTICE Boilermaker Ray Matthews, who joined the Department this year, last month returned to his old school—Altona North Technical School—to receive a Duke of Edinburgh Award. Consisting of a medal and a certificate, the award is presented for excellence in academic work, athletics and hobbies. In Ray's case, it was, of course, presented for his achievements last year at the school. Candidates for the award must go for a 20-mile hike with pack; run a set distance to time; and qualify in discus throwing, shot putting or similar athletics. Ray, incidentally, is a member of St. Stephen's Harriers.

Apprentice Ray Matthews

Vacancies for apprentices

THE Department is inviting applications for 276 apprenticeships in 24 different trades. The closing date for receipt of applications is October 25; and the lads will begin their apprenticeships on January 17 next year. Nineteen of the vacancies will be at Bendigo and 17 at Ballarat.

A SCRAPBOOK HISTORY OF APPRENTICESHIP TRAINING IN THE VICTORIAN RAILWAYS

1965 - 2

APPRENTICESHIP WEEK
V.R. DISPLAYS DRAW CROWDS

AS the employer of approximately 1,000 apprentices, covering 25 trades, the Department makes a noteworthy contribution to Apprenticeship Week. It shows the public the wide scope and excellent opportunities that railway apprenticeships offer; and those parents whose sons are already apprenticed in the Department can see at first hand the care and attention given to their training and welfare.

In a more compact display than in previous years (confined to the V.R. Technical College and adjacent apprentice training centres) visitors saw apprentices at their training work; there were fascinating technical displays, 1/12th scale models of rolling stock, and other trade exhibits that showed clearly the vital role of apprentices and tradesmen in the running of trains. As well as the day sessions, the displays were open during the evenings from 6.30 p.m. to 9 p.m.

Other contributions made by the Department to the Week, were window displays in the Victorian Government Tourist Bureau (Collins Street) and at shopping centres in Geelong, Ballarat and Bendigo. There was also an exhibit at Storey Hall in the Royal Melbourne Institute of Technology.

Altogether, about 3,000 visitors went to the V.R. College displays, including groups of first-year railway apprentices from Ballarat and Bendigo.

Appreciation

Eloquent testimony to the value of the displays and their effect on visitors can be seen from appreciative letters received.

Mr. N. S. Abbott, 72 Prince's Highway, Pakenham East, writes:

"In response to an invitation from the Railways Technical College, Newport, my wife and I were able to visit the training establishment where our son is a first year apprentice.

"We would like to express our delight with the cordial reception we received from the staff, especially Mr. S. Curwood and Mr. J. Mitchell of the fitter and turner's department. Their enthusiasm and skill was most impressive and their kindly interest in the lads in their charge seemed to extend beyond normal calls of duty. We were impressed with the facilities and conditions existing at the

At the V.R. Technical College, Apprentice S. L. Baker demonstrates the use of a bench micrometer.

Apprentices who have won Commissioners' first prizes for three consecutive years are congratulated by the Chairman of the Staff Board, Mr. C. S. Morris (second from right) and the Principal of the V.R. Technical College, Mr. H. Siinger (right) Apprentices are (from left): Messrs. P. R. Bond, R. B. Jones, F. B. Woodford G. R. Baldwin, and M. F. O'Dea.

84   The Victorian Railways News Letter

training centre, and feel that when Victorian Railways claim this to be the best apprenticeship training available in the country, they make no idle boast. As we toured the rooms and inspected exhibits we spoke to many of the apprentices and sensed their pride in the school and satisfaction with the real opportunity to become first class tradesmen.

"We feel moved to offer this appreciation for publication in your journal not only as a well deserved tribute to all concerned but perhaps as an assurance to parents who may not realize the opportunity afforded their lads or know of the interest and care displayed in them.

"Country parents in particular may rest assured that boys living away from home have responsible people awake to their needs out of working time, and it is good for parents to feel that their lads are being trained in an atmosphere of kindly discipline, and understanding, with first-class technical facilities.

"To those who despair of modern youth and are only aware of the antics which receive so much publicity, we would suggest a visit to this hive of industry at Newport and we think, they too, would share our conviction that here will be produced some good, talented citizens for tomorrow, a credit to their instructors and ready to enjoy an assured place in Victorian Railways."

Writing to the Principal of the V.R. Technical College, Mr. C. R. Pittock,

Mr. W. O. Galletly, Chief Mechanical Engineer, (*right*) admires awards that were presented to V.R. apprentices at the Melbourne Town Hall, by the Governor of Victoria, Major General Sir Rohan Delacombe. (*From left*) Apprentices N. Yuille and R. Bennett (the year's outstanding apprentices in their respective trades) and M. F. O'Dea (the year's outstanding apprentice at the V.R. Technical College).

Principal of Sunshine Technical School, says: "The trip we had over your school and associated shops was outstanding. Not only the staff but our students also, were impressed tremendously with the high standard of work you have obtained. The equipment made us envious of both staff and students . . ."

WILD CATS OF FLINDERS STREET

THE *wild cats* of Flinders Street are not a rock 'n roll group. They are just a bunch of loveable, frolicsome kittens that make the permanent way at No. 11 (St. Kilda) platform, Flinders Street, their stage for a morning and evening show that intrigues and delights train travellers.

The kittens were born and reared in the shrubs that grow on the River Yarra embankment at the side of the line. This little piece of railway land has become a sanctuary for them.

Father of the kittens—he has two families, one at the down end the other at the up end of the platform—is an outsize in Tom cats. He resists all attempts at friendship. Approach him and he'll crouch, bare his fangs, snarl and hiss. Not a friendly type at all.

Mother of the large family is not often seen on the tracks. She is a much more placid type than husband Tom and prefers to remain very much in the background.

No household pets could be better fed than the *wild cats* of Flinders Street. Platform staff say that three women take it in turn, morning and evening, to feed the kittens. Some train travellers bring them scraps of food from the breakfast table, or the remains of a midday lunch. Delicacies– such as chicken bones from a Sunday dinner– are sometimes tossed to the kittens scampering along the permanent way. They drink from small plastic saucers that have been tossed to the side of the tracks by their admirers. The saucers are occasionally filled with water by station staff.

The only ones to resent the presence of the cat colony are the seagulls who try to swoop down on the morsels of food, but the darting paws of the kittens make them wary of the consequences of coming too close.

The kittens almost appear to have a premonition of the approach of a train. So much so that one of the station staff jokingly remarked that "they seemed to know the timetable". When a train crosses the railway bridge spanning the river and approaches No. 11 platform, the kittens scamper into the bushes, and after the train has left, they venture forth again to finish the meal.

A regular St. Kilda line traveller– an animal lover– took a particular fancy to one of the kittens and asked one of the station staff to get it for her as she would like to take it home and bring it up as a family pet.

He tried to corner the kitten, but found it too fast and tricky for him and had to give up the chase.

A SCRAPBOOK HISTORY OF APPRENTICESHIP TRAINING IN THE VICTORIAN RAILWAYS

THE YEAR 1966

NEW APPRENTICES: These lads were among the 210 new apprentices who were officially welcomed to the Department last month by the Chairman of the Staff Board, Mr. C. S. Morris. They are seen here with the Supervisor of Apprentices, Mr. R. Curtis (left), and the V.R. Technical College Principal Mr. J. Kain (right).

Apprenticeship opportunities

THIS year the Department is offering 254 apprenticeships in a range of 24 different trades. Applications close on October 24.

These vacancies are available to eligible junior railway employees and sons of railway staff as well as to young applicants from the general public.

Information booklets and application forms have been distributed to most railway stations and may also be obtained from the Employment Officer, Room 215, Railways Administrative Offices, Spencer Street, Melbourne. Members of the staff can co-operate by encouraging inquiries about apprenticeships and advising those interested how to obtain information.

Officers-in-charge of stations can help by ensuring that information booklets and application forms are available, to meet any requests stimulated by railwaymen and through Departmental advertising. Additional copies can be obtained from Room 215, Head Office, auto. 1678 or 1780.

Railway tradition

SEVENTEEN-YEAR-OLD Allan Douglas Morffew who was among the 210 new apprentices who began last month is certainly adhering to a family tradition. His father is an electric train driver; his mother was a typiste in the Department; and his grandfather (Mr Les Pope) is a foreman blacksmith at Newport Workshops.

Apprentice Morffew

Allan's great uncle was also a blacksmith in the Workshops; his great-grandfather was an electric train driver; and his great-great-great uncle was a foreman in the Williamstown Railway Workshops away back in 1890! Allan, himself, has been a scout for five years, and is now a Queen's Scout.

This group of apprentices were presented last month with prizes won for their work during 1965. In the centre of the front row are (from left): Messrs. J. Kain (Principal of the V.R. Technical College), R. M. Wright (Actg. Chairman, Staff Board) and R. Curtis (Supervisor of Apprentices).

1966 - 2

My Apprenticeship Years 1966 – 1971: Norm Swanwick

I can remember being interviewed for an apprentice electrical fitter's position at the VRI hall building near the Geelong railway station. My application was successful and I commenced my five-year apprenticeship training with the Victorian Railways on 17 January 1966. As I would be undertaking my first year at the Newport Railway Workshops, I decided to board away from home. Most of the apprentices from Geelong would travel back & forth each day. The Victorian Railways paid our board and many of my fellow apprentices came from the country. There were four of us boarding at a Melbourne Road Newport boarding house, two in each room. The house was directly opposite the workshops. The house was fairly old and the roof leaked like a sieve. If it was raining at night we would wake up in the morning with either a wet bed or pots all around the floor to catch the drips. Every Monday night we would borrow the landlord's old car and go to the local Albion Drive-in. It didn't matter what the movie was or what the weather was like. With the Landladies family, there were nine of us living in the house and with only one bathroom, there was always a queue every morning to get into the bathroom but somehow we managed to squeeze in breakfast as well and get to work on time.

On that first day, 210 of us gathered at the VRI Hall located at Spencer Street station where we were officially welcomed by the Chairman of the VR staff board. We were then escorted to the manual training centres located at the Newport Workshops. The manual training centre for electrical apprentices was located in half a workshop on the west side of the workshops near the Melbourne Geelong railway line and known as West Block. It was established around the same time that the new Victorian Railways Technical College which opened in 1961. We had to walk some distance to the other side of the workshops to attend the technical college. The other two manual training centres for the mechanical trades were located near rear of the college.

During these first twelve months, we undertook routine bench work, and machine work learning to operate lathes, drills, grinders etc. On another day we would be trained on practical work involving electrical wiring. During the week we would also attend the technical college to undertake various theory classes. Once a week we would undertake chipping which involved chiselling and filing away on a great block of cast iron (see item below).

Extract from "Once Upon a Train" by Dennis Denman: The bloody block

Another task to which every generation of ETC apprentice would have common recall was the infernal chipping block. Every comment would undoubtedly revolve around the frequency of attendance at the shop's nurse with hand abrasions and worse. Why it had previously been overlooked as skill errors or collateral damage I'm unsure, but I viewed it differently. In my eyes, a skill that should have been relegated to previous centuries was still on the books.

A SCRAPBOOK HISTORY OF APPRENTICESHIP TRAINING IN THE VICTORIAN RAILWAYS

The task involved chipping about a half inch (10 mm) from a 5-inch (100 mm) square cast iron block, an outdated skill where machine time and labour were today's main ingredients (in other words, the cost of labour to do the job).

The compromise was to use the 'shaper' machine to minimise the block's surface with the remainder to be hand chipped. The chipping skill maintained; the instances of hand abrasions declined. The continued sight of band-aids prompted the thought of first aid. Our industry has a long history of first aid practitioners and ambulance competitions. The first aid finals were a calendar highlight held annually at Mt Evelyn. Teams and individual competition were supported from statewide locations. Not only in-house but competitions were also held between other State railways.

OUT INTO THE BIG WIDE VR WORLD - ON THE JOB TRAINING

JOLIMONT WORKSHOPS:

After completing my first twelve months at the Newport training centre I was appointed to the Rolling Stock branch of the Victorian Railways and sent to the Jolimont Workshops which were the maintenance workshops for suburban trains and where I remained for the next 12 – 18 months.

I can remember the "sign on" clock which had a large rotating arm with holes around the circumference. You lined the arm up with the hole indicating your staff number and punched it. There was a character who would come in and punch a whole stack of numbers no matter if they were in or not. At shift end the workforce lined up to use the time clocks (two in number) much like a sheep run, the image of the jostling and rush to depart the premises at day's end remains a distant but clear memory. The time clock is now held at the VR Museum at Williamstown.

I can remember working in the lifting shop where, in the morning, we would climb into the pits below the carriages to carry out maintenance on the various relays and electrical equipment. In the afternoon we would all climb up into the carriages for an afternoon nap or play cards. The foremen were aware of the practice and on occasion would join us.

By the mid-1980s the Metropolitan Transit Authority (successor to the Victorian Railways) drew up plans for the closure and decentralisation of the Jolimont Workshops, with new railway facilities to be built around suburban Melbourne. The workshops finally closed in April 1993. Track and overhead were removed by November 1993, with the demolition of the workshops approved in May 1994, and the inspection and paint shops demolished by August 1994. The land was used to expand the Melbourne Park tennis centre, with the opening of additional outside courts to the north of Rod Laver Arena.

A SCRAPBOOK HISTORY OF APPRENTICESHIP TRAINING IN THE VICTORIAN RAILWAYS

Jolimont workshops, lifting shop circa 1960's

Jolimont Workshops circa 1980's

Another view of the lifting Bay probably taken during the 1950's

BACK TO NEWPORT:

From the Jolimont Workshops, it was back to the Newport. During this period I decided to move back home and travelled each day from Geelong. We only paid quarter fare for our train travel and on holidays we were given free travel. At Newport, I moved around between the various workshops spending a few months in each. I can especially remember working in the East Block Wheel shop where the electric diesels were maintained. The cabs would be partly lifted above the bogies and we would have to crawl between the two to disconnect the bogie motors from the main body of the engine. It was very dirty work, for which we were paid a dirt allowance and claustrophobic to boot. The tradesman I worked with we called Mumma Cass. He was a big Slavian guy who grunted and growled at you. You kept hoping that the diesel's cab would not slip and crush you under it. I was glad the day came when I moved on to my next section. Some of the other shops I worked in included the Plant Shop carrying out routine electrical maintenance and the Drawing Office where I spent most of the day wandering around the various shops looking for drawings long lost and never to be found.

During the first two years of on-the-job training, we would periodically return to both the Technical College and manual training centre to further our knowledge and skills needed for our trade.

TRAIN LIGHTING DEPOT:

At some stage during my training, I was located at the train lighting depot in Dudley Street, West Melbourne opposite Festival Hall. Four of us, all railway apprentices (Brian, Keith, Ian and myself) decided to share a flat. At the train lighting depot, we would undertake maintenance work on the VR passenger rolling stock. Part of our duties was to accompany a tradesman on the Spirit of Progress and the Intercapital Daylight Express as train electricians. We would travel from Melbourne to Harden and back monitoring the power van, air-conditioning and if we wanted free eats, helping the dining car crew by washing the dishes, emptying the bins etc. The dining car crew would change at Junee and we would continue on to Harden arriving around 3.30 pm where a NSW electrician would take over. There was a large railway barracks at Harden where we would get some sleep and be up at 2.00 am to catch the Spirit back to Melbourne. Some of the guys would over sleep and miss the train back to Melbourne so they eventually had a station assistant come across to the barracks and check that we were awake.

TLD Aerial View 1962   **TLD Aerial View more recently**

MY FINAL YEAR AS AN APPRENTICE:

After the Train Lighting Depot, I then returned to Newport workshops and in 1969 I was selected as the outstanding apprentice in the Victorian Railways for 1968 and received a medallion from the Governor of Victoria at an Apprenticeship Week Awards night. I completed my apprenticeship in January 1971 back at the train lighting depot and a month later in February, I left the railways to undertake an electronic engineering traineeship with the Department of Defence. Some great friendships and fond memories of the best years of my working life.

1966 - 5
1966 OPEN DAY

A "MUST" FOR PARENTS

who want a promising technical career for their sons, is a visit to the annual Apprentice Week Display at the V.R. Technical College, Newport.

During his inspection of the display at Newport Technical College, the Governor, Sir Rohan Delacombe, was interested in a demonstration of equipment testing by Apprentice Electrical Fitter John Vloedmans. (From left) Mr. G. F. Brown (Deputy Chairman of Commissioners), Mr. R. Curtis, (Supervisor of Apprentices), Sir Rohan, and Mr. J. Kain (Principal of the V.R. Technical College).

THERE they can see the many advantages of a railway apprenticeship—the wide scope offered by 31 trades from which to choose; the thorough instruction given to the youths, combining theoretical training in the College with practical work at the training centres; and the fatherly care that the Supervisor of Apprentices gives to the career of each lad. In addition, the high standard of skill acquired by the apprentices is made obvious by the superb craftsmanship in the displays, and the pride in their work shown by the apprentice demonstrators. And parents who have a son already apprenticed may discuss his progress with the instructors.

There are exhibits covering every trade, and apprentices may be seen at work in their manual training centres. This year's display at the College was inspected by the Governor, Sir Rohan Delacombe, and, altogether, it attracted over 2,600 visitors, including groups of first-year railway apprentices from Ballarat and Bendigo Workshops. It was open from May 10 to 12 until 9 p.m. each night.

In addition to the V.R. Technical College displays there were others by the Department in the Victorian Government Tourist Bureau window (Collins Street) and at shopping centres in Geelong, Ballarat and Bendigo. There was also an exhibit at Storey Hall in the Royal Melbourne Institute of Technology.

Indicative of the success of the displays are such comments as the following from the V.R. College visitors' book:

"Impressed by the confidence and ability shown by the boys demonstrating." (J. Kepert, Chief Inspector of Technical Schools)

"Very high standard of work shown, very impressed by the help given to visitors by apprentices and their ability to communicate with people." (B. Brown, ICIANZ Apprentice Training School)

"Wonderful apparatus; guides and demonstrators—excellent." (Brother Bouchard, St. John's College, Braybrook)

"An excellent grounding for future tradesmen." (E. J. Barker, Principal, School of Mines and Industries, Ballarat)

A visitor, Mrs. J. Tainsh, has the operation of a spectrometer (used to determine the refractive index of a material) explained to her by (from left) Apprentice Fitter and Turner J. R. Barry and her son John, who is an Apprentice Electrical Mechanic. At right is another interested visitor, Miss Lorraine Payne.

A SCRAPBOOK HISTORY OF APPRENTICESHIP TRAINING IN THE VICTORIAN RAILWAYS

Mrs. E. Pleydell (left), a typiste in the office of the Supervisor of Apprentices, and Mrs. B. Downs, a typiste in the V.R. Technical College, obligingly pose against locomotive boiler plates that have been welded to an oil tank end.

At the conclusion of His Excellency's inspection, he was presented with a writing pad and stand made by the apprentices. The presentation was made on their behalf by Robert Arklay (right), the V.R. Technical College's outstanding apprentice for 1965. (From left) Sir Rohan, Messrs. J. Kain and G. F. Brown. (The following evening, Sir Rohan presented to Robert a bronze medallion during the annual presentation of awards to the State's leading apprentices at Melbourne Town Hall.)

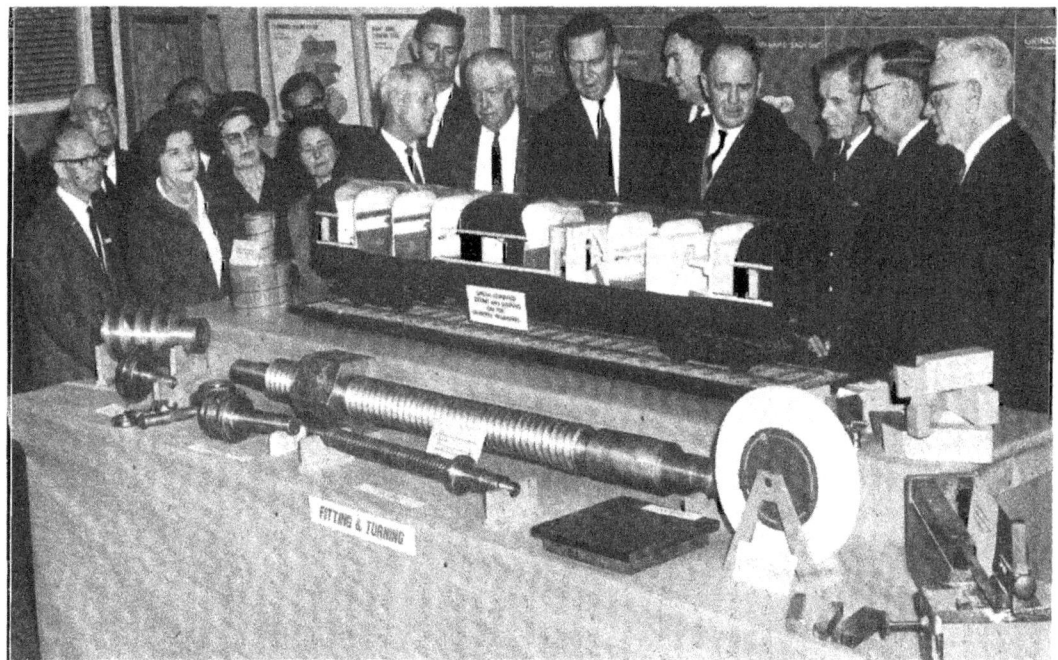

Members of the Advisory Council on Technical Education also inspected the display at the V.R. Technical College. (The Chairman of the Advisory Council is Mr. G. F. Brown, Deputy Chairman of Commissioners). (Left to right) Messrs. J. Kain, G. Thompson*, Acting Principal of the Royal Melbourne Institute of Technology; Mrs. H. T. McKern; Mr. R. Curtis; Mrs. V. E. Vibert; Mr. G. Barton*, Manager, Victorian Division, Bradford Cotton Mills Pty. Ltd.; Miss M. Cahill (V.R. Stenographer); Messrs. W. Chapman, Manager of Newport Workshops; J. Barker*, Principal of School of Mines and Industries, Ballarat; E. Boland, Apprenticeship Commissioner of New South Wales; H. T. McKern*, Managing Director of H. T. McKern and Sons Pty. Ltd.; J. Watson*, Manager of Training and Development, General-Motors-Holdens Pty. Ltd.; G. F. Brown*, J. Kepert*, Chief Inspector of Technical Schools; H. Beanland*, Principal of the Footscray Technical College; and V. E. Vibert*, of E. J. Vibert Pty. Ltd.
(* Member of the Advisory Council on Technical Education)

June 1966

THE YEAR 1967

APPRENTICES WELCOMED: Apprentices at the V.R.I. Ballroom were welcomed to the Department last month by Mr. C. S. Morr Board, on behalf of the Commissioners. Officers who accompanied Mr. Morris included Messrs. G. Godfrey (Chairman of the App: J. Kain (V.R. Technical College Principal), R. Curtis (Supervisor of Apprentices), and R. Baggott (Acting Secretary V.R.I.). Altoget: taken into the Department.

APPRENTICES: Accompanied by Mr G. F. Brown, Chairman of Commissioners (left) Apprentices L. Jewell (centre) and J. Brincat are shown after attending a ceremony at the Melbourne Town Hall where the Governor, Sir Rohan Delacombe, presented the apprentices with awards they had won. Apprentice Jewell was the outstanding apprentice coppersmith in the State, and Apprentice Brincat the outstanding apprentice in the Victorian Railways. Mr. Brown is holding the employer's certificates presented by the Governor.

FROM NAURU came Apprentice Fitter and Turner Paul Aingimea. There he was advised by Mr. Arthur Watson, a former Victorian Railwayman and now a British Phosphate Commission foreman, to learn his trade in the Victorian Railways.

FROM RAILWAY FAMILIES: Among the 47 new apprentices who came from families with close railway associations were Robert Wignall (left) and Geoff Odgers.

Robert's father, Mr. H. L. Wignall, is the Assistant Ambulance Officer, and there has been a railwayman in every generation back to Robert's great-great-grandfather, Mr. G. E. Wignall, who was a driller at Newport Workshops.

Geoff Odgers' father, Mr. W. H. Odgers, is a Spotless Train driver; an uncle, Mr. C. Odgers, is an electrical instructor at Newport Workshops, and a great-grandfather, Mr. W. Odgers of Wodonga, is a retired driver.

1967 -1966 Prize winners

A SCRAPBOOK HISTORY OF APPRENTICESHIP TRAINING IN THE VICTORIAN RAILWAYS

1967 - 2

1967 APPRENTICESHIP WEEK

APPRENTICESHIP WEEK
V.R. DISPLAYS DRAW CROWDS

Underwater cutting of steel plate is about to be demonstrated by Apprentice Boilermaker Allan Rees.

Paying his first official visit as Chairman of Commissioners to the V.R. Technical College, Mr. G. F. Brown watches Apprentice Boilermaker Grant Bovell oxy-propane cut steel plate.

Craftsmanship of the carpenter is shown by Apprentice John Ashton as he squares the leg of a welder's stool.

Apprentice Upholsterer John Coleman is at work on a van back. He received an honourable mention certificate for a group project at Prahran Technical School.

As usual, the Department's main contribution to Apprenticeship Week—the 3-day display at the V.R. Technical College and Newport Workshops' Manual Training Centres—provided one of the most interesting events of its kind during the week. The wide variety of railway work—by 26 different trades—resulted in a display that was almost a complete cross-section of modern industry. And skills that were revealed ranged from the age-old and exacting craftsmanship of the joiner to the complexity of the work done in today's electrical trades. The quality of the exhibits and the enthusiasm of the young demonstrators spoke volumes for the instruction given to railway apprentices.

The hours during which the Newport display was open—9 a.m. to 5 p.m. and 6.30 p.m. to 9 p.m.—facilitated visits by parents of apprentices, and others who might be considering such a career for their lads.

Those who have not seen this annual display should make a point of visiting it next year; it's both rewarding and interesting—even if there's no potential apprentice in the family.

Over 3,500 visitors attended the display—1,000 more than last year. As well as groups from technical

June 1967

A SCRAPBOOK HISTORY OF APPRENTICESHIP TRAINING IN THE VICTORIAN RAILWAYS

Students from Footscray Technical College listen to Apprentice Electrical Fitter John Semple as he explains the operation of a mobile radio. This radio, which is fitted to V.R. road vehicles by apprentices, enables the operator to converse from his vehicle to any telephone on the V.R. system.

(*Top right*) Apprentices from Bendigo Workshops watch Apprentice Antonio Falvo demonstrate drilling of a bore for ball and socket.

(*Right*) Teaching of safety begins right at the outset of a railway apprentice's career, as these blackboard cartoons indicate. They were some of those done by Mr. K. Stanley, senior teacher at the College.

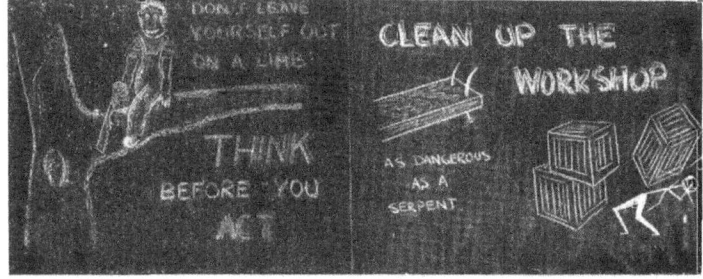

schools and railway centres, they included members of the Advisory Council on Technical Education, municipal leaders, and representatives from the Naval Dockyard, the United States Navy, State Electricity Commission, and large industrial organizations. Appreciation of the excellence of the display and the keenness of students was freely expressed by the visitors, whose feelings are perhaps best summarized in the letter received by Mr. J. Kain, V.R. Technical College Principal, from Mr. H. Ely, Principal of the Broadmeadows Technical School, who wrote:

"Please accept our grateful thanks for a most enjoyable and informative day. The courteous manner in which we were received, both by members of your staff and your students, was very much appreciated. The patience exercised in explaining repeatedly the many complicated exhibits, and the organization behind the tour guiding was splendid. Many of our students expressed their desire to be a part of a team that could attain and show such a pride in craftsmanship".

During Apprenticeship Week there were also other V.R. displays—with the theme of *Trained Tradesmen*—in the Lower Melbourne Town Hall, the Victorian Government Tourist Bureau in Collins Street, and shopping centres at Bendigo and Geelong.

THE YEAR 1968

APPRENTICES WELCOMED

TWIN GREETS TWINS: Among the 210 new apprentices who were welcomed to the Department last month, by Mr. C. S. Morris, Chairman of the Staff Board, and other senior officers, were the twin brothers Lillico. Mr. Morris (left) is pointing out features of the Flinders Street station area to John Lillico and his twin brother Alan. Incidentally, Mr. Morris is himself a twin; both he and his twin brother (now headmaster of Ararat High School) began in the Department as junior clerks at the Melbourne Goods Sheds, 43 years ago.

Outstanding apprentice

Apprentice Fitter and Turner Santo Chiodo is the outstanding apprentice among those who attended the V. R. Technical College last year. Santo began his apprenticeship with the Department in January 1965, after gaining his junior technical certificate at Collingwood Technical School. He was awarded a special prize as best apprentice in his training centre during 1965, and gained first prize in his class, for examination results, in each of the two succeeding years. Santo's hobbies are fishing, and repairing car engines.

Mr. Chiodo

Prize winners

V.R. apprentices who received prizes last month. With the apprentices are, (in front row, centre) Messrs. J. B. Kain (Principal, V.R. Technical College), C. S. Morris (Chairman, Staff Board), and R. W. Curtis (Supervisor of Apprentices).

1968 - 2

VACANCIES FOR APPRENTICES

The Department will have vacancies for 234 new apprentices, covering 20 different trades, in 1969. Most of the vacancies will be in the metropolitan area, but some will be at Bendigo and Ballarat.

Applications for the apprenticeships will close on October 21, 1968.

No industry in Australia has more experience in the important business of training apprentices than the Victorian Railways.

The first Railway apprentices started their training at Williamstown Workshops in 1860, and since then the Department has taken a justifiable pride in its training methods in producing first-class tradesmen.

A 14-page full colour booklet, with illustrations and details of the present wide range of trade training in the Railways, has been produced for interested school-leavers and parents.

The booklets and application forms are available at all staffed railway stations in the state, and can also be obtained from the Employment Officer, Room 215, Railways Administrative Officers, Spencer Street, Melbourne, 3000, or by ringing auto. 1910.

FLINDERS STREET DEVELOPMENT

As *News Letter* went to press, it was reported that Meldon Properties Pty. Ltd., which has the option to develop the Flinders Street station site, has, for more than a year, been making a feasibility survey of the site. The option for that site was previously held by H.K.J. Pty. Ltd. Lend Lease Corporation Ltd., a partner in Meldon Properties Pty. Ltd., was soon expected to make a firm proposition to the Government on its plans for the redevelopment. (See *News Letter* Nov. 1967, p. 162, and June 1963, p. 86).

The Victorian Railways News Letter

Scholarships for apprentices

Railway apprentices with passes in suitable Form 5 subjects will be considered for full-time scholarships for Diploma in Engineering after only one year.

These scholarships will be in addition to those available to apprentices who attained this educational standard by the end of their second or third years.

Successful completion of the academic portion of the Diploma means appointment to the engineering staff of the Department.

APPRENTICESHIP WEEK:

This month, Apprenticeship Week will bring to public notice the excellent opportunities open to apprentices. The Department will have displays at Newport Workshops, the Victorian Government Tourist Bureau in Collins Street, the Lower Town Hall, Melbourne, and at Geelong, Ballarat and Bendigo. At the V.R. Technical College, the display will be open from 9 a.m. to 5 p.m. and 6.30 p.m. to 9 p.m. on May 28, 29, and 30. Visitors are cordially invited. They will see an interesting range of exhibits and the work of young railwaymen such as Apprentice Painter John Crouch who is shown on the front cover painting the cut-outs on a polyurethane-coated tallow tank (see story on this page).

Apprenticeships rushed

More than 1,000 applications have been received by the Department to fill the 234 apprenticeships in 20 trades available for 1969. This was one of the best responses from prospective apprentices for the past 20 years.

About half the applicants were from country areas. Although some apprentices will train in the country at Ballarat North and Bendigo North Workshops, most will work in Melbourne.

Successful lads will start their apprenticeships next month.

A SCRAPBOOK HISTORY OF APPRENTICESHIP TRAINING IN THE VICTORIAN RAILWAYS

1968 – 3 OPEN DAY

APPRENTICESHIP WEEK

At the V.R. Technical College display, Apprentice Electrical Fitter John Coward (*above*) is adjusting a high frequency mobile radio, and (*right*) Apprentice Upholsterer Peter Wilson is working on a motorman's seat for an electric train.

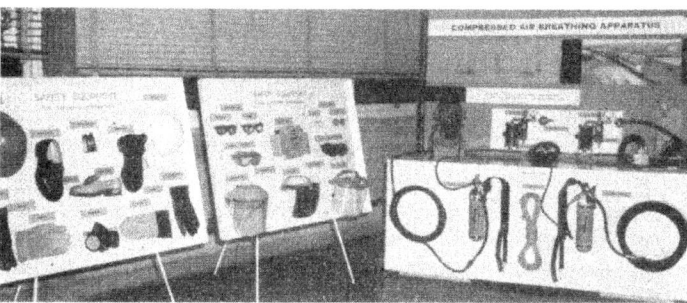

Safety display (*above*) and electroplating display (*below*) at the V.R. Technical College.

ONE of the best free shows in Melbourne must surely be the Apprenticeship Week display in the V.R. Technical College and Manual Training Centres at Newport Workshops. The exacting standards of craftmanship revealed, and the variety of exhibits—by 24 different trades—would fascinate any visitor, no matter what his or her age.

About 4,000 visitors saw the display during the three days, May 28-30, that it was open. Among them were 1,600 students from metropolitan schools, parents and friends of railway apprentices, and representatives of educational and other organizations, trade unions, municipalities, and Government Departments.

Visitors saw apprentices at work on their normal trade training exercises, and also saw a slide presentation of fitting and turning work.

On May 27, annual prizes totalling nearly $850, were presented by the Chairman of the Staff Board (Mr. C. S. Morris) to 73 railway apprentices who had won student awards in their various trade courses. Among them was the Department's outstanding apprentice, Santo Chiodo, who, on May 29, was a guest at a Rotary Club luncheon, and, two days later, accompanied the Chairman of Commissioners, Mr. G. F. Brown, to the Melbourne Town Hall where Mr. Brown received the employer's certificate from the Duke of Edinburgh, and Santo was presented with a bronze medallion.

A SCRAPBOOK HISTORY OF APPRENTICESHIP TRAINING IN THE VICTORIAN RAILWAYS

THE YEAR 1969

1969 Apprenticeship Week

APPRENTICESHIP WEEK DISPLAYS

The Department's contribution to Apprenticeship Week (May 25-31) included a 3-day display and public inspection of the Technical College and Manual Training Centres at Newport Workshops.

Nearly 4,000 visitors saw the display and trade exhibits. More than a third of the visitors were students from metropolitan schools; others included parents and friends of railway apprentices, and representatives of educational and industrial organizations, and trade unions.

Exhibits at the College and training centres showed the relationship between the theory and practice of each of the 29 different apprenticeship trades in the Department. And the exhibits were not only fascinating in themselves, but spoke volumes for the skills imparted and thorough training given to railway apprentices. Visitors also saw apprentices at work on their normal trade training exercises.

Other railway activities during Apprenticeship Week were special displays, having the theme *Trained Tradesmen*, in the Lower Melbourne Town Hall, Victorian Government Tourist Bureau, Collins Street, Melbourne, and in shopping centres at Bendigo, Ballarat, and Geelong.

(*Top, from left*) Apprentice Telephone Technicians I. Ralph, J. Whittington, and P. Bourke show how teleprinter distortion is measured.

(*Left*) The functioning of a point operating mechanism is demonstrated by (*from left*) Apprentice Electrical Fitters (Signal) M. Hall, W. Gear, K. Maher, P. Walton, and J. Broughton.

PRIZE WINNERS

These V.R. apprentices were presented, last month, with prizes totalling $900, by Mr. C. S. Morris, Chairman of the Staff Board. With the apprentices are (*in front row, centre*) Messrs. J. B. Kain (Principal, V.R. Technical College), C.S. Morris, and R. W. Curtis (Supervisor of Apprentices).

June 1969

A SCRAPBOOK HISTORY OF APPRENTICESHIP TRAINING IN THE VICTORIAN RAILWAYS

1969 - 2

Top apprentices

Apprentice Electrical Fitter Norman Swanwick (from Norlane) won the award as the top apprentice attending the V.R. Technical College, and Apprentice Coppersmith Phillip Wenn (from Heidelberg) was the outstanding apprentice in his trade in Victoria. On May 30, both youths were presented with bronze medallions by the Governor of Victoria, Sir Rohan Delacombe. They accompanied the Chairman of Commissioners, Mr. G. F. Brown, who, at the same time, received the employers' awards at the ceremony in the Melbourne Town Hall.

Mr. Swanwick

Mr. Wenn

The youths were presented with Railway prizes they had won, on May 26. Two days later, they were guests at a Rotary Club luncheon.

ITIM camp was held at Halls Gap in May 1969.
Apprentices N. Swanwick and P. Wren were sponsored by the Victorian Railways

Corio News June 1969

A SCRAPBOOK HISTORY OF APPRENTICESHIP TRAINING IN THE VICTORIAN RAILWAYS

THE YEAR 1970 APPRENTICE AWARDS

Wins scholarship

Apprentice Letterpress Machinist John Noonan, shown starting a letterpress machine at the V.R. Printing Works, has been awarded a Bank of New South Wales post-apprentice scholarship. This award, valued at $100, is presented to the seven outstanding fourth year apprentices for post-apprentice studies at the Melbourne School of Printing and Graphic Arts. John's father and a younger brother work in the Ballarat North Workshops, and he also has other relatives in the Railways.

First student member

Mr. Douglas Hayhoe, a final year civil engineering student in the Way and Works Branch, has been elected the first student member of the Warrnambool Institute of Advanced Education Council. Since 1967, Mr. Hayhoe has been engaged on a civil engineering course at the Warrnambool Institute of Advanced Education under a scholarship granted by the Railways.

Copy of history wanted

A copy of the Railway history—"V.R. to '62"—is urgently required by Mr. G. Waterhouse of 11 Trudgeon Avenue, Reservoir, 3073, (telephone 478-2743). Mr. Waterhouse has informed *News Letter* that he will pay up to $14 for a copy in good condition.

Apprentice awards

As well as being the top apprentice attending the V.R. Technical College, Apprentice Boilermaker Ernest Betts also received the 1969 award for the outstanding apprentice in his trade in Victoria.

At a ceremony in the Melbourne Town Hall, last month, Ernest was presented with a silver medallion by the Governor of Victoria (Sir Rohan Delacombe). Ernest was accompanied by Mr. G. F. Brown, Chairman of Commissioners, who, at the same time, received the employer's award. On May 27, Ernest was a guest at a Rotary Club luncheon, he was also among the 77 apprentices who received student cash awards from the Railways.

Mr. G. F. Brown, Chairman of Commissioners, *(left)*, congratulates Apprentice Boilermaker E. Betts. In centre is the Assistant Chief Mechanical Engineer, Mr. A. J. Nicholson.

Reunion

Intending to make a visit to England, Mr. M. Hughson, Manager of the Dining Car Depot, decided to see if he could meet the crew with whom he flew in Wellington bombers during the Second World War. While still in Australia, he put his request in *News of the World*. It was successful, and on reaching England, Mr. Hughson was able to have a reunion with the other five members of the crew. They came from different parts of the country, travelling hundreds of miles, and the story was featured in the press.

Prize winners

Railway apprentices who were presented with prizes, last month, by Mr. I. G. Hodges, Chairman of the Apprentices Advisory Committee. With the apprentices are (in front row, centre) Messrs. R. W. Curtis (Supervisor of Apprentices), I. G. Hodges, and J. B. Kain (Principal, V. R. Technical College).

THE YEAR 1971

1971 Apprentice of the Year

Top apprentices

Railway apprentices again figured in State-wide apprentice awards. Apprentice Electrical Fitter John Lucas (what better name for that industry), *above*, won the award for the best apprentice at the Railway College as well as the award for the best apprentice electrical fitter in the State. With John is Mr. Commissioner Hodges, before they left to receive the award from the Governor, Sir Rohan Delacombe.

At right, Apprentice Upholsterer Peter Wilson, shows Mr. G. F. Brown, Chairman of Commissioners, the early-Victorian chair he upholstered to win the State's Craftsmanship Award. Peter was also declared the best apprentice upholsterer in the State.

Both are from the country—John from Robinvale and Peter from Wangaratta, where he plays football for Greta in the Ovens & King League.

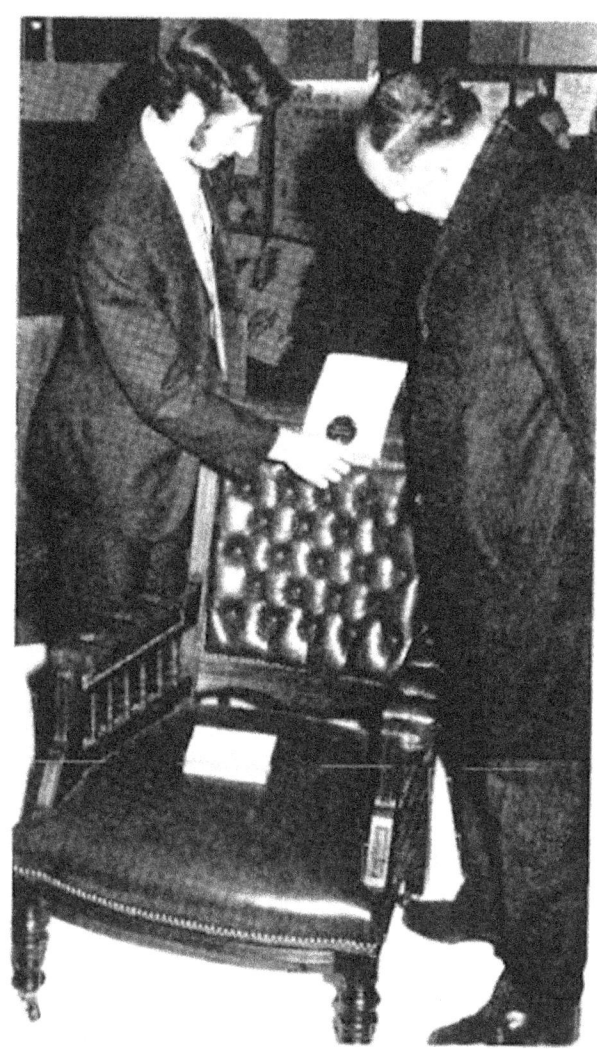

A SCRAPBOOK HISTORY OF APPRENTICESHIP TRAINING IN THE VICTORIAN RAILWAYS

THE YEAR 1972

Prize-winning apprentices

Cash awards totalling $669 were distributed to 65 Victorian Railway apprentices last month for outstanding craftmanship. Chairman of the Victorian Railways Staff Board, Mr. R. M. Wright, (*front, centre*) told the prize winners that by balancing their time between fun and study and keeping up their good work, they could advance to high levels within the V.R. administration. "Two of our three Commissioners—Messrs. G. F. Brown and I. G. Hodges—started as apprentices in the Victorian Railways," he added.

The long and the short

Apprentices come in all shapes and sizes. The longest and the shortest accepted for this year's apprentice intake are seen here with Driver K. Hodgson. Shortest is 17-year-old Karl Weil, who is only 4 ft. 7 in. Biggest is Alan Moore, who, at 16, nudges 6 ft. 4 in. Both will be apprenticed in fitting and turning. Despite his size, Karl wields a mean tennis racquet and has won an open B-grade competition at Geelong. Alan's sports are rugby and spearfishing.

Trained 1,000 apprentices

The 46-year V.R. career of Jack Connelly, a Manual Training Instructor for apprentices, came to a close on May 19. Starting as a lad labourer Jack later excelled as a boilermaker and, after years of training apprentices at workshops throughout the system, he was made an Instructor at the Manual Training Centre at Newport Workshops in 1962.

"I can't speak highly enough of the standards here," he told *News Letter* with pride. "Many overseas visitors have been through our set up and said that it is the best in the Southern Hemisphere. They've taken back with them many sketches and technical drawings for use in similar schemes."

In recent years, Ern Best, one of Jack's pupils, took out the coveted award of best apprentice in the State for oxy-welding.

In younger days, Jack was a keen rower and water polo player. He was later an umpire for the Victorian Amateur Football Association, and has been, for many years, the organist at his local church.

Training over 1,000 exuberant youths has never been a trouble to Jack who sums his years of teaching philosophically by saying: "They try to use their psychology on me, but by treating them as young men and using psychology back on them, we've got on well."

There's more than 1,000 ex-apprentices who would agree, too.

Saturday, May 20, was a happy day for typist, Patsy Shortell—she married 20-y Maurie Benton. Mary McManus, the A was bridesmaid and Fred Newman of th manned the camera to really r

Morden tradition ends

Another name well known to the older V.R. sporting fraternity—Bonding Section Ganger Clem Morden—disappeared from V.R. time sheets on May 19.

Retiring Instructor, Jack Connelly, (*centre*) with some of his pupils on his last day.

THE YEAR 1973

Only one relevant item appeared in the 1973 editions of the Railways Newsletters.

Prize-winning apprentices

Cash awards totalling $669 were distributed to 65 Victorian Railway apprentices last month for outstanding craftmanship. Chairman of the Victorian Railways Staff Board, Mr. R. M. Wright, (*front, centre*) told the prize winners that by balancing their time between fun and study and keeping up their good work, they could advance to high levels within the V.R. administration. "Two of our three Commissioners—Messrs. G. F. Brown and I. G. Hodges—started as apprentices in the Victorian Railways," he added.

Apprentice of the Year award suspended.

It appears that the award for Apprentice of the Year was not awarded between 1973 and 1977 when it was reinstated when all apprentices in the Victorian Railways were eligible to be considered.

A SCRAPBOOK HISTORY OF APPRENTICESHIP TRAINING IN THE VICTORIAN RAILWAYS

THE YEAR 1974

Apprentices Awards

After being presented with their awards, the V.R. Apprentices face the camera, behind the official presentation party.

The official party (*front row, left to right*) is: P. Gibb (Manager Spotswood Workshops); A. Nicholson (Assistant Chief Mechanical Engineer); E. Rudolph (Assistant Chief Electrical Engineer); R. Gallacher (Assistant Chief Civil Engineer); R. Wright (Manager, Personnel); R. Kain (Principal, V.R. Technical College); J. Baillie (Supervisor of Apprentices); L. Rolls (Manager, Newport Workshops); R. Jones (Industrial Chaplain); R. Hannam (Lighting & Power).

Prizes have been awarded to top V.R. apprentices The awards are made after results for final examinations for 1973 at the V.R. Technical College, Ballarat School of Mines, Bendigo Technical College, Royal Melbourne Institute of Technology, and other metropolitan training schools, have been obtained.

Prizewinners at last month's presentation ceremony at the VRI Ballroom, Flinders Street, were:

Boilermakers — 1st. year.
1st. — L. J. Britton, Newport, 2nd. — M. Ferrari, Newport.

Boilermakers — 2nd. year.
1st. — R. Groves, Newport, 2nd. — J. Young, Newport.

Boilermakers — 3rd. year.
1st — J. Redfern, Ballarat, 2nd. — D. Potter, Newport, 3rd. — G. Bovell, Newport.

Electrical Fitters — 1st. year.
1st. equal — A. Armstrong, Jolimont, 1st. equal — P. Levy, Sig. and Communications, 2nd. — M. Cox, Newport, 3rd. — P. Vegter, Electrical.

Electrical Fitters — 2nd. year.
1st — W. Wilson, Electrical, 2nd. — K. O'Dea, Electrical, 3rd. — G. Leighton, Sig. and Communications.

Electrical Fitters — 3rd. year.
1st. — D. Johnstone, Electrical, 2nd. — R. Smith, Electrical, 3rd. — W. McStay, Electrical.

Electrical Mechanics — 1st. year.
1st. — S. Hudson, Electrical, 2nd. — J. Anderson, Electrical, 3rd. — A. Slee, Electrical.

Electrical Mechanics — 2nd. year.
1st. equal — G. Bryce, Electrical, 1st. — equal A. Loriggo, Electrical, 2nd. — I. Hames, Electrical, 3rd. — P. Kendall, Electrical.

Fitters and Turners — 1st. year.
1st. — D. Ryan, Newport, 2nd. — I. Thompson, Newport, 3rd. — S. Maiolo, Spotswood.

Fitters and Turners — 2nd. year.
1st. — K. MacKenzie, North Melbourne, 2nd. — N. Brinsmead, Spotswood, 3rd. — S. Mattievich, Newport.

Fitters and Turners — 3rd. year.
1st. — P. Redding, North Melbourne, 2nd. — G. Watts, Newport, 3rd. — D. Hedges, North Melbourne.

Carpenters and Joiners — all years.
1st. — K. Clarke Spotswood 2nd. equal — R. Bowen, Spotswood, 2nd. equal — G. Jurey Spotswood.

Motor Mechanics, Coppersmiths, Moulders, Watchmakers, Instrument Makers — all years.
1st. — F. Cini Jolimont, 2nd. — K. Black Newport, 3rd. — P. Roberts Jolimont.

Car and Wagon Builders and Upholsterers — all years.
1st. — D. Morton Newport, 2nd. — R. Clarke, Newport, 3rd. — G. Smith, Newport.

Painters, Carpainters, Signwriters — all years.
1st. — J. Murphy, Newport, 2nd. — D. Thorpe, Newport.

Plumbers and Gasfitters — all years.
1st. — K. Nolan, Way and Works, 2nd. — R. Kinney, Way and Works, 3rd. — G. Tullett, Way and Works.

T/S and S/M Workers — all years.
2nd. — N. Ford, Newport, 3rd. — G. O'Brien, Spotswood.

Telecom Tradesmen — 1st. & 2nd. years.
1st. — A. Grech, Sig. and Communications, 2nd. — P. Lawrie, Sig. and Communications, 3rd. — G. Douglas, Sig. and Communications.

Bendigo — All Grades — all years.
2nd. equal — C. Kennedy 2nd. equal — A. Phillips 3rd. — D. Hall.

Ballarat — Boilermakers — all years.
1st. — I. Harris, 2nd. — N. Rose, 3rd. — D. Drew.

Ballarat — all other trades — all years.
1st. — M. Petrie 2nd. — P. Roberts 3rd. — P. Geddes.

1974 - 2

SUPERVISOR OF APPRENTICES RETIRES

"Uncle Roy"—Victorian Railways Superviser of Apprentices for the past 36 years—retired on February 21. Roy Curtis, of McKinnon, has looked after the welfare of 6000 railways apprentices since he was appointed to the post in 1937. Those that have "gone through his hands" include the present Deputy General Manager of the Railways (Mr. I. G. Hodges), two heads of branches and three assistant heads of branches.

Mr. Curtis described himself as "the liaison between the apprentice and management". In addition, he was the representative of parents.

Frequently, he was called upon to arrange board and lodging for country lads and by close contact with a chaplain helped "nudge the boys in the right direction".

Asked his thoughts of the future of the Apprenticeship system, Mr. Curtis said that the scheme would continue for many years, even though revision was under way.

"In fact, I would say there is no other way of producing a skilled tradesman," Mr. Curtis added.

Starting as an apprentice fitter and turner in 1926, at the beginning of the depression, Mr. Curtis became a tradesman at a time when the only work offering was labouring.

"The business people of Geelong established an unemployment scheme and the Department of Labour asked for me to run the centre," said Mr. Curtis.

After the depression, it was back to the Railways at a time when the railway apprentice scheme was re-established and Mr. Curtis was given a trial in the newly created position of Supervisor of Apprentices.

"They told me I was too young at 27 for the job, but I have been there ever since," Mr. Curtis added.

Seen with "Uncle Roy" is his wife and a gathering of Railways apprentices—both old and new.

Two visitors study details of apprenticeship opportunities with the Railways. The display was held at the Melbourne Town Hall last month during Apprenticeship Week.

Apprenticeship Week VR display Melbourne Town Hall

Letterpress Machinist Danny Rigbye (left) and Coppersmith Michael Petrie (right) with VR General Manager Mr. I. G. Hodges, after being presented with apprentices awards.

Danny, who works at the VR Printing Works, North Melbourne, and Michael, from Ballarat North Workshops, topped their trades for the State for 1973. Mr. Hodges received the employer's certificate at the ceremony last month at the Melbourne Town Hall, from the Governor of Victoria, Sir Henry Winneke.

The awards are conducted on a State basis by the Apprenticeship Commission of Victoria.

A SCRAPBOOK HISTORY OF APPRENTICESHIP TRAINING IN THE VICTORIAN RAILWAYS

THE YEAR 1975

TOP MARKS — 55 WIN VR AWARDS

Fifty-five VR apprentices won prizes after their final exams for this year.

Last month *Rail Ways* reported the unexpectedly large number of relatives who came along to the presentation ceremonies, and we now feature the full list of awards for 1975.

BLACKSMITH, CAR & WAGON BUILDERS—All Years

1st—Richard Clarke (Rolling Stock); 2nd—Graeme Smith (Rolling Stock); 3rd—Dennis Morton (Rolling Stock).

BOILERMAKERS—1st Year

1st—Klaus Weber (Rolling Stock); 2nd—Peter Reilly (Rolling Stock).

BOILERMAKERS—2nd Year

1st—Lionel Britton (Rolling Stock); 2nd—Keith Parr (Rolling Stock).

BOILERMAKERS—3rd Year

1st—Trevor Down (Way and Works); 2nd equal—Peter Downey (Way and Works), and John Young (Rolling Stock).

ELECTRICAL FITTERS—1st Year

1st—Nenad Topic (Electrical Engineering); 2nd—Vince Circosta (Electrical Engineering); 3rd—Vito Menchise (Electrical Engineering).

ELECTRICAL FITTERS—2nd Year

1st—Brendon Sidebottom (Way and Works); 2nd—Phillip Wegter (Electrical Engineering); 3rd equal—Alan Armstrong (Rolling Stock), and Christopher Portingale (Electrical Engineering).

ELECTRICAL FITTERS—3rd Year

1st—Wayne Wilson (Electrical Engineering); 2nd—Vaclav Prib (Way and Works); 3rd—John Gibson (Way and Works).

ELECTRICAL MECHANICS—1st Year

1st—Vincent Tonna (Electrical Engineering); 2nd—Robert Nolan (Electrical Engineering); 3rd—Ian Nankervis (Electrical Engineering).

FITTERS & TURNERS—1st Year

1st—Ronald Williams (Rolling Stock); 2nd—Leslie Nichol (Rolling Stock); 3rd—Daryl Fiddian (Way and Works).

FITTERS & TURNERS—2nd Year

1st—Salvatore Maiolo (Way and Works); 2nd—Peter Gray (Rolling Stock); 3rd—Joseph Borg (Rolling Stock).

FITTERS & TURNERS—3rd Year

1st equal—Gregory Magill (Rolling Stock), Silvio Mattievich (Rolling Stock); 2nd—Kenneth MacKenzie (Way and Works); 3rd—Mark Younger (Rolling Stock).

PLUMBER & GAS FITTERS, ELECTRO-PLATERS—All Years

1st—Rodney Kinny (Way and Works); 2nd Kevin Nolan (Way and Works); 3rn Garry Tullett (Way and Works).

CARPENTERS & JOINERS, UPHOLSTERERS—All Years

1st—Kenneth Clarke (Way and Works); 2nd—Gray Jurey (Way and Works).

PAINTERS, SIGNWRITERS, PATTERNMAKERS—All Years

1st—Kenneth Clark (Way and Works); 2nd—Keith Decker (Way and Works).

MOTOR MECHANICS, COPPERSMITHS, MOULDERS, WATCHMAKERS, INSTRUMENT MAKER T/S & S/M WORKERS—All Years

1st—Wayne Theisinger (Rolling Stock); 2nd—Kendal Black (Rolling Stock); 3rd—John Browne (Rolling Stock).

PRINTERS—All Years

1st—Steven Bright (Stores).

TELEPHONE TECHNICIANS—1st Year

1st—Phillip Savige (Way and Works); 2nd—Raymond Clark (Way and Works); 3rd—Christopher Welgus (Way and Works).

TELEPHONE TECHNICIANS—2nd Year

1st—Gary Douglas (Way and Works); 2nd—Arthur Grech (Way and Works); 3rd—Peter Nolte (Way and Works).

BALLARAT

ALL TRADES—All Years

1st—Peter Roberts (Rolling Stock); 2nd—Kim Baxter (Rolling Stock); 3rd—Peter Geddes (Rolling Stock).

BENDIGO

ALL TRADES—All Years

1st—Brian Paterson (Rolling Stock); 2nd—Mark Waters (Rolling Stock).

September 1975

1975 - 2

Apprentice prize winners for 1974 (presented in 1975)

A SCRAPBOOK HISTORY OF APPRENTICESHIP TRAINING IN THE VICTORIAN RAILWAYS

THE YEAR 1976

Apprentices — bosses of the future

Take a close look at this picture .... one of these boys could be running VicRail in the year 2000.

They are all VicRail apprentices.

A quick look around the place shows it's not uncommon to find former railway apprentices in the top jobs.

VicRail General Manager Mr Ian Hodges was an electrical apprentice, Deputy General Manager, Lindsay McCallum, was an apprentice fitter and turner.

Other former apprentices include Les Rolls, assistant chief mechanical engineer, Jack Brodie assistant chief civil engineer and Alan Firth, Chief Electrical Engineer.

Our picture was taken at the 1976 Apprenticeship Award presentations held in the VRI Ballroom.

They used to be held in the boilermakers' canteen at Newport, but with the great interest shown by parents and the apprentices themselves a larger venue was needed.

VicRail now has approx 620 apprentices in 22 trades.

Deputy General Manager, Mr McCallum told apprentices that they had the opportunity in the railways to go as far as possible in their careers.

"There are opportunities for scholarships; if you try hard enough, they are there for you.

"We are anxious to provide a future for you.

"The future can only be for the better for Railways, this is the trend right around the world," he said.

Cheques from $10 to $30 were awarded to the prizewinners.

Suggestions adopted

- Extra door near Electrical Workshops welding shop $30
- Built in integrator with standard peak meter $10
- Distribution cut for special country race circulars $35
- Change in Melville car water supply system $10
- Eliminating low tension wire in carbon file regulators $10
- Use of pop rivets on Y class traction motors $25
- Relocating train indicator board at Oakleigh $10
- Albion signal power supply $10
- Strengthening KS motor flooring $15
- Peak hour passenger poster $10
- Briquette delivery at Ararat signal box $10

Victorian Rail Ways

A SCRAPBOOK HISTORY OF APPRENTICESHIP TRAINING IN THE VICTORIAN RAILWAYS

THE YEAR 1977

Top marks to VicRail apprentices

Over 40 apprentices from all over the state received prize money at last month's apprenticeship awards at Victorian Railways Institute Concert Hall, in Flinders Street.

Apprentices came from Ballarat School of Mines, Bendigo Technical School, Royal Melbourne Institute of Technology and Telecom Australia Training School.

Highest marks went to telephone technician at VicRail's Head Office, Evan Craig *(above left)*, who averaged 95% and an electrical fitter at Spencer Street workshop, Andrew Wheatland *(top right)* averaged 93%. Both apprentices received $20 prize money.

VicRail Boilermaker and Welder, Peter Morgan *(above)* won an Australian Welding Institute award for top marks in his trade last month at Newport Technical College.

It was the first time such an award has been given. Each year the Australian Welding Institute will offer nine regional awards to top third year apprentices.

Principal of the College, Mr. K. Hall, presented Peter with his award for the highest marks in the western region.

Peter, 19, works at the Newport workshop making body components for Ford vans and rail wagons.

126 *Victorian Rail Ways*

THE YEAR 1978

• The boys' lined up for their photographs after the presentations were made at the Concert Hall. In the centre of the second row are, from left: Mr. Alan Firth (Chief Electrical Engineer), Mr. K. Hall (Principal of the Victorian Railways Technical College), and supervisor of apprentices, Mr. Bob Bailey.

He's the 'class' of '77

• Apprentice of the Year, Andrew Wheatland, of Bentleigh, proudly shows the certificate presented to him by Mr. Ian Hodges, VicRail General Manager.

Andrew Wheatland, 21, is VicRail's top apprentice for 1977 — he gained 95 per cent at his end of the year exams in electrical fitting.

As a matter of fact, in his three years of training, Andrew has always scored more than 90 per cent in his exams.

And as Apprentice of the Year, he was presented with a framed certificate and a cheque for $100 by General Manager, Mr. Ian Hodges.

Altogether, 77 apprentices won awards for their year's work.

Andrew is at sub-station maintenance in Batman Avenue, and is also studying industrial electronics at Footscray Technical College. His father is an electrical engineer with the railways.

The apprentices were presented with their awards at the VRI Concert Hall on July 5, and their parents were also invited to attend.

The exams were held at the Victorian Railways Technical College, the Ballarat School of Mines, Bendigo Technical School, RMIT, Telecom Australia's training school and other metropolitan technical schools.

August 1978

1978 - 2

Jenny (second from left) and three of her classmates learn the reading of signals from enginemen's instructor Len McPhan (left).

Expert supports Vicrail

Mr Harold Lawrence, a transport consultant living at Templestowe, wrote a letter to The Age recently in support of VicRail.

We thought the public praise pleasant and rare enough to reprint for all our readers. Mr Lawrence said:

Recent publicity given to railway losses, particularly in relation to suburban electrified operations, have once more focused attention on the vast and growing disparity between cost of providing this type of service and the revenue which can be obtained from fares.

The Victorian Railways' financial problem is not unique. It is matched by the major metropolitan transport operations in other Australian and overseas cities — the bigger the city the bigger the deficit.

Carping criticism by amateur experts will not alter the facts of life, and it may be of interest to serious students of the subject to know that a survey taken in Europe recently showed that in 20 major cities, less than half the cost of operating the public passenger transport was met from fares revenue.

The summary of this survey is:

France (four cities), fares revenue as percentage of operating costs, 40-75; Germany (4) 50-75; Italy (2) 15-20; Denmark, Norway, Sweden (4) 40-60; Austria, Belgium, Holland, Switzerland (6) 50-55.

Thus, actual costs of operating in these cities were slightly more than double the amounts collected in fares.

These facts do not detract from the need for the authorities here to act in a responsible financial manner, but they do show that governments — and in the long run that means the people generally — must be prepared in all major cities substantially to underwrite the costs of providing adequate public passenger transport.

AWARDS TO 77 APPRENTICES

Seventy-seven apprentices were presented with cheques worth a total of $1270 by the General Manager, Mr Ian Hodges, at a ceremony at the VRI Concert Hall on Wednesday, July 5.

The boys, from Rolling Stock, W and Works, Electrical Engineering a Stores Branches, topped their exams l. year.

They are:

Blacksmiths (all years): Gregory Har son, Timothy Edwards. **Boilermakers** (1 year): Raymond Box, William Crum (2nd year): Peter Neilson, Alan Bla (3rd year): David Bell. **Car and wago builders** (1st year): Anthony Sievers, No Robinson, Phillip Ferguson, (2nd and 3 years): Emmanual Catania, Mark Hamme Anthony Van Someron, Robert Hame

Electrical fitters (1st year): Jam Warwick, Jeffrey Hilder, Neville Hoga (2nd year): Mark Humphries, Paul Clissol (3rd year): Andrew Wheatland, John V de Garde, Colin Rutledge. **Electric mechanics** (1st year): Brian Micalle Christopher Quinn, Dale McCurdy; (2r year): Stuart Thomson, Philip Jone Johanne Van Eyk; (3rd year): Geoffre Heron, John Anagnostou.

Fitters and machinists (1st year Emmanuel Pavgouzas, Adolfo Bellegant Trevor Reeves; (2nd year): Warric Barker, Phillip McIlroy, Noel Harve (3rd year): Owen Beckham, Saran Sariklis, Peter Ringberg, Joseph M

Carpenters and joiners (1st year Robert Tangee, Ian Clarke, Andre Atherton; (2nd and 3rd years): Dav Colbourne, Andrew Prosser, Ian Fro **Motor mechanics, coppersmiths, tinsmith sheet metal workers and electroplaters** (years): Kurt Meyer, Barry Wood, Pet Nunn. **Plumbers** (all years): Domen Marino, Wayne Hobbs, Brendon Ratclif

Telephone technicians (all years Harry Van Someron, David Edmonc Steven Williams, Bruce Smith. **Upholstere** (all years): Daryl Jeacle, Brian Quinn, N Gillett. **Printers** (all years): Brian Galv

Ballarat Workshops — Boilermake (all years): Andrew Hammond, Neil Dea Graeme Hill, Shane Kennedy. **Car ar wagon builders** (all years): Robert Lythg Russel Venn, Geoffrey Baulch. **All oth trades** (all years): Neil Glover, Gr Watson, Ian Walker.

Bendigo Workshops — Boilermake (all years): Allan Gard, Gregory Borser Wayne Bell, Thomas Slattery. **Car ar wagon builders, car painters, coppersm** (all years): Neil Andrews, William Ma **Fitters and turners, upholsters** (all years Graeme Cocks.

1978 - 3

1978 Intake

It was their first day at "school" for 1978, and these likely lads were caught by our cameraman before classes. They are some of the 160 apprentices taken on by VicRail at the Newport workshops this year.

THE YEAR 1979

This year's apprentice awards

This year's VicRail awards for apprentice achievement were presented recently at the VRI Concert Hall in Melbourne by General Manager, Ian Hodges.

Apprentices who were given awards were involved in many sections of the rail industry. These included boilermakers, car and wagon builders, electrical fitters, electrical mechanics, fitters and machinists, carpenters and joiners, telephone technicians, painters and signwriters and plumbers and upholsterers.

Another function was also held at the Dallas Brooks Hall where Outstanding Apprentice Awards were handed out. Our representatives at this evening were Deputy General Manager, Lindsay McCallum and Director of Personnel, Peter Stuart.

Congratulations are extended to all award winners, particularly Apprentice Coppersmith, K. D. Meyer, who also attended a special luncheon organised by the Melbourne Rotary Club.

Above: Award winning apprentices are shown with (centred front row, left to right) Bob Baillie (Supervisor of Apprentices), Alan Firth (Chief Electrical Engineer) and Ken Hall (Principal of the VRTC).

118   *Rail Ways*

A SCRAPBOOK HISTORY OF APPRENTICESHIP TRAINING IN THE VICTORIAN RAILWAYS

THE YEAR 1980 – 1979 APPRENTICESHIP AWARDS AND VICTORIAN RAILWAY TECHNICAL COLLEGE CLOSES.

APPRENTICESHIP PRIZE WINNERS OF 1979

For the first time VicRail apprentice prize winners were presented with a medallion in recognition of their achievements.

At a ceremony held at the Melbourne and Metropolitan Board of Works theatre, Spencer Street, 77 of our apprentices received either gold, silver or bronze medals for their 1979 efforts.

At the presentation, held at the end of July special guest was Michael Meszaros who designed the medal.

Apprentice of the Year, Jeff Hilder (featured in August RailWays) along with the past apprentices of the year Andrew Wheatland (1977) and David Colbourne (1978) received larger plaques.

The prizes were presented by Deputy Chairman, Mr. Ian Hodges, himself a former VicRail apprentice.

Above: Deputy Chairman, Mr. Ian Hodges with 1978 Apprentice of the Year, David Colbourne, (left), Andrew Wheatland (1977, centre) and 1979 winner Jeff Hilder (far right).

Below: 1979 prize winners from Ballarat.

1980 - 2

Above: Bendigo 1979 apprentice prize winners. Left: As well as receiving first prize for third year apprentice boilermakers Ray Box also received an award from the Australian Welding Institute for the best arc-welding in Melbourne's western region.

THE DESIGNER

VicRail thinks so highly of its apprentices and their potential for the country's industrial growth that it commissioned one of Australia's leading sculptors and medallists to commemorate this year's Apprentice of the Year Award.

Michael Meszaros, who has emerged as one of this generation's best sculptors in bronze, has created a plaque and a series of bronze medallions for VicRail's top apprentices.

This design, in common with Michael's other medallions, reflects his ability to sum up the essentials of a particular profession or industry and translate them into small graphic works of art.

The medallion features a hand holding a file and a puzzle piece, the piece being part of a jigsaw depicting a railway line.

This is how Michael sees the way various and diverse skills and trades, represented by the jigsaw pieces, are brought together to form one cohesive unit for the running of the railways.

The track was chosen as the symbol of the railways, because it is the one basic and eternal element common to all railway systems.

Michael believes sculpture should efficiently transmit an idea and uses the human form in both free-standing sculpture and in relief to put across a message.

September 1980

A SCRAPBOOK HISTORY OF APPRENTICESHIP TRAINING IN THE VICTORIAN RAILWAYS

1980 - 3

NEW NEWPORT COLLEGE SET TO OPEN

After nearly 60 years of teaching our apprentices, the Technical College at Newport Workshops will close its doors later this year.

At present only the electrical trades are still conducting classes at the old college. They will transfer over when new equipment in installed.

All other apprentices from the old college have transferred to the new $9 million Newport Technical College.

Built on six hectares of leased railway land in Champion Road, the College will be used exclusively by apprentices working in the western region of Melbourne.

Railway apprenticeship training has certainly come a long way since the first classes were conducted in 1905.

These classes were run by the Working Men's College (now the R.M.I.T.) on behalf of VicRail, with two afternoon and one evening classes per week.

In 1923 the first VicRail College opened, near Newport station. This was demolished when the Melbourne Road overpass was built in 1959.

The present Technical College near North Williamstown station was opened in July 1960 and over 5000 apprentices have passed through its doors in 20 years.

There is however one link between the old and the new. Newport College takes over VicRail's College's school number 7270.

Above: One of the new class rooms in use at the new Newport Technical College.

Below: Two of the last classes to be held at our Technical College. Both are electrical trade classes.

1980 - 4

After twenty two years Don leaves school

After spending the past 22 years working in the office of the College, Don Cox believes that with its closure it is time for his retirement.

Don was recruited from England in 1950 as a Blacksmiths striker. He transferred to Newport Workshops office the following year and to Head Office in 1957.

In 1958 he made his final transfer, to the Technical College, he has seen over 5000 apprentices through the school.

Above: A class at the new College. Below: Don Cox (left) and VicRail College Principal Ken Hall.

September 1980

NEWPORT COLLEGE OF TAFE

The Newport College of TAFE was formally established in November 1982 when the Newport Technical College separated from the Footscray Institute of Technology. It also incorporated the Victorian Railways Technical College, which had provided apprentice training for the Victorian Railways. The Newport College of TAFE provided courses in areas such as electrical fitting, motor mechanics, fitting and machining, building studies and metal fabrication and welding.

The college reputedly on a 99-year lease was situated fronting Champion Road on acres within the western boundary of the Newport workshops near the Geelong railway line. A new vision of training was now in place as our apprentices joined private and other community wide apprentices.

Newport College of TAFE was headed first by Ken Hall, who had overseen the separation and transition from being a division of Footscray Institute of Technology and into the first year of the College's existence. After his retirement in 1983, Lloyd Morris became Acting Director, a position he would hold for two years.

When it was established, the Newport College of TAFE provided primarily apprenticeship courses in a variety of areas. These courses were soon expanded to include pre-and post-apprenticeships, technicians' certificates, and community-based short courses. It also commenced access courses in areas such as English for migrants, basic literacy and typing and shorthand.

After a long search and selection process, Ian Daykin was appointed as Director in 1985. He remained at Newport for two years, and again there was some time before a new Director was appointed. Ken Latta was appointed Director in 1988 and remained as Director until 1991, overseeing the amalgamation with Footscray College of TAFE.

In 1989, following a Ministerial Review of TAFE provision in the Western Metropolitan Region, the Minister Responsible for Post-Secondary Education decided to merge the Newport and Footscray Colleges of TAFE. For the first months, Newport opposed the amalgamation, stating that it was unnecessary and that the essential characteristics of Newport would be lost. However, it soon became clear that the Minister was determined to amalgamate the two TAFE Colleges despite strong opposition. 1990 and early 1991 was taken up primarily with preparing for the amalgamation.

TIMELINE: 1980: Opened division of Footscray Institute of Technology. May 1991: Renamed Gellibrand College of TAFE. August 1991: Renamed Western Metropolitan College of TAFE. 2012: Teaching ceased and closed. 2015-2020: Owned by Freemantle Media and used as a TV film lot. 2021: Demolished.

A SCRAPBOOK HISTORY OF APPRENTICESHIP TRAINING IN THE VICTORIAN RAILWAYS

Demolition of Newport TAFE College Circa 2014

New college ready for 1979

The first stage of the $9.4 million Newport Technical College will be ready for students early next year, an Education Department spokesman has told Rail Ways.

The new college will eventually replace the Railway Technical School, which opened its doors to apprentices in 1922.

Stage two of the project is expected to be finished by January 1980.

Work on the $3.8 million L-shaped stage one block began in June last year, and the exterior is now almost completed.

About 340 metal, welding and machine tool trade apprentices, and 40 teachers and other staff are expected to move into the building next January.

The Education Department recently called tenders for the $5.6 million stage two block, which will cater for carpentry, joinery and electrical trades.

The new college will be able to cater for more than 1000 students, and will cover 11 acres of land beside the workshops in Champion Road, Newport.

The technical schools' division of the department has signed a 99-year lease on the VicRail land.

The stage one facilities — one and two-storey buildings — include classrooms, an auditorium, plant room, staff and administration section and a computer room.

Students and staff in trades covered in the stage one block will transfer from the railway school to the new college next year.

Student grants

Mr Dick Mills, VicRail's rehabilitation officer, says student family allowance review forms are now available from the Department of Social Security.

The forms enable the department to decide whether a family is eligible for an allowance this year. All of last year's student family grants were suspended after the December instalment.

The allowances are available to the parents of fulltime students aged between 16 and 25.

Once a parent completes and returns the form payment will be restored as soon as possible from the January instalment — if the entitlement still exists, Mr Mills said.

Where there are also dependent children under 16 years of age in the family, the family allowance and the student family allowance payments will be made together.

Since June 1976, the rate of payment for student has been between $14 and $28 every four weeks, depending on how many other children there are in the family, and the student's position in the family.

"It should be mentioned that this payment will not be made if the student is either not studying on a fulltime basis, or is bonded to a prospective employer," Mr Mills said.

THE YEAR 1981

Apprentice Achievement

Over 70 VicRail apprentices were awarded prizes for high scholastic achievements, both academic and practical by the Chairman, Mr. Reiher, at the 1980 Awards presentation held in June.

The prizewinners came from the metropolitan area, Ballarat and Bendigo, with representation from most trades.

The Apprentice of the Year Award was won by Douglas Gavin, apprentice carpenter and joiner in the Way and Works Branch, Batman Avenue. Doug also won first prize in the Building Studies Technician's Award presented by Preston College for 1981.

A large audience was in attendance, mainly mums and dads, who proudly clapped as their sons were called on stage to receive their medallions from Mr. Reiher. Each received a bronze medallion designed by sculptor, Michael Meszaros.

Mr. Reiher said the young men in the audience were the greatest asset for the growing future of railways in Victoria.

These apprentices from Ballarat were among those who won prizes at VicRail's annual Apprentice Awards. Each received a bronze medallion designed by sculptor, Michael Meszaros.

From Left: Apprentice boilermakers, Steven Cody, Robin Eastick and Glen Taylor, apprentice upholsterer, Stephen Thompson, Ballarat Workshops Manager, Mr. John Barry, apprentice car and wagon builder, James Irving, Mr Reiher, apprentice car painter, Alexander Day from Ararat and apprentice car and wagon builders, Peter O'Donnell and Ricky Atkinson.

For Safety

Safety Achievement Awards were presented to members of the Electric Trains Maintenance Depot at Jolimont recently. Out of a total of 28 sections 14 received a safety award for the first time since the depot was subdivided into 28 sections in 1979.

For the year 1980 — 81 accidents were reduced by about 10 percent and, hopefully, next year will see an even greater reduction in lost — time accidents. Here one of the recipients of the awards, Roy Hanley, from the Inspection Shop Mechanical Car Maintenance Section, presented with his first — year Safety Achievement Award by Depot Manager, Mr. Len Waters, in the presence of Acting Assistant Chief Mechanical Engineer, Mr. Bill Maguire, and Inspection Shop Foreman, Mr. Ken Hancock (right).

Douglas Gavin, VicRail's Apprentice of the Year for 1980 after the recent presentation.

VicRail News

A SCRAPBOOK HISTORY OF APPRENTICESHIP TRAINING IN THE VICTORIAN RAILWAYS

1981 - 2

THE YEAR 1982

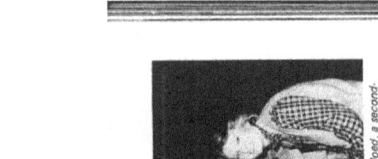

1982 - 2

The Camberwell Civic Centre reverberated to the sounds of hard rock and the gentler tones of old-time music at the recent VicRail Ball.

With the amalgamation of VicRail with other transport groups next year, this annual get together, held this year on July 23, marks the last VicRail Ball as such.

VicRail Ball Committee President, Jack Conheady, explained that the Railway Ball was started back in 1956 to "give our people and friends a social identity and create a venue in a social atmosphere where barriers could be broken down between Branches and make liaison between staff in their ordinary working day a little easier."

In this respect he thanked those in management who had lent their support to make the Railway Ball such a success over the years, and in particular, this year's Ball Committee Secretary, Bryan Stanley from the Personnel Branch, and others that ensured the 1982 ball would be one long remembered.

Enjoying themselves at the ball were . . .

(from left) Lorna and Phil Knight, Barbara and John Dowell, and Marliese Stanley, wife of Committee Secretary, Bryan.

VicRail Ball Committee President, Jack Conheady, thanked all who had worked so hard to make this year's evening such a success.

September 1982

Apprentice craftsmen display their skills

VicRail was well represented at the Craftsmanship Exhibition held last month at the Exhibition buildings to mark Apprenticeship Week this year.

In contrast to previous years when our apprentices built static displays to give the public some idea of the trades employed by the railways, this year our apprentices presented a series of working models to illustrate the type of equipment made and used by VicRail.

The models were designed and built by apprentices attending the Electrical Branch's little publicised Signal Maintenance Technicians' Training Centre at Caulfield. The only full-time school of its type in Australia, the centre trains second, third and fourth year apprentice electrical fitters (signals), as well as offering, with the introduction of new equipment, post-trade courses, orientation courses for engineers and a host of subjects for guards, signal assistants, gangers, supervisors and technicians.

The four exhibits made entirely by the students featured models of a simulated track circuit, of relay interlocking on a set of points, of a signal box panel, together with a full size boom barrier.

Each model was the work of a group of students in one particular year and to ensure continuity of work one apprentice in each group was in charge of each project.

Apprentices (from left) Paul Hockey, Michael Royal, Bradley Wooding and Andrew Richards got together with instructors (in front) David Ffrost and Wayne Collins with the boom barrier built by students at the Signal Maintenance Technicians' Training Centre for this year's Craftsmanship Exhibition held last month to mark Apprenticeship Week.

Instructor, Wayne Collins, praised the 30 students who took part in the exercise for their work, pointing out that the apprentices designed the models and made them up, in the process of working with carpenters and welders, ordering materials and dealing with the various branches within the organisation.

Only when someone got "bogged down" did he turn to Wayne, or one of the other two instructors at the centre, David Ffrost and Les Hill for guidance.

The two projects undertaken by the fourth year apprentices consisted of an interlocking board which showed the operation of a set of points and a simulated track circuit model incorporating a coded Jumont track circuit designed to detect the presence of trains on the rails, the basis of our safe-working system.

One group of third year apprentices constructed a model of a signal box panel, while others got together with second-year students to produce a full size boom barrier which operates on a time delay system.

One of the highlights of the display was an audio visual presentation which gave a brief history of the signalling system and the type of training undergone by the apprentices in this section.

This interesting presentation was the work of apprentices Michael Ampt and Martin Elliott who not only took 35 mm slides to illustrate the display, but wrote and typed up the script, and recorded the narration.

A SCRAPBOOK HISTORY OF APPRENTICESHIP TRAINING IN THE VICTORIAN RAILWAYS

THE YEAR 1983

1983-2

Taking out the honours

A railway apprentice described as "unquestionably the best electrical fitter for his year in the Signal & Communications Division" was awarded a silver medallion at this year's State-wide Apprenticeship Awards.

Antonino Comperatore, who last year completed his apprenticeship, was one of five finalists judged to be an Outstanding Apprentice by the Ministry of Employment and Training which each year honours young people who have excelled in their chosen trade.

Antonino missed out on the Apprenticeship Of The Year Award but did take out top honours from both the Metal Trades Industry Association, who in August presented him with its Apprenticeship Achievement Prize for 1983, and from V/LINE where he is the organisation's own Apprentice of the Year. As a finalist in the State awards Antonino also received a cash award from the Minister for Employment and Training, Mr. Jim Simmonds, for the high standard of his scholarship and craftsmanship over the years.

The national Apprentice Of The Year Awards were held in Brisbane in November this year.

Antonino Comperatore, receives a silver medallion from the Minister for Employment and Training, Mr Jim Simmonds, in recognition of his skills as an electrical fitter.

A SCRAPBOOK HISTORY OF APPRENTICESHIP TRAINING IN THE VICTORIAN RAILWAYS

THE YEAR 1984

V Line's Apprentice of the Year — A career in the making

V Line's Apprentice Of The Year, Trevor Furness, was presented with his award by the Chief General Manager, Workshops, Dick Terrell. Trevor, who received a bronze medallion by sculptor, Michael Meszaros, is now a fitter and turner at Newport Workshops. Scholastic achievement seems to run in the Furness family, which hails from Beena near Korumburra. Trevor, like his brother, Alistair, now a technical officer with the Transport Operations Division, won a scholarship last year to study for his Certificate of Technology.

Trevor Furness joined an illustrious group when he won V Line's Apprentice Of The Year Award recently. By completing his apprenticeship in fitting and turning with top honours this young man from Gippsland not only acquired a trade, a valuable asset in a technology-hungry society, but he joined the ranks of those railway apprentices who have made it to the top both in the organisation and in outside industry.

Those who rose to senior levels of management in the railways both in its past and present structure, include Chief Manager Workshops, Frank Uhe, Bob Arkiay and Bill Butler, Managers of the Newport and Electrical Workshops, respectively, Metrail's Group Manager Rail Engineering, Graham Swift, and one of V Line's most senior engineers, Les Rolls, to name just a few. Many will also remember former VicRail executives Deputy Chairman, Ian Hodges, General Manager, Bob Gallacher, and Assistent General Manager, Jack Brodie and Deputy General Manager, Lindsay McCallum, all railway apprentices who, like many of V Line's present senior engineers, continued their studies, usually on a scholarship, to technical college or university to become professional engineers and to make it to the top of the corporate ladder.

The first apprentice intake goes back to 1860 at the old Williamstown Depot, later replaced by the present Newport Workshops. Training was on-the-job and covered a multitude of trades reflecting the industrial self-sufficiency promoted by the railways at a time when it was the major employer in Victoria.

The main trades taught then were blacksmithing, boilermaking and fitting, together with skills no longer needed by a modern transport system, such as sail making, tin smithing, bricklaying and french polishing. Theory was taught at the various metropolitan and regional technical schools throughout the State.

With the opening of the Victorian Railways Technical College at Newport in 1960 manual skills of the four main trades — boilermaking and structural steel fabricating, electrical fitting, electrical mechanics and fitting and turning — were taught at an accelerated rate, in line with the curriculum set by the technical colleges.

The wide range of other skills offered by the organisation — blacksmithing, moulding, cooking, car painting, upholstering, electrical linework and plumbing — continued to be taught, as they still are, on the shop floor, while country boys learn their trade at the Theory for all apprentices is now taught, with the closure of VR's Technical College in 1960, at the nearby Newport College of TAFE.

At present we have almost 500 apprentices learning varying trades at V Line, long recognised as providing one of the best trainings a would-be tradesman could acquire.

This recognition was echoed by Chief General Manager, Workshops, Dick Terrell, at this year's apprentice prize presentation when he said he, as a newcomer to the organisation, had met tradesmen in the railways whom he believed were second to none.

For those young people thinking in terms of their future Dick pointed out that tomorrow belongs to those prepared to gain technological qualifications, promising them real satisfaction if they go down that road taking pride in their work and in so doing landing pride in themselves.

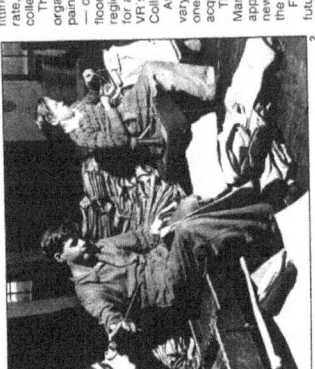

1. The Machine Shop at Newport Workshops, 1894 style.

2. A skill no longer required by today's railways. Apprentice sailmakers sew up bags which were used s sheathfs for the metal roneturners provided in most country trains.

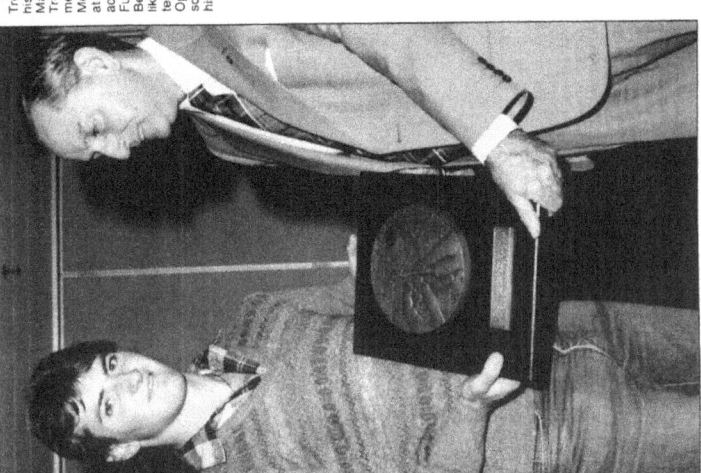

A SCRAPBOOK HISTORY OF APPRENTICESHIP TRAINING IN THE VICTORIAN RAILWAYS

THE YEARS 1988-1992

Succeeding the Victorian Railways, the State Transport Authority was established in 1983 operating until 1989. It operated under the trading name V/Line which today operates the regional passenger train services throughout Victoria. In addition, V/Line is responsible for the maintenance of much of the Victorian freight and passenger rail network outside of the areas managed by Metro Trains Melbourne and the Australian Rail Track Corporation.

By 1988, the Newport Workshops had virtually closed down with sections gradually being handed over to private contractors. The intake of railway apprentices had been greatly reduced in numbers. Four-year apprenticeships in Boiler Making, Fitting & Turning, Electrical Fitting and Painting were still being offered by V/Line. Theory training was undertaken at Newport TAFE Technical College and practical training for a period was at the Newport Workshops before heading off to one or more of the suburban workshops or special training facilities such as the Caulfield Signals Centre.

Scott Gould commenced his electrical fitter apprenticeship (signals) in 1988 and recalls:

"I started at Newport in January 1988 as a 16-year-old kid from Bendigo, in the trade of Electrical fitter, Signal Maintenance. We did most of the first year in the electrical wiring, fitting, and fitting and metalwork workshops, before the four of us in the Signals group headed off to Caulfield to do our signalling specific training.

Newport TAFE was where we did the schooling side of things.

Merv Carson was the Fitting and Turning Instructor, Lindsay Hately, George Saliba, and Boris?? Were in Electrical, with Graham Copeland the head instructor. Arthur Sandilands was one of the TAFE instructors, who had been a signalling apprentice years earlier.

I remember my first pay was cash, lining up at the window to get my little yellow envelope with $398 per fortnight in it- being a country kid we got a living away from home allowance, which basically meant we were on the same money for I think the first three years.

Being in Signals, I didn't spend much apprenticeship time in any of the fun bits of Newport - loco shop, 7 Road or Jolimont, but did go to the at the time new Spotswood workshops for some armature winding, motor overhaul, and making up loco jumper cables.

The Adderly St. workshop was another one I spent time in, working on fitting two-way radios to cars, overhauling 1500V DC circuit breakers, and signalling relays.

One thing I do remember of Spotty was being there when the tradies were on strike, but the Labourers were still there, and a couple of them thought it would be a great idea to put the crane hook through the back of my overalls, and hoist me up.

I was fortunate enough to get a first, and third place in the Apprentice of the year awards for Signal Maintenance during my tenure, complete with the medallions of the jigsaw puzzle.

36 years later, I'm still on the job, now as Signal Maintenance Manager for Metro, something I'd never even thought about when I first started."

Scott couldn't recall there being any form of staff magazine and there was no formal presentation of the awards he and others received, hence the lack of any photographs. It would appear that the V/Line Apprentice of the Year award for all trades had been abolished.

1985 AND BEYOND – THE GREAT UNKNOWN

Unfortunately, I have been unable to find any formal records regarding apprenticeship training in the Railways after 1985 and have to rely on drawing on the recollections of those who undertook their apprenticeship training in these later years.

I contacted several individuals and organisations I thought may be able to assist but have not had any success with little or no response. The National Library in Canberra holds most copies of the V/Line magazines 1983-1991. These magazines contained very little staff news and were more like a travel magazine so did not help with my research.

With the complete closure of the Newport Workshops in 1992 and the handing over of the maintenance work to private industry, I would expect that the training of apprentices was gradually wound down and possibly ceased completely in the early 90s. However, I believe there must have been some training of apprentices most likely after 1984 and wouldn't have ended so abruptly.

In 2016 a Rail Academy was established on part of the Newport Workshops site. I did contact them but they advised me that they did not train apprentices. They were established to provide specialised training in signal maintenance and other rail and tram infrastructure. See the item below:

From the History of the Rail Academy Newport:

"The Rail Academy Newport is one of Australia's leading rail training facilities, located 13 kilometres west of the Melbourne CBD. The Academy offers educational spaces for training providers serving the rail sector and other industries. The Rail Academy Newport does not provide direct training."

2007 – The Rail Skills Centre Victoria was established to offer specialist training and assessment facilities for Victoria's rail and tram sector.

2009 – The Rail Skills Centre Victoria was established to meet the needs of the Victorian Transport Plan, addressing the demand for industry-specific skills, an ageing workforce and expanding infrastructure of the Train and Tram Industry.

2016 – The Department of Economic Development Jobs, Transport and Resources (DEDJTR), now the Department of Transport (DOT), through the Level Crossing Removal Project (LXRP) leased the site from VicTrack. It rebranded the site as the Rail Academy Newport to ensure the continued investment and development in training for Rail and Tram infrastructure.

NEWPORT RAIL ACADEMY

APPRENTICES OF THE YEAR

Top Apprentices attending the Victorian Railway Technical College:

1960	Anthony Davis	Fitting and Turning
1961	Allen G Bourquin	Fitting and Turning
1962	Robert John Stewart	Electrical Fitting
1963	K. R. Pepperell	Electrical Fitting
1964	M. F. O'Dea	Unknown
1965	Robert Arklay	Unknown
1966	J Brincat	Unknown
1967	Santo Chiodo	Fitter & Turner
1968	Norm Swanwick	Electrical Fitter
1969	Ernest Betts	Boilermaker
1970	John Lucas	Electrical Fitter

The award for Apprentice of the Year at the VR Technical College appears to have been abolished and replaced with awards being presented to apprentices from all areas of the Victorian Railways.

1971 – 1976   No individual award.

Apprentice of the Year award was re-established and covered all areas of the Victorian Railways.

1977	Andrew Wheatland	Electrical Fitter	
1978	David Colbourne	Carpenter & Joiner	
1979	Jeff Hilder	Unknown	
1980	Douglas Gavin	Carpenter & Joiner	Batman Avenue
1981	Graeme Clarke	Electrical Mechanic	Bendigo Workshops
1982	Antonino Comperatore	Electrical Fitter	

V/Line Apprentice of the Year

1983	Trevor Furness	Fitter & Turner	Newport Workshops

State Awards Top of their Trades:

1964	N. Yuille	Unknown
1964	R. Bennett	Bricklayer
1968	Phillip Wenn	Coppersmith
1970	John Lucas	Electrical Fitter
	Peter Wilson	Upholsterer
1974	Danny Rigbye	Letterpress Machinist
	Michael Petrie	Coppersmith

Reflections

I read in a magazine about the closure of the Newport Workshops and wondered what had happened to the Victorian Railway Technical College. I got a bit nostalgic and thought I would do some research. The realisation struck me that thousands of young men had embarked on their careers through the apprenticeship programs offered by the Victorian Railways. For many, this experience was not only a formative chapter in their working lives, but also a legacy that shaped their futures. I have put together a 'Scrapbook History of Apprentice Training in the Victorian Railways.' Some great friendships and fond memories of the best years of a working life.

Norman Swanwick 2025

This collaboration is dedicated to the many men in blue overalls who shared their trade skills, knowledge and stories. Along with others in grey coats, they formed our mentors. They helped shape generations of youths as they progressed from their shadows to master new technologies and the processes of the future.… our appreciation and thanks.

Each story is unique 'time capsule' of their experience as an apprentice in the Victorian Railways.

To my old man Joe Denman, who never had the advantages of a tertiary education or an apprenticeship but plied his trade as a wheel tapper and undergear repairer.

Dennis Denman 2025

Notes

Notes

Notes

Notes